Insanity Begins at Home

Insanity Begins at Home

Surviving Ma and the Road

A Therapist's Memoir

KEN LUDMER

INSANITY BEGINS AT HOME
SURVIVING MA AND THE ROAD

iUniverse books may be ordered through booksellers or by contacting:

iUniverse
1663 Liberty Drive
Bloomington, IN 47403
www.iuniverse.com
1-800-Authors (1-800-288-4677)

ISBN: 978-1-4917-3978-5 (sc)
ISBN: 978-1-4917-3981-5 (e)

Library of Congress Control Number: 2014913001

Printed in the United States of America.

iUniverse rev. date: 07/30/2014

To Alice Liebl, my Ma, you said I could say anything about us once you were gone. Here it is. I finally got the last word. A first.

This book was written with the love and support of two women. Jill Elliot, my partner, who believed in me and encouraged me to go to the cave and write it. Mia Seddio, my dear friend, who said, "Male therapists don't write about their mothers, and you need to share the life battle you had with yours." I want to thank Amy and Ken Ferris for their guidance in the initial stages of the book formation. Their loving advice was well heeded. Elizabeth Law helped shape the developmental process and her expertise is greatly appreciated. Gotham Writers Workshop encouraged me to write it and showed me how to do it better. Then there is Krista Hill at I Universe who is my gem, a rock solid professional, who guided me through the rough waters of publication, with total honesty, great skill and warm hearted support. I sincerely thank you all. To the readers.. I hope you laugh, cry and feel everything as you go on this journey, because that is what this life is all about. I learned very young that I did not want to have the aha phenomenon on my death bed, when one realizes that they really did not live at all.

Ken Ludmer Westfield NJ July 2014

Contents

Life Begins … with a Headache

My mother tells the story that on the last day of January 1942, the month following the attack on Pearl Harbor, the United States was testing its air raid sirens for the first time. Not being up on the news due to her very late-stage pregnancy, she heard the two-in-the-afternoon sirens and thought there was another real Japanese attack underway.

She ran around in this small second-floor apartment, not knowing what to do first. She finally hopped into her bed and hid under the covers. She became further upset because my father had just taken the car, along with my sister, to do the family's weekly errands, and this had left her all alone. Then her water broke, and she went into full panic mode, as the delivery was to begin. She called her friend Mazzie Dillon, who came over immediately and said that they needed to get to the hospital, pronto. Mazzie then called my mother's doctor, who told them he would meet them at Margaret Hague Hospital in Jersey City. They left a note for my father.

This was to be my mother's second child, so she knew the routine. She got into Mazzie's car, and they headed to Jersey City. About one mile into the ride, my mother screamed that the baby was on the way. They realized they would never make it to Margaret Hague, and so they redirected to nearby Christ Hospital.

The doctor was already en route to Margaret Hague. When they arrived at the emergency room at Christ Hospital, the nurse confirmed that the baby was ready to be born. But no one there wanted to deliver the baby without the doctor being present. A call was placed to Margaret Hague, telling them to reroute the doctor to Christ Hospital.

In the meantime, the nurses tied my mother's legs together with a sheet. This was common practice back then but a surefire lawsuit these days. I was in final position for the ride down the canal. When I arrived at the opening, it was blocked. All of nature was pushing me up against this artificial barricade, and my head way getting squashed. The doctor finally arrived and the sheet was untied, and I was permitted to emerge.

The nurses announced that it was a carrottopped boy—who was a red-faced screamer—and he did not look at all happy. I was labeled Caruso by the staff because I was as loud as the Italian opera star. My mother swears that being blocked at birth is the reason I have always been impatient with waiting.

She proclaimed that I came out with a headache and, from that day forward, gave one to everyone else.

The Beginning of the End

Many decades after my siren debut, I was in my house preparing dinner when my phone rang. I answered, "Hello."

"Mr. Ludmer, this is Gina Mirth. I am the nurse at Cedar Crest, and I have some bad news to tell you."

That is never something you want to hear as an opening to a phone conversation, so I went straight to the worst news possible.

"Did she die?" I asked.

"Oh, no. She's quite alive, but she did fall, and broke her hip."

"Aaah, where is she?"

"She's at Pompton Plains Hospital, and they are operating on her now."

"Thank you, Gina. I'm on my way."

And so it began, the long, arduous fight to keep her life. Ma was now ninety-one years old and every bit as feisty as she was for every day of those ninety-one years. She was still clear in her thinking and stubbornly independent. We did, however, move her, one year ago, to her own apartment in a top-of-the-line senior facility after her second husband, of forty-two years, died, as she could no longer stay in their apartment.

"The memories are too painful," she would say. This is the same man she criticized for every day of their forty-two years together, but that came along with the turf with my mother. It was exceptionally painful for me to have to move her out of that apartment, because it sat on top of the Palisade Cliffs and had an unobstructed view of the Manhattan skyline, from the Verrazano to the George Washington Bridges—virtually the entire New York City skyline, which is the view chosen for postcards of New York City. We loved it there and would watch everything related to that skyline and river, including every big ship that came up the Hudson and berthed in the West Side piers, for over forty years. All family and friends loved that apartment and its view. It was a major loss for everyone.

Ma had watched as New York built and rebuilt its skyline. She had seen the rise of the midtown skyscrapers and the World Trade Center, as it rose floor by floor, and she saw it live when the planes flew into it. After that day, she would leave her drape closed on the south part of her balcony, so she could not see the emptiness below Canal Street. It was too painful.

So here she was, twenty-five miles northwest in a senior citizen community, with all the frills and services she could ever want. She lived independently in her own apartment, but as part of the complex, there was assisted living and a hospital, if necessary. It even had a hospice unit. The complex included a dining hall and a movie theater, and it provided bus trips to the casinos, which she loved prior to moving there. All were part of the everyday activities. There would be many people with whom to eat meals; she would not be alone. The complex also had medical offices, pharmacy services, a library, and live entertainment with comedians and even karaoke. They had card games, roulette wheels, and a swimming pool, all at her disposal.

She decorated the apartment with her usual upscale gold, beige, and brown motif and said she felt very comfortable there. That lasted one month.

"I hate this place. I hate it. Doesn't have a view."

Once you leave the New York skyline, it's tough to find another as its equal. She now lived on her own and ate some of her meals in the community dining room, but that didn't last long. My mother was old school, and women did not go out unescorted, and she just could not get used to not having a partner with whom to eat a meal.

She did not want to be one of "those fucking old ladies," which was how she referred to the senior-citizen widows who ate in the dining room. My mother had been married to my father for twenty-six years before he died, when she was forty-four, and then she was with her second husband, Geno, for forty-two years. She rarely ate alone.

When I arrived at the hospital, Ma was postoperative in the recovery room. Amazingly, her heart held up during surgery, and I was told she had a few pins in her hip to hold it together. The surgeon stopped by later and told me she had done very well. He expected her to make a full recovery, but she would need rehab and therapy.

I told him I knew the drill, as she'd had elective knee replacement surgery three years ago, at age eighty-eight, and I'd taken her to rehab three times a week.

"Then she's in good hands," he said.

I waited by her bedside, and she awoke a few hours later and immediately asked for medication, which the nurses gave her. I was told she would sleep for quite a while and that I should go home and come back the next day, when she was more stable. When I returned, she was awake in her own semiprivate room.

I have never been comfortable with hospital odors and was struggling with recurrent and painful hospital memories.

She greeted me with, "Son of a bitch, I fell and broke my goddamn hip."

"How you feeling?"

"Okay. I need some water." As I poured her a big glass, she said, "These drugs are wonderful. I don't feel anything."

"Funny to hear that coming from you," I said.

"Right, but they are not the drugs you use."

"Used to use."

"Yes, thank God."

"Since when do you thank God?"

"A lot these days."

"Afraid of dying without one?"

"Kinda, I guess."

I patted her hand and told her, "Don't worry, Ma. You gave up your chance for heaven years ago, and this new God of yours probably knows it's just a long-shot insurance plan on your part."

"Can't hurt."

"Why would you want to go to heaven anyway?" I asked.

"My mother will be there."

"That is true. Nanny was the world's kindest person." I put some cream on her hands and asked her, "Do you remember what happened with your fall?"

"The damn bedpost. I bumped into it and fell and just must have landed wrong. Cracked it pretty good, they said."

"I am sorry for that, Ma, but the doc says you'll make a full recovery."

"I hope so, but don't bet on it."

"Why not?"

"I've seen it too many times. It's usually the beginning of the end, either with infections or pneumonia or something, as old people go downhill after a hip is broken."

"Well, you are not like everyone else."

"We'll see, we'll see."

I pointed to a box that I had brought, saying, "Look, Ma—chocolate cherries."

"Ah, Sonny Boy, ain't you something."

"Who'd have thunk it, huh, Ma?"

"Amazing, after all we've been through, just amazing. You are really a good son to me."

"Thanks, Ma, it's nice to hear you say that."

She reached out, squeezed my hand, and gave me her warmest look. I smiled back at her, and we had our moment—peaceful, warm, and close, like it had been all those many years ago.

The Early Years …
Insanity Begins at Home

On my next visit to Ma in the hospital, she was sitting up in her bed while reading the newspaper.

"Hi Ma, what's up?"

"I dreamt of Manny last night."

"Wow I haven't heard you mention him in years."

"Well he was your father wasn't he?"

"What did you dream?"

"None of your shrink shit, and I'll tell you."

"Deal"

"I dreamt he came home from the War, with a red fire engine and a Japanese woman."

I said, "I remember that he did bring me a red fire engine."

Ma continues, "I told him to take the woman to Remo or Julio as they needed one. Then he said he has a time machine on his heart."

"That's so true, he did," I replied.

"Then he went out and comes back drunk with a bunch of sailors who stayed at the house and I couldn't get rid of them. Isn't that crazy?

"Not really, but crazy is a good word for those years, Ma."

"Says who?"

"Says me,"

"Bullshit."

"Have you forgotten what it was like?"

Ma wrinkled her brow as if she didn't have the faintest clue what I was talking about.

"What are you talking about?"

"Well for starters I use to think my house was perfectly normal until I started going to other houses."

"Other houses?"

"Yeah, normal ones."

"You are nuts"

"Let me remind you how it was."

Ma fell asleep as I was reminding her about our early years.

That was back in the 1940's during the last years of WW2. My father was overseas in the Navy. Ma was 28 at the time and she was considered quite a good looking woman. She fed me, and changed my diapers. My ten year older sister also was there and she would always squeeze me a little too tightly, a sure sign of her ambivalence to my presence in the apartment. My grandmother, "Nanny" visited all the time. When I was three, this man appeared. It was very early in the morning, when I went to Ma's bedroom and there he was, next to her. I woke her and asked, "who's that?"

"That is your father."

"Oh."

"Now go back to bed."

Simple, quick, to the point. That was Ma.

My father turned out to be a pretty neat guy. He had returned from the war and gave me this huge red fire engine. He was always with the kisses. He also took me places with him, like the barber shop. I was three and a half and hadn't been to one. My long, reddish blonde curls were his first order of business.

"This is a boy," he said to the assembled crowd, at this barbershop, "now let's make him look like one."

I didn't understand then, why Ma cried when she looked at me when we returned home. But my dad managed to bring home one curl, which he put under the glass, in a framed blown up picture of me. Believe it or not, it is legend within my family, that this lock of hair, changed color over the years as mine did. From reddish blonde to light brown to mixed. I still have this picture, but the curl is having trouble with this latest lack of color I have developed.

So, my normal family, was a 1945 post WW Two, American working class family. My father was thirty three years old when he was drafted into the Navy, three months after Pearl Harbor, to go fight the Japanese. He went all the way around the world to some Island off the coast of the Philippines, and that is where the Japanese shot him in the chest from an airplane. He had to go to a hospital for a long time and now although he looks ok he is not allowed to climb stairs or walk fast. He had to go to doctors all the time, and he is not allowed to work. These men came to the house to see him, and I was told never to talk to them. They were some kind of detective people from the Veterans Administration, and they were never to know that my father secretly worked in an office, because he had a Service connected disability, which meant the family received money each month from the government, because he was too sick to work.

Let me widen the view of who these people really were. My mother's parents were born in Germany in 1883 and 1889. My grandmother "Nanny" was Hochdeutsch, and spoke high German, born in Hanover to a northern German middle class family. In her house there was classical music, many books, art, and they drank white wine with dinner and ate veal and vegetables. They were Protestant.

My mother's father was Pladtdeutch and spoke lower German, and he was born in Munich, in southern Germany to a farmer family. In his house were hummels and beer steins. The music was polka, and they drank beer and ate sausage, with bread and potatoes. He was Catholic.

They met at Ellis Island and stayed together for almost seventy years. Amazing, in its own right. Pop-Pop was a picture framer who commuted two and a half hours by horse drawn carriage, ferry and trolley from Hoboken NJ to New York City each day for fifty nine years. Nanny ran the small picture frame shop which had a two room apartment in the rear.

My father's parents were born in Austria, in the Carpathian Mountains. This part of the world appears as Austria-Hungary and at other times Russia, depending on who invaded who at the time. The were farmers and their land was being taken by the Prussians, who did not like the Jews. Nothing new there. My father's family were Orthodox Jews, who came to New York, not by choice, and settled in Brooklyn, by Prospect Park.

The oldest son, Morris, was eventually able to buy an embroidery machine that made lace, and this business was in New Jersey. One by one the younger siblings followed him to New Jersey, and that is where my father met *"the shiksa,"* as my mother was referred to by his family. Once they married, the family sat *"shiva"* for my father. To the non Jews, this is a custom, when a Jew dies, the community comes to the bereaved house and sits *shiva* for a week. During this time, ungodly amounts of food, cakes, breads and everything else is brought, so that the family does not have to prepare any meals. They treated him as if he were dead.

His first born, my sister, made no impact on them whatsoever. But ten years later when I was born, it signaled hope for the family name, as I could marry a Jewish woman and restore the name to its Jewish roots. They came to see me from that day on. This, to my mother, was offensive, and she never forgave them, although she was told that this was not personal, and was their religious teachings.

"Bullshit" was her favorite phrase, when any mention of this previous hiatus period was brought up. My mother believed being Jewish was ok, but they were *too Jewish*. A concept all in itself. So with the cast of characters assembled let us proceed to the insanity.

My father left his religion and family in order to acculturate, which was the enemy of Orthodox Jews. He felt Jews had no chance in 1916, when he got here, to advance into any productive job. Jews were herded into small communities, with mainly the garment and restaurant businesses, open to them if you did not have the money to go to college. My father figured he could blend into the wider American community, if he was not, visibly, a Jew. So he never joined a temple, and he let my mother send me to a Protestant church, although neither she, nor he, ever attended. More about that later.

But, he would take me to Jewish deli's, and I learned to eat chopped liver, matzo ball soup, borscht with sour cream, dark breads and those great brisket sandwiches. Not to mention the corned beef, pastrami and pickles. I knew what a knish was. I ate potato kugel and drank Dr. Brown's Cream Soda. If we were in New York, it was always an egg cream, and we never forgot to bring home the bagels and lox. Some weird Jew, my father.

So lets see, Christmas, and Easter were Christian holidays we celebrated with Nanny and Pop-Pop. Passover and Yom Kippur were Jewish holidays that we didn't celebrate, but we went to Brooklyn to sit and eat at the family table, which was in a dark and scary cramped room. I also had to kiss my Aunt Yetta, a tiny wrinkled up old woman who had hair growing out of a mole on her face. She, I found out years later, had some learning disability and suffered from seizures and was never sent to school. It was at uncle Fishel's table, that I uttered the phrase that was heard throughout the entire Brooklyn Jewish community, I asked my mother a little too loudly, "do they have any milk?"

Orthodox Jews keep kosher, which means you don't mix meat and dairy. You don't even put them on the same plate. *Ever.* This particular reminder that I was not being raised Jewish caused my aunt Hilda to flee the table muttering

"Oh vey" to herself.

Cousin Lionel said "It's ok, but he should learn."

From then on, I was instructed on the do's and don'ts of non religious, but religious meals, in Brooklyn. I learned when it was the right time to cut the Challah. I never asked for butter for matzoh. I learned to not eat when uncle Fischel was reading from the Torah. Oh yes Chanukah, which usually coincides with Christmas, was never recognized by the Orthodox as a holiday, as it was thought to be for the Reformed Jews, who did not want to be left out of gift giving, and they were just like Protestants, to my Brooklyn relatives. So Chanukah was never in play at my house. We had Santa.

So back at home there was my German mother yelling at my Jewish father that he cannot tell her what to do. This had nothing to do with religion as neither one of them practiced it. This had to do with who was in charge. She was, by the way, a *Free Thinker,* and would have been a *Flapper,* if she were old enough. she was an original women's liberationist. He being a conservative man, did not want her out at night, with her friends, because they liked to dance. These types of battles progressed over the years to the clashing of wills, with my mother accusing my father of being

"Hitler in the house."

"Hitler in the house"

The words still cause my brain to jam. She's the German, he's the Jew...Hitler in the House. Hitler in the House. The German calling the Jew "Hitler" was just crazy. My feelings of insanity had begun, at home.

The floor nurse entered to give Ma her medicine and had awakened her. Ma snapped to attention as I was finishing my recollection of Hitler.

"You still yapping about Hitler? it wasn't my fault, your father was a tyrant, and you, Smart-ass, you shouldn't have been listening anyway."

"Ma, people just didn't grow up with Hitler in their house, they don't even like to use the word. It brings out very painful memories.

"Big deal, get over it. Nurse, is my dinner ready?"

The Wooden Spoon

Ma made progress in the hospital and more color returned to her face. I told her so. "Hey, Ma, lookin' good."

"Hello, Sonny Boy. Get me the hell outta this damn hospital."

"Only one getting you outta here is you."

"I know, but I hate the damn rehab. Same crap as with my knee."

"But you are almost done. Once you can walk the ramp and use the stairs, you can go back to the apartment."

Actually, no one worked harder than she did—she was determined to get back to her apartment. Then she said something that almost knocked me down.

"Well, if that goddamn doctor doesn't sign off on my rehab soon, I'll use the wooden spoon on him."

Ma meant this as a joke, but for me, it brought back some deep-seated and painful memories.

I didn't think my mom was different from most moms who were raising children after World War II. These women went back to their kitchens and laundry rooms, happy to have their men back from the war. They focused on family life and getting on with the new stability that followed the war.

There I was, back at home with Ma, day after day. I would stand at the front window, watching the other kids go to and return from school. Envy filled me as I pleaded with Ma to let me go also.

"Not yet" was her reply, over and over again. I was bored with the routine in the house. I was allowed to go to the corner to await my father's bus and his return from work each day.

Ma and I did get to walk three blocks every week to the Laundromat, and I loved watching the washers and driers spin their loads in a circled frenzy. Ma would let me use the big scooper to pour the white laundry powder into the chute above the washer. The best part of laundry day was the trolley ride we took while the last load was drying. We would take it to the transfer station and then switch for the return trolley. It would clang when it started and stopped. I loved the smell of the trolley—kind of musky wood—and I loved the rattan seats. The conductor had his official uniform and hat, and I hoped that one day, I would drive the trolley car.

Back at the Laundromat, Ma would let me fold the clothes and then pull the cart for the journey home. Life was simple and good but a little boring. I think it was then that I devised the game, in order to fill the void in my very young and narrow life.

The game involved getting my mother to chase me. It started simply enough, when I just asked her if she would do so.

"No, I'm too busy," she answered.

I would persist, and she would become increasingly frustrated with my nonstop begging, pleading, and cajoling. One day, however, I saw I was getting to her. She told me that if I did not stop begging, she would put me back in my room. I no longer remember the reason, but on that day, I pushed the envelope farther than ever before, and she charged. As she came after me; I ran. I think that on the third time around the circle that covered the kitchen, my bedroom, my sister's bedroom, her bedroom, and the hall connecting to the kitchen, we both realized that I had gotten her to chase me. She became even angrier as I started to laugh, which was a capital offense in those days. You never taunted a parent.

Ma was furious, frustrated, and feeling outfoxed by a five-year-old. She went to the next level. I had seen the wooden spoon and knew she used it for cooking. It lived in the big hinged compartment that was part of every stove I had ever seen. She went right for it, rattling around in the mix of cooking utensils that also lived in there. She emerged with it. Now armed, she began the chase in earnest, all the time mumbling louder and louder to herself.

This was serious. I took off, cutting the corner in my bedroom with great speed, and flew through her room in a flash. I thought she was really slow, not even visible in my backward glances, but as I rounded the turn for the kitchen, I ran straight into her. Crash. Foiled by the wits of an adult. End of game. She put me on the floor, took down my pants, and applied the wooden spoon, at first to my rear end and then, when I did not respond correctly, she upped the ante by going for the back of my upper legs. Whack, whack, whack—the blasts came faster, and they increasingly, stingingly smarted. I wailed for her to stop. When she did, her fury was spent, and my legs were bright red. Defeated, beaten, and outsmarted, I was sent to my room to learn from the errors of my ways.

I still liked the chase part, but this spoon had to go. So, as a major battlefield strategist, I hid the spoon in my toy box when she wasn't looking.

It didn't take too many days for me to torment her enough to get her to chase me. But she was a battle-worn veteran, who had raised my sister ten years earlier. They never played "chase me," but my mom had learned from her strategic errors. This time, she changed her pattern and went directly for the spoon. I was shocked that she did not try to chase me first. I bravely stood at my bedroom door, watching her thrash through the oven compartment, muttering to herself, "Where is the goddamn spoon?"

I broke into gleeful laughter, and that, of course, was the worst possible crime. She gave up on the spoon and came after me, unarmed. It seemed like a blissful eternity as we raced from room to room, with her stopping and switching directions, and me, now perfecting my craft by listening for foot noises and also switching directions. It went on forever. I eventually tripped on the bedpost in her bedroom and went cascading into the hall door, where I came to an abrupt stop. She pounced. With an open hand, the blows to the legs came swiftly. She promised to stop if I revealed to her where the spoon was hidden. I told her. She then hid it herself. During the next round, which I also lost, she had it.

I don't know if I waited longer than usual or if she lost track of time, but as she was just finishing her next installment of spoon therapy, we both heard my father, who had come home early and was now slowly climbing the stairs to the apartment.

She panicked and bolted back to the kitchen, where she threw the spoon into its original spot in the stove. He entered, and I just lay there, with my pants down below my knees. His eyes widened, and the way he looked at me, I knew I was all right. He bent over and saw the red welts on my legs. His face appeared different than I ever had seen as he asked me what had happened.

"Ma beats me with a wooden spoon when you are not here."

He went nuts. No asking what I had done, no conferring with Ma—this was the male-dominated forties. He just raced to the kitchen and asked one question: "Where is this wooden spoon?"

I didn't wait a second. From the hall, I blurted out, "It's in the stove."

What happened next forever changed my relationship with my mother and my father. He got the spoon, and without one iota of hesitation, he took off in her direction. She cried, begged, pleaded, and did anything she could to get him under control. He would have none of it. He pushed her onto my bed and whacked the daylights out of the back of her thighs. He then asked her, "How did that feel?"

He then proclaimed that from this day forth, "If he gets it, you get it."

Wow! Dad—my hero! The great defender of beaten kids everywhere. There had been no parenting huddles to talk it out, just swift justice. An eye for an eye. Thigh for a thigh.

Life was different for me and Ma after that day. She no longer chased me—she barely spoke to me. I was more bored than ever. I had won the battle but lost the war. Luckily for me, school came that fall. They didn't have any wooden spoons there. For fifty-nine years, Ma never mentioned that wooden spoon ... until today in her hospital room.

Living with Hitler

O n my next hospital visit, I brought up the wooden-spoon issue and asked her how she felt about the whole incident. She knew it was wrong to beat a kid, but she truly felt it was the right thing to do (until she was the recipient). She said it was different back then, as everyone hit their kids. That was true. I thought for a moment and then tried to talk to her about the one facet of my childhood that took me a lot of therapy and maturation to fully understand. I asked her if she knew how painful it was for me to hear her call my father "Hitler."

She looked me in the eyes and said, "It was wrong of me, and I apologize."

It took her fifty-six years to say that. Hearing those words felt somewhat unreal but very satisfying nonetheless.

My father was an Eastern European man of small stature who had much self-doubt. He came to this country as a Yiddish-speaking seven-year-old with no English skills. He paradoxically adopted an authoritarian stance, as most men did in their pre–women's-liberation marriages. From Ralph Kramden in The Honeymooners, bellowing that he was "the king of the castle," to every Hollywood movie showing the little lady in the kitchen, with daddy coming home to his dinner served promptly, the scenario was that women asked men for permission for everything—for example, on how to spend the money, or if they could go on vacation this year, or if they could get a car. That was the way it was back then.

Women were not in the boardrooms or on the Supreme Court. For every Margaret Sanger, Margaret Mead, or Eleanor Roosevelt, there were tens of thousands of housewives who existed under the rule of the male-driven world in which they lived.

But the German shiksa my father married wasn't your average housewife who did her daily duties without bemoaning her lot in life. Not Alice Liebl. She was a firestorm of her own making, a ruthless control freak, who had to have it her way—or else. She ruled her roost, and the problem was that he didn't listen to her. Her mode was always attack. I knew that from my basic training with her, when we ran the circle of rooms back in the wooden-spoon days. If she couldn't get you overtly, she would lie in wait, like a lioness in the wild, and at the precise moment, she would pounce.

Now, deprived of her spoon in her battle with me, she armed herself with a week's worth of my violations and presented them to my father, after she had provided him with God-knows-what in the bedroom.

Oh, she was good. She would smile as he gave me the lecture. Then, with the cutting edge of a sword, she would administer the coup de grâce by saying, "You know this is killing your father. He is a sick man, and he cannot keep being upset by your behavior."

Zing—direct hit. Oh, my God, I thought. I'm killing my father, and if he dies, it'll be my fault.

She used this once too often, and being a fairly good counter-puncher, I learned how to duck this effective right to the chin by going directly to my father myself. This way, I could get in my side of the story and tell him she was driving me crazy and that she acted differently toward me when he wasn't there. That got to him, for he knew that was true. So now her weekly crimes reports were met with my father's saying, "I know. I talked to him about it already."

Hah. One for the good guys. I was learning that living with "Hitler" wasn't so bad. He actually listened and didn't yell very often or very loudly. He also had a sense of humor. When I would go with him to the barbershop, or Corsi's Garage, or to Michael the tailor, he always laughed with them. They all told me that my father was a very kind and funny man.

No one ever said that about Ma when I accompanied her to the Laundromat, or the butcher, or the pharmacist. Old Tom at the ice cream parlor would giggle with her, but I never knew what that was about. So for years, I heard her tell my father that he was "Hitler."

Then somewhere around fourth grade, my class was studying history, and we had to watch a film about a crazy, scary man in Germany who tried to kill all the Jews, and his name was Hitler.

The depth of my internal crazy bell at that moment must have rendered me totally numb, and I developed the shakes. My mind was on tilt. I could not find words and sat there forever, until they made me go home. My kind, caring, gentle father … Hitler? This concept was beyond my ability to process it. This was the name my mother called my Jewish father—the name of the worst mass killer ever, and he killed Jews? How could she use that word in his house?

I had missed the call to dinner. This had to be serious, because I never voluntarily missed a meal. I was in my bed under my pillow. My father came into the room and asked if I was sick. I gave no response. He asked numerous other questions without getting any responses from me. Ma yelled from the kitchen, "Dinner's ready. What the hell is going on in there?"

My father rolled me over onto my back and saw my tears. As gentle as in any quiet moment between a father and his son, he softly said, "What is it Kenny? You can tell me."

"I know who Hitler was. He killed Jews."

He looked at me, and he could tell how painful this was for me. He hugged and kissed me and said, "You will never again hear that word in this house."

And I never did.

"Mud Puddle"

It was Ma's fifteenth day in the hospital, and when I arrived that day, she greeted me, beaming from ear to ear, with, "Well, the doctor signed off on rehab. I'm free. Let's get the hell outta here"

"Great news, Ma," I responded.

She took the mandatory wheelchair ride to the hospital exit and then walked fairly steadily to the car.

"I did it!" she proclaimed. "Now let's get a goddamn lobster."

"A lobster it is," I agreed.

We had to get support services for Ma, and that meant Thelma entered our lives. She was large black woman from the South in her midfifties. She was kind and thoughtful, and she was firm with Ma but also good to her. I told Thelma that she would have to get used to Ma's critical and demanding personality, and she did a great job of letting Ma's acerbic comments pass her by. A month passed easily for Ma back in her apartment.

On my next visit, Ma was sitting at the kitchen table, peeling carrots. She started a rant about my sister's selfish and sneaky ways. This was a common theme, as my mother had recently gained a new appreciation of me, I believe, mostly due to her concurrence with

Thelma, who shared her own view of the differences between Ma's children.

"Okay, Ma, fair enough," I said, "but please keep the bashing to less than five minutes."

"Well, mister, at least I wasn't called to school because of her bad behavior."

"Ouch, low blow."

"What did he call you?"

"Mud puddle."

"That's right. Mud puddle," she said, and she began to laugh.

I remembered "mud puddle" like it was yesterday.

It seemed like an eternity until I was able to join all the kids that walked past my house each day on their way to and from school. I had missed the cutoff and was now five and a half, going to my first day of school with all the other kids. No more being cooped up in the house with my mother. I was now part of the herd of kids who had someplace to go. My mother was never big on warm nurturing, and if she could get out of any chore that had to do with taking me from place to place, she would jump at the chance. After two days of her walking me to school, I told her she didn't need to walk me any longer; I could go with other the kids.

There were moms at the corners, and safety was not an issue. No one at the time had ever heard of missing children. I was only afraid of the boogeyman, and he came out at night to get kids who wouldn't go to sleep, so that put me in the clear.

Once we kids arrived at school, we waited outside for the bell to ring. We flipped baseball cards, ran around, and compared our cereal-box rings. When it was close to bell time, we would line up by grade level, little kids first and the older kids following in succession. It gave one real status to go in last. One day, I would be a bigger kid and be able to watch all the little "puny kids" walk in first.

For now, I reveled in my kindergarten status; at least I was at school and not at home. We all wondered if little Gerard Heather was going to cry and make it through the entire first morning. His mom quivered when they pulled him off her legs and made him walk him inside, both seemed to worry that he would pee in his pants. The assembly of other moms hugged Gerard's mom; they understood her feelings. Well, he did pee in his pants and then began to cry. Such were the perils of separation.

On line each morning was a huge third-grader named Kenny File. He was the Scut Farkas of our day. Scut Farkus was the bully from the movie A Christmas Story who ambushed little Ralphie and his brother Randy on their way to school. Well, Kenny File didn't like my name—or me. I really didn't know the kid. All I knew was that he lived two blocks over on Shippen Street, and was tall, and wore glasses. For the last three days, he had been coming up to me, looking down, and calling me "mud puddle" in front of all the other kids on line. The origin of his particular name-calling was easily discernible. My last name is Ludmer. To Kenny File, Lud sounded like mud. Mud puddle was a third-grader's way of turning my name into a belittling put-down.

On this fifth day of kindergarten when he tossed "mud puddle" at me, the other kids started to laugh and began mouthing it themselves. I felt a bubble build up inside me, and it got very painful. The next thing I knew, I was jumping up in the air in order to unleash a huge right-hand roundhouse shot, which landed above Kenny File's nose and broke his glasses in two.

His face was bleeding, and he was crying and screaming that I had broken his glasses and that I was now in real trouble.

The teachers came and took me to the principal's office, and I had to sit on a hard bench and wait until my mother came for me. They had called her, and I was sweating every moment until she arrived. I thought, I have just blown school.

Ma yanked me by the arm and dragged me home, while yelling at me, nonstop.

It was a very long day, as I waited for my father's return, and I worried more and more as the day dragged on.

When he finally came home, my mother recounted my offense in great detail and said how embarrassed she was having to go to school to retrieve me. To my utter amazement, he simply said, "A third-grader called him that? Served him right."

A smile came ever so slightly to my face, but my mother's look got more intense. I was not out of the woods yet, as everyone had to go to school—Kenny File and his parents and me and my parents.

And you know, the people at school said exactly the same thing. They admonished Kenny for picking on a kindergartner, and his reputation was forever tarnished among his peers for being "whupped" by a kid three years younger. I had to listen to a strong lecture about how he could have been seriously injured if the glasses had broken in his eye, and that did scare me. But I'd never thought about hitting him and barely remembered that he wore glasses. The last I knew, there was his face looking down at me and calling me mud puddle, and after that, a bubble burst, and there was a lot of chaos and confusion.

I promised never again to hit any kid wearing glasses. My father disagreed with my mother about having to pay for his new glasses. My father thought it was his parents' obligation to teach their young bully that he couldn't go around name-calling without consequences. But my mother prevailed, and we paid for his new pair. From that day on, he always took off his glasses when he passed me in the halls. Justice.

Ma's Man

How's the Queen [the family name for Ma] today?" I asked, as she was misting her small nursery of flowers and plants. Ma had taught me how to care for plants, and I felt good watching her mist them.

"I dreamed of Manny again."

"Wonder why he is on your mind."

"You're the shrink," she said. "You tell me."

Ma had a softer look today. We both enjoyed telling the old stories, as she had grown impatient with TV and preferred good ol' talk. So I took the cue and asked her to tell me about Manny, my father. She jumped right in.

She told me the story of her first meeting my father. She was a freshman in high school, and he was a senior. She and her girlfriends flipped when they saw him. He was such a dapper dresser—always good-looking with his sleek black hair and a thin mustache.

"Who made the first move?" I asked her.

"My girlfriends said he was the football team's manager, and we should go down the field and just loll around there. We did. So when he walked past us, I must have said something to him. He turned around and just looked at us, and then he looked directly at me and asked my name. I answered so weakly that he had to ask again. That's when my friend Marion said to him, 'Her name is Alice Liebl, and she's a freshman.' He laughed. I almost died." Ma still seemed a bit embarrassed as she recalled the story. "I was so young, Kenny, and he seemed like a grown man".

"What happened next?"

"He started talking to me in the halls, and then he joined us one day after school at the soda fountain. I was nervous all the time around him, as he was so handsome. Your father had the best manners and was a gentleman all the time. He even paid for my soda. He asked if he could meet my parents, so that it would be all right for him to take me out. I did not want him to see how poor I was or meet my father, so I lied and said that I could meet him wherever he wanted, that coming to my house was unnecessary. I didn't realize that his family was as poor as mine or that they could never accept me."

"Because of the Jewish thing?"

"Correct. He never told them he was seeing me, and I never told my parents. Everyone in town knew about us except for our parents. It took almost two years for them to find out." Ma stopped misting the plants, and I could see she was really picturing those early days of innocence and bravery. She continued. "When he graduated, he got a job in New York City for Metropolitan Life Insurance Company, and I thought it was the greatest thing to have a secret boyfriend who went to New York each day."

"When I graduated, he gave me a ring and said he wanted to get married. It was very hard telling Nanny that I had kept this from her for all that time, but she said if I loved him, then I should follow my heart. I didn't realize how hard it was for your father to leave his family, but he almost never talked about them, as he said they were 'old country' and 'this is America.' He wanted new, and they were an embarrassment to him, as they were poor, uneducated, and spoke minimal English."

"We had a simple, small wedding, and only his youngest sister came to it. She swore on the life of her unborn children to never tell that she was there. There were not many mixed marriages back then, but I did not give a damn about religion. Boy, did that one bite me in the ass."

Ma shook her head as if to say how naive she was. "We rented a small apartment, and I got a job as a secretary, and we were fine. Ten months later, your sister was born. I was totally shocked when his family refused to come see the child, but he never complained about it."

Ma seemed almost embarrassed as she said, "It was the Great Depression, and people were lucky if they had jobs. Your father was a good worker. Everyone at Metropolitan liked him, and he even got promotions and salary increases. Considering how others were doing, I was happy that we had enough to pay our bills."

I asked, "Were there any difficulties in the marriage?"

"Sure, his family. I knew it bothered him, but he would never say anything about it. Also, he was prone to gambling, with those damn poker games at Corsi's Garage. I even had to go there one night to see if he was really playing cards, as someone had whispered to me that a floozy-looking woman was seen coming out of there."

"Find anything?"

"No, but the other men were nervous. There was something there, but I could never prove it. My main problem with your father was that he would try to tell me what I could and could not do."

"Wasn't that the way it was back then?"

Ma got up, started to leave the room, stopped, and put her hands on her hips. "Well, not in my house. I was the only one of my friends who stood up to her husband. They thought I was taking a big risk, but secretly, they wished they could say what I said."

"Women still are fighting that battle today, Ma."

She proudly stated, "I was way ahead of my time—way ahead. Your father was a hard worker and determined to get us a house. He had an insurance route, which meant he walked from house to house, seeing his clients and trying to get new ones. By the time your sister was of school age, we moved to Weehawken, because of the better schools. Life was good. We were a young couple in love. We had lots of friends, and there were plenty of children." Ma's face softened when she spoke of those years, and it seemed to reflect a real happiness.

Her brow wrinkled as she continued. "But times got very difficult as the Great Depression worsened, and people had less and less money to spend. I wanted another child, but your father was firm and said we could not afford another one."

I patted her hand and asked, "So what changed his mind?"

"Nothing. I was twenty-eight, and your sister was almost nine. So on the right day, I got him drunk and got pregnant."

"What?"

"You heard me. Listen, if it wasn't for that, we would not be having this conversation. Once I was pregnant, he was fine with it. Then the war broke out, and everything went bad. He got drafted just after you were born. He spent three years away and came back all shot up and disabled."

"How awful."

"Then he had the heart attacks and could no longer work at Metropolitan, and we stayed poor and never got the house."

I felt very bad for her and said, "Geez, Ma, that was hell for you."

"That is life, Sonny Boy, one shot after another."

She sat down and we just sat quietly for a minute or two.

"Tell me," I said, "was it true that he was the last man to be drafted from Weehawken?"

"Yeah, he was thirty-three and had two kids, and they still took him. Can you believe that? Now it's twenty-five or younger."

"Terrible."

Her face drained, and she added, "He was not the same man after the war. He couldn't dance anymore and that ate him up. He felt terrible that he couldn't play ball with you, as he tired too quickly. It was tough on everyone, his being so sick. The doctors kept telling me he was at risk, but I could never stop him from what he wanted to do, as he smoked those Lucky Strikes. We all paid the price when he died at age forty-nine."

"So sad."

"It was the war and cigarettes that did him in."

"Damn both of them."

The Big One

M a was in the kitchen, cooking, and the wonderful aroma of her veal stew filled the air.

"Smells great, Ma," I said as I joined her in the kitchen. "How's the girl today?"

"Not bad, except those old fucking ladies are going to drive me nuts."

"Why?"

"All the bitching about their illnesses and their dead husbands. I don't want to hear any more about heart attacks."

"You certainly had to deal with many heart attacks."

"Fucking-A right. Your father had five of them."

"I know, the second one was when he was with me, on the way to Yankee Stadium."

"But it was the first one that was the really big one."

"I don't think I ever heard the full story."

She stopped stirring the stew, sat down, and began to tell the story.

"It was 1947 during a horrific winter snowstorm. Your father had been back from the Pacific for two years. He had recovered from the Japanese bullets to his chest but was now 90 percent disabled, according to the Veterans Administration. He was trudging through the snow, coming home from work, and it was just too much for his heart. He collapsed on the steps, coming up to our door. He was thirty-eight. It took forever for the ambulance to get there and take him to the hospital. The doctors didn't think he would make it. He stayed in the Veterans Hospital for six weeks."

"I remember going to the Bronx with you to see him there."

"Remember, Kenny, this was post–World War II, and the hospitals were full of amputees and permanently disabled veterans. You were five years old and the sights you saw then I'm sure weren't good for you, but you wanted to see him."

"Right, I remember after that, I could not look at war movies or anything connected to blood. Even the smells of ammonia or cleaning fluids upset me."

"Your father was told he could not climb stairs, and as we lived up one full flight after ten porch steps, it was out of the question. So we had to go to Florida for his post-recovery, and you went to live with Nanny."

That turned out to be a wonderful time for me. Nanny practiced unconditional love, very different from Ma's obedience-or-else model. Nanny hugged and kissed me all the time. She played with me. She talked to me. She let me help with making cookies, and I learned to peel carrots and potatoes. I used the hand mixer for the batter for cakes. We played marbles and pick-up sticks. At the end of every day, Nanny came to the couch where I slept and told me a story from old Germany, from when she was a child.

She read me the postcards from Florida, and I had a heavy heart when Nanny told me I would be going back home as Mom and Dad were coming back. After that, I would go to Nanny's from school before I went home, and sometimes she let me stay for dinner. I even got to stay over on Friday or Saturday nights. Whatever goodness or kindness I now possess, I attribute it directly to Nanny, who showed me love and warmth and how to feel for others. Ma returned to the veal stew but then paused and said in her most earnest voice, "I think it was good for you to be with Nanny. She loved you like crazy, and you kept wanting to go over to her apartment all the time."

"I loved living there."

Ma scowled. "I did, however, have to set her straight about who was the mother."

"Lucky for me."

"Knock it off."

Up the Lake

When I arrived at Ma's, she was looking through old pictures. She laughed when she pulled one out and showed it to me. "Look—you and Omah and Nanny, 'up the lake.'"

"There's no place like 'the lake' anymore."

Ma answered decisively, "You always loved it up there. For the life of me, I don't see what you liked about that hole-in-the-wall cabin with no electricity and no bathroom."

"It was about Nanny, Ma. She was so kind and loving."

"Well, it was good, because I got a break from you," Ma said, without any thought of how that might sound.

"I was a kid, Ma, and kids want to do things, not sit around on a curb and play with the soft asphalt. Up the lake, I could go on adventures and find stuff, and Nanny let me help her in that primitive kitchen she had. It was wonderful sleeping on the screened-in porch and listening to the animals. I looked forward to those summers with Nanny and Pop-Pop."

Ma added, "But it did begin with that torturous ride."

"You should have been in the backseat."

If you lived in New Jersey in the late forties, getting anywhere was not easy. The roads mainly had one lane, with constant traffic lights. People generally went one of two places for vacation: to the mountains, or "down the shore," which was a forever drive to the Atlantic Ocean. This was before they built the Garden State Parkway. "A fool's venture," said my not-too-clear-thinking father about the Parkway. "They pay to sit in traffic, and I don't." Little did he realize that in a few years, the ride to the shore would be just about cut in half when they finished the road.

But we went "up the lake," which was another torturous ride.

We rode on local streets until we hit Route 17 North, which was just about the main thoroughfare to the Catskill Mountains. New York State hadn't built the thruway yet, but they were blasting the rocks of Bear Mountain to make way for it. Ma was in the front passenger seat, admonishing my father on every aspect of driving, although she didn't drive. Nanny and Pop-Pop were in the back with me. We didn't say much due to the tension level and cursing that was going on in the front. We passed places like Sloatsburg, which had a light that permitted the New York traffic that had come over the Tappan Zee Bridge to merge onto 17 North. My father hated the New Yorkers, and every time we got to the Sloatsburg light, we would hear how "the damn New Yorkers slow down the ride."

By the way, my father's family lived in Brooklyn, and they came over the Tappan Zee and merged with "damn Jerseyites, who should go down the shore anyway."

Next town was Tuxedo Junction—not much of a place but they had a train stop and a great song named after it. Once we cleared Tuxedo Junction, the road signs started appearing for the Red Apple Rest ("Only 7 miles to the RAR"). I could not contain myself and started telling everyone what I was going to eat: two hotdogs with mustard and sauerkraut and French fries and a Nehi soda.

"That's true," Ma concurred as I reminisced. "You were impossible after you saw that sign."

Everyone in the world who took this forever-ride stopped at the Red Apple Rest. Years later, they built another roadside rest stop, called the Orseck Brothers, about five hundred yards farther along. Real aficionados like us, however, only went to the RAR.

Once we were full of hot dogs or hamburgers and French fries or onion rings, we went about two hundred yards past the RAR and took a left, to a single-lane road that headed …

"To the mountains," my father would proclaim.

There was then a fork in the road, and we went right onto a bumpier road that wound itself up the mountain. At some point, there was a left-hand turn directly into the woods onto a road that was dirt and rock and had a hump of grass in the middle. The road was made by car tracks, and we had to blow our horn if we were to enter, because there was only room for one car, either going in or coming out, and if we failed to blow our horn, we would be the one who had to back out. Many heated discussions took place over who blew and who didn't.

"I made sure your father hit the horn hard," Ma said.

The road made a huge Z through the woods until it opened into the grand courtyard, where everyone parked their cars. This place was called Mombasha Lake, a private community of about twenty cabins scattered beyond the courtyard, along with a second tier of cabins. My grandparents had been coming here for years, "to get away from life for a while."

They rented the bungalow, which consisted of a kitchen, two small bedrooms separated by a three-quarters wall, and a tiny screened-in porch. There was no electricity or running water and no bathroom. The "outhouse" was in the courtyard, but only the brave went into it, as it had wasps, and the summer odor was something not to be believed. I preferred the woods. I had my two favorite rocks to stand on, and I always brought a shovel with me.

The water came from a deep artesian well in the courtyard. We brought our own pails and poured the water from the well pail down the spout into our pail. It was easier to bring two pails for balance on the hundred-yard walk back to the bungalow. My parents would stay for the weekend and then leave me with Nanny and Pop-Pop for my summer.

I slept in the screened-in porch, which I thought was the greatest place in the world. It felt like I was outside, because I could smell the rain and hear all the night animals, but I was protected by the screens, except when the wind blew the rain in sideways, and we had to roll down the awning.

The kitchen had a metal plate, which in the early years had to be heated by firewood. There were now propane tanks, and Nanny could cook on a real stove. The icebox was our refrigerator, and the ice man came twice a week with two huge sheets of ice, which were placed onto the bottom rack of the icebox.

Our milk was set directly on the ice. A drip pan was under the icebox and needed constant attention. Light in the cabin came from a kerosene lamp, which had a huge wick that could be turned up or down.

The Dugans' truck came twice a week with milk, eggs, bread, butter, and cakes. Mr. Dugan also had ice cream sandwiches, which we really had to eat the first day or they would melt.

There were one or two cars in the courtyard during the week, so we had to go to Monroe with whoever was driving to get the rest of the supplies, like meat, vegetables, soap, and toilet paper. We had a battery-operated radio, and we could listen to Jean Shepherd, broadcasting his storytelling hour. It was a life hard to imagine these days—no TV, cell phones, Internet, stereos, or iPods. We had a deck of cards and some board games like Parcheesi and Chinese checkers, as well as pick-up sticks and a yo-yo.

I looked across the table at Ma and said, "It was wonderful, Ma. Life was so simple then."

"Yeah, and simpletons went there."

"Ma!"

I remembered that in the evenings, everyone would sit in a big circle in the courtyard, with a beautiful fire in the center. If we were lucky, we could get a stick and roast marshmallows, while the adults talked and drank beer. On the weekends, when the other families arrived, we would have softball games. Later on, they assembled a rustic backboard and basketball hoop. Frank Grather was my favorite dad from the families who joined us, as he brought a BB rifle and would let us set up the beer cans for targets. The mothers would yell that we'd shoot our eyes out. Never did.

I learned the path over the mountain and down the other side to the lake, and Pop-Pop would fish for trout. We swam in this murky lake, and played with one raft that always was tilted to one side, making it hard not to fall off. I loved the evening thunderstorms and the smell of the fresh grass and herbs that grew in the wild. Deer were a common phenomena, and no one seemed upset with them. The rabbits were the enemy, as they ate the community vegetable garden, which never really produced much anyway.

Those summers were my time away from Ma and under the loving care of Nanny, who always played cards with me and scratched my back. When she told stories of her childhood in Germany, she said the lake reminded her of it. We would sit in chairs outside at night and just look at the beautiful sky, all full of stars, and wait for the meteors. It was a time of simplicity and family and love. I am glad I had those summers, because that world—and Nanny—are long gone now.

"Yes, your time with Nanny was good for you," Ma said kindly.

Down the Shore, One and Done

Ma was talking on the phone to her last surviving friend, Lola, when I entered her apartment. She raised a finger, indicating I should wait.

When she got off the phone, she laughed, saying, "Lola was talking about going down the shore."

"Oh no, not the shore," I retorted.

The word "shore" sent me on a bad memory. In addition to going up the lake, my father wanted his vacation down the shore.

My parents, one summer, rented a nasty little bungalow, and off we went in the car—mother and father up front, and my teenage sister next to me in the back. No Nanny and Pop-Pop, because they were up the lake.

We were packed to the rafters for our week "vacation" in a mosquito-ridden, dirty, little shingled bungalow near a swamp.

My parents hadn't yet discovered the real shore, which was the Atlantic Ocean, because they didn't want to drive that far, so we found the Atlantic Highlands on bayside. It's one of the first towns you come to once you cross the bridge over the Raritan River, which separates North and South Jersey. Because it was the bayside, it had an unbelievably bad smell at low tide, and the mosquitoes had built condos to live in while they ferociously fed on the tourists.

It was a ride from hell to get there—one lane each way, and a million little towns with traffic lights and trucks, and with my mother's nonstop direction giving, It was as tense as the final furlong of the Kentucky Derby. We went over the Raritan Bridge that took forever. Kids today can't appreciate that little bit of nostalgia, because the ride to the shore is seven lanes over the same bridge, and these kids have headphones and earpieces to drown out the parental noise.

When we got to our vacation bungalow, my mother was already cursing that the place was filthy and that she would have to get on her hands and knees and scrub the "damn place" clean.

And she did. I wondered why anyone would choose to go to a place that you know was going to be filthy, which you then had to clean, as well as shop for all the food, cook, and clean up, and call it a vacation.

I would ask her why we had to stay in that place and why we couldn't get a motel.

"Shut up" was all she said.

In addition to its being dead-ugly and dirty, smelling bad, and having mosquitoes and no air conditioning, it was so humid that we would stick to everything.

The first night was spent mending screens as best as we could, because the lotion my mother put on me seemed to attract the mosquitoes rather than repel them.

We had to go to the pharmacy in the morning to get medicine for the bites, and I was told to stay out of the sun. Honestly, it was as crazy as a Kafka play. By the afternoon, my mother relented and let me go find some kids to play with. It was not hard to find them, as bungalow row seemed to have kids in every house. There was a big ball field across the street where kids playing some form of baseball. I joined in, as I was a baseball nut. We had fun, and the kids said we should all meet up after supper and go for a walk along the bay.

I hoped it would be high tide, so the smell would be gone. After dinner, I told my parents that the kids from the other houses were going to walk along the bay to find stuff. My mother, happy to be rid of me, said okay but cautioned me, "Be back before the sun goes down. We'll go for ice cream then, if you're not late."

I met up with about seven kids, and we started our walk to the bay and along the water's edge. We found tin cans, shells, and even pieces of car tires. There were glass shards and plenty of rocks of all sizes. We even found a dead bird. We came to a long log that was stuck in the sand, and hanging from its underside was a huge rusty chain about five feet long. We worked on it for about fifteen minutes until we were able to yank it free. Whoever took a turn with it would find his hand had turned orange-brown and had to rub like crazy with the bay water to get it off. We continued on our way, looking for other fun things.

The group had stopped to look for stuff, and I leaned over to pick up something from the sand—a shiny bracelet-looking thing with blue glass in it. At the same time, this kid, Robert, started twirling the rusty chain around his head, like a cowboy with a lasso. As I stood up to show my newfound treasure, the chain was in full motion. It hit me directly on my left eyebrow and opened up a huge gash. The kids panicked and ran away, and I put my hand over my eye and saw it was completely bloody. Between the tears and the blood, I could barely see, and the walk/run to my bungalow seemed to take a thousand years. My mother started screaming before I even told her what had happened, and we got in the car and went to the hospital to have my eye sewn up. It seemed to take forever in the emergency room, but in the end, I got needles and stitches and a big lecture from my mother. I had the second biggest headache of my life and was told I could not get my eye wet until the stitches came out the following week. The next morning found my left eye completely swollen and black and blue. I looked like I had been in the ring with Rocky Marciano, the current heavyweight champ.

I spent my vacation week not being able to swim, or run around, or do anything fun. The next year, I opted to go up the lake with Nanny and Pop-Pop and did so for every summer after that. I had no interest in down the shore.

I heard Ma's voice say, "Hello? Sonny Boy? Where did you go? You were staring." I just looked at her and she knew. Shaking her head, she said, "Show me your eye."

"Glad I still have one to show you."

The Decline

When the phone rang and the caller identified herself as Gina Mirth, the nurse from Cedar Crest, my response was, "Your calls are never good."

"I know," she acknowledged. "I am sorry to tell you that your mom has suffered a heart attack and is back in Pompton Plains Hospital. She is in ICU, and they tell me she is stable, but the next twenty-four hours are critical."

"Okay, thanks, Gina, on my horse."

In the car, I thought, This is what Ma was talking about—once a hip is broken, old people start to decline rapidly. We had been going to outpatient hip rehab three times a week for about a month now, and she was slowly getting stronger. She moved slowly, but she was determined not to be bedridden or in a wheelchair.

"Gotta keep it moving," she would tell me as we walked up the little rehab ramps and the five-step obstacle course. She sat in the car seat at the facility and practiced getting in and out and used the three-pronged walker for balance. "I hate being here," she said, "having to listen to all these other people. They are nothing but gripers."

She probably griped more than anyone, but I had to hand it to her—no one worked harder at recovery. She would have completed outpatient in three days if all had gone well. Now, the heart attack would probably stop that plan.

When I got to ICU, she was awake but groggy.

"Sonny Boy, get me the hell out of here."

"Ma, take it easy, you just had a heart attack, and they want you to rest."

"Is that what happened? Je-sus Christ, I remember a lot of people, and then it gets all fuzzy."

"They tell me it wasn't a very big heart attack and no surgery is necessary, but you have to rest, and then we'll see about getting you out of the hospital."

Over the next week, it was evident that my mother had weakened considerably, and there was concern about her ability to use the walker without falling. They wanted her to get a wheelchair.

"Bullshit," she snorted. "I am going to walk out of here."

We continued the rehab for her hip while she was hospitalized, but she was noticeably slower and got tired very easily. I consulted with everyone, and the consensus was that it was better for her to keep moving, but there were significant risks involved. I told her that she had to show everyone here that she could navigate ramps and doors and that would determine if she could go back to her apartment.

In the world, there were few like Ma, as she possessed an inner strength that at times went against all the odds. Within a month she was almost back to pre-heart attack strength, and she walked out again from the hospital door to my car.

"Well, Sonny Boy, I did it. No damn heart attack or hip is going to stop me," she proudly proclaimed.

"Nobody like you, Ma."

"This was harder than the goddamn knee, but I needed that knee done."

"I remember. Not many people replace their knees at age eighty-eight."

"I was going to Russia for my ninetieth, and the old knee would have stopped me."

"And you did it and drank vodka in Kremlin Square."

"I sure did and had some caviar and crackers with it. Made me damn proud to be there on a good knee. Too bad there was no more czar, as that Moscow is one grand place, with its elegant ballrooms and grand old hotels."

"Ma!"

In the days to come, she would move slower but as deliberate as ever.

When I visited her, now back again in her apartment, I made her walk to the community dining room, just so she would get out. To her credit, she got fully dressed—makeup, wig, and jewelry.

"This is my son," she would tell the assembled seniors. "He drove me crazy for years, but he is true blue."

"Ma, knock it off," I'd admonish her. "No one gives a damn about that stuff."

She always thought I had good looks, and I think she was getting some secondary gain from being seen with me. Of course, it had to do with her, because who else produced this being but her?

She seemed satisfied with being back in the apartment and soon told me she did not need the nurse or the aide any longer, because she had passed the independency test.

We modified the schedule; we kept Thelma for daytimes but made Ma wear a first-alert button. This button connected to the emergency nursing staff of the facility, and they had trained EMTs to answer the alarm.

She was back in her apartment, and everything, once again, was running smoothly.

46

I Have No Luck at Funerals

Ma was doing well and seemed to have adjusted to walking slowly. She made sure she got her exercise every day. When I got to the apartment, she gave me her usual shopping list. I went to the local supermarket and came back with her food for the week.

As we put away the food, she asked, "What do you think is going to happen at my funeral?"

I knew where she was going with this, as the family history with funerals was bizarre. I just played along. "When are you going to die?" I asked.

"Whenever I choose."

"Whatever season it is will determine my answer," I told her.

"Oh, okay, this winter, if I'm lucky."

"Then there will be a crippling blizzard that day."

"Right, what if I make it to spring?"

"Then it will be the worst rainstorm seen in fifty years."

"This is good, and if its summer?"

"Now you are setting me up. You know it will be 106 degrees with high humidity, and there will be a monstrous traffic jam caused by all the overheated cars."

"Love it. Wouldn't have it any other way." she said happily.

"And if you make it to the fall, then it will be the worst hurricane ever recorded in New Jersey."

"Nothing but the finest to send me out."

"And as a bonus, if you make it to next winter, it will be so cold that day that none of the cars will start, or if they do, the road will be full of ice, and the hearse will smash into a guard rail."

"Now you're talkin'."

Our conversation was deadpan and fun. Let me tell you what we actually have been through at funerals.

I awoke on the first day of spring in my sixteenth year to a heavy, wet snowstorm. The schools had already closed for the day. My father, stubborn in his proud way, was getting dressed to go to work. I was afraid he would have another heart attack if he went in today.

His second heart attack had been especially brutal for me, as he and I were on the D train going to a Yankees game, when he grabbed his chest and fell to the floor. I got him out of the train, with help, onto the platform, and waited until the police and the emergency paramedics took him by ambulance to Saint Claire's Hospital. I was ten years old. I went in the police car, terrified and alone, and waited in the hospital emergency room by myself, until my mother arrived. I don't know how long that took, because I was still suffering from trauma from my earlier hospital visits and did not want to look at anyone. This time it felt exceptionally cruel. For a long time after that, I could not go into the subway or hospitals.

Dr. Fialk, my father's doctor, had an office in Union City, New Jersey. We went there religiously, my father and I. It was a dark office, with closed-in windows and heavy dark drapes. Fialk was a tiny man with a mustache, like my father. At the end of the cursory examination, Fialk, puffing on his cigarette, would look across the desk, lean in toward my father, and say, "Ludmer"—cough, cough, cough, throat clear—"you have to stop smoking." His hoarse voice crackled.

Normally, this would be a funny Saturday Night Live bit, and everyone would laugh. But this was real. On the way out one day, I said to my father, "If it's no good for you to smoke, why is he still doing it?"

My father just answered honestly, "I don't listen to him."

And there you have the doctor and the patient in a nutshell.

My last memory of my father is his standing at the top of the stairs on this first day of spring. I was begging him not to go to work. The boss knew of his heart condition, and he was under doctor's orders to not walk in snow or sand, as it was too taxing for his very-beaten-up heart. My mother admonished him also that it was "too hard a day to go," but he forcefully brushed me back with his left arm and went down the stairs. Forty-five minutes later, the police rang our bell to tell us that he'd had another heart attack, this time in the Port Authority Bus Terminal in New York, and had been taken to St. Claire's Hospital. Again.

This would be my last trip to St. Claire's Hospital, because when we got there, we were told that he was already dead. The next week, Ma made me go to his New York office and get all the things from his desk. I wondered if I was really old enough for this and feared it might damage me somehow down the road.

The funeral was a haze for me, as it was three days of fear, crying, and periodic panic attacks. Each friend who entered Leber's Funeral Home brought on another wave of tears. Most of the time, my main feeling was numbness, as if it were not actually happening but more like a dream or a movie, in that I was just watching the people walk by with their mouths moving, but I couldn't hear them. My father was well known in town, as was my entire family, and the crowds were huge. He and I were very popular local people. I was recognized for my sports ability and as the kid who was on the Happy Felton's Knothole Gang, the baseball competition show that aired before every Brooklyn Dodger home game. (The day I was on the show, I met all the players, including Gil Hodges, Pee Wee Recse, Roy Campanella, and Duke Snider, and Jackie Robinson gave me his bat.)

My father was a man with an ever-present smile and was thought to be kind and considerate; a good man.

What made this funeral over the edge was my mother's lifelong friend, Edith Greene, wife of King Features Syndicate general manager, Ward Greene, who was my father's boss. (Ward wrote Lady and the Tramp, which was made into a Disney movie.) Edith came to the first night of the wake and then, on her way home from the funeral parlor, was killed in a head-on crash with a drunk driver. So after we buried my father, we went to Aunt Edith's funeral.

Ma was a wreck, and years later, some said that she never was the same again. I felt numb for a long time and wondered if two deaths in two days was just bad luck or if something more mystical was in play. Living with Ma was difficult after that, as she barely spoke or got out of bed. She stayed that way for almost two years. Life turned so quickly for me after my father's death that I really did not know what to think. I only knew that we were poor, and I had lost my support in my survival battle with my mother. My future? Fat chance.

Nanny was next. She had lived a long and fruitful life and was eighty-three when she died of kidney failure. I loved Nanny with all my heart, and this loss was very difficult for me. Now, my mother had to go to Florida and make arrangements for Nanny to be brought back to Leber's.

As it turned out, there was a problem on the day Nanny was to be buried: the hearse drivers were on strike. This was a delicate conversation between the funeral director and the family. He knew our family and after asking how we all were doing, he tried to explain the situation. We could not use the union drivers, he told us, and no other driver would cross the picket line—this was New Jersey, and the Teamsters Union, the local 560, a noted Mafia-infested union (which later was indicted for pension-fund violations) was making the ruling.

So Mr. Harry Leber, the longtime friend of the family, had to get a personal guarantee from the union official, so that we could go bury Nanny.

They agreed to let a nonunion driver do the task if we paid "a union waiver fee", which we agreed to do. It was then arranged that we would take Nanny to the cemetery the following day.

When we arrived at the funeral parlor, however, the director called us into the office. Now there was a problem at the cemetery. The grave diggers were on strike. We could go to the cemetery, but they would not lower Nanny. They would put Nanny near her resting spot, and she'd be covered by a tarp—under the watchful eye of no one—and when the strike was over, we could return, and they would lower her. We had to go the next day, because the union had said, "No bodies come in or go out of the funeral parlor after tomorrow." We agreed; we went to the cemetery and left Nanny on the ground and went home.

The look in Ma's eyes was priceless. No one needed to say a word. Two days later, we returned—a free ride from the funeral director— and we watched as Nanny was lowered.

My feeling about funerals was already formed, and I knew anything could happen at funerals. Ma kept shaking her head.

Pop-Pop was next. He died one year later, at age ninety, because he did not want to live without Nanny. The funeral director at Leber's told us how sorry he was about the fiasco with Nanny. We all hoped that this one went off without a hitch. We had begged Pop-Pop to live to his ninetieth birthday, as he had said three months after Nanny died that he wanted to die. He promised to live until his birthday, which he did, and then died within eighteen days. (Both he and my mother knew there is an internal switch that you can flip.)

This time, there were no union problems or strikes, and the wake went off as planned. The funeral director whispered to my mom as we left with Pop-Pop that he was glad there were no problems.

My mother and I were very calm on the ten-mile ride to the cemetery. Compared to what we had been through at the other funerals, this one was easy.

We were on Route 4, going to the cemetery in Paramus, when the back left tire of the hearse blew out. Ma and I just laughed. We pulled over to the side of the road, and they called for backup. After a thirty-five minute wait, the service vehicle arrived. They had to take Pop-Pop out of the hearse and lay him on the side of the road while they changed the tire. To make matters worse, it started to rain.

We sat in the limo, watching the horror on the faces of passing motorists. Some look so pained that we felt bad for them. Others had their hands over their mouths, although we didn't know if it was because they didn't want to laugh or were so stunned at this sight that they did not know how to react. We were calm and tried to figure out what it was with this family and funerals.

Once the tire was changed, they put Pop-Pop back in the hearse and delivered us to the cemetery. We told Nanny that Pop-Pop didn't want to be upstaged by her. He always had to have the last word anyway. Not many families laugh on the way home from a funeral, but we did.

We hadn't had a funeral in the family for twenty years after Pop-Pop died, when my father's youngest sister, Helen, died at the age of ninety-two. She was Jewish, and I made the arrangements with her rabbi. It would be a simple matter of picking up the body at the funeral parlor and driving to Queens for her burial. In the back of my mind, I knew something was going to happen. I did not know what, but I would have bet on it; something would happen, even though this one looked like it had the best chance to be normal. The family met the rabbi in northern New Jersey. There was the limo for the family that would follow the hearse, across the George Washington Bridge to Flushing, Queens, near the site of the World's Fair and old Shea Stadium. We lined up at the funeral parlor and waited for the hearse to pull away.

Out of the funeral parlor came the rabbi, who walked to the driver of the hearse and leaned over to speak with him. I said to everyone in the limo, "Here we go again."

After the rabbi and the driver conferred, the driver got out, and the rabbi came back to the family car. "There has been a mix-up," he told us. "This hearse driver was not supposed to do this run, because he was to drive another hearse. The replacement driver is on his way, but don't worry. Your limo driver is free to take you to the cemetery and you can meet up with the hearse there."

"You mean we're to leave now and go to the cemetery without the body?" I asked.

"Yes," he said. "The replacement hearse driver will most likely catch up to you, or pass you on the way, as he is very reliable."

"Really?"

"Most assuredly, it will be fine."

We left for the cemetery, but as you might have guessed, the replacement driver never showed. They had to scurry to find yet another backup, and he ran into midday traffic. So we sat at the cemetery for ninety minutes, awaiting the body.

It's not every day that a bereaved family claps when a relative's dead body shows up at a cemetery. But you have to admit, I just don't have any luck at funerals.

War Begins

Ma and Thelma were eating cake when I arrived, and they offered me a piece.

"Sonny Boy," Ma said, "Thelma cannot believe that you and I ever were at war with each other. She is amazed by how much you do for me, and you don't seem to mind."

"And?" I prompted.

"And how can that be if we were at war?" Ma finished.

"Did you tell her about it?" I asked.

"No, I don't remember all the specific details."

"That's right, Mr. Ken," Thelma said. "I can't believe you two ever had bad times, as you are two sides of the same sandwich."

"Whoa, Thelma, stop right there," I said. "Too much comparison to her will have me back in therapy! It took years for me to overcome my feelings about Ma, but all I will say is that was then, and this is now."

"Oh, stop with the dramatics and save that for your sister," Ma scolded. "Just tell what happened, okay?"

"You sure you want to hear this, Ma?"

"Let 'er fly, Sonny Boy."

"Okay, then ..."

Our war began in 1958, as Ma was depressed and angry at being alone at age forty-five. She had buried her husband and her best friend within four days. Who, except a trained professional with a bag of not-yet-existent antidepression medication, could help her? Certainly not her barely sixteen-year-old son. When she wasn't crying or sleeping in her bed, she was yelling at me. Not that I was a bad kid, but my timing was different than hers, and a few months after my father died, I started to mobilize and live my life, which had a big upside potential and a confusing, isolated, and fearful downside.

I needed her, and she just wasn't there. Looking back as an adult, I can see it clearly. Then, as a confused sixteen-year-old, I needed a mom, and there was none to be found, and I was angry. First I lost my father and then my mother. She was not available for anything. It really hurt, as she wouldn't even watch baseball with me, which is something that was very centrally connected between us. It was my mother, not my father, who introduced me to baseball. I still can see her setting up the ironing board in the living room and putting on the TV to watch the Yankees in the World Series. She explained all the rules and knew all the players. She would point out Joe DiMaggio to me and yell, "Joltin' Joe!" when he came to the plate.

We had a special bond and could talk baseball with the best of them. She loved the game and encouraged me to play. We talked baseball all the time.

In high school, I started on the varsity team. She dragged herself to my games, but the life was missing in her, and then we stopped talking about the games. Then she stopped watching the Yankees. It was a very big loss for me.

She told me about two months after my father died that she had nothing more to give me, as I knew right from wrong, and I'd just have to find my own way. She told me I had to learn how to be a man.

I was sixteen. I said I understood, but I did not really grasp what she was saying. What she meant was that she was lost and overwhelmed and was just about able to care for herself. Taking care of me was just too much for her.

I had no other males to turn to for help. I was surprised that my father's older brother did not try step in, but he didn't. Neither did any of the men on my father's side of the family. My mother's brother was "slow," so he wouldn't be any help. My mother's father was now in Florida, and he was no help to me growing up, except for showing me how to fish when I was a kid. Plus, Pop-Pop couldn't read. So there was no one.

And then our war began.

I would ask Ma to get out of bed. Then I would plead with her to get out of bed. Then I would try to entice her to get out of bed as I filled the kitchen with aromas from my newly developed skill of cooking. Nothing worked. Then I would scream at her to get out of bed. She screamed back. Then we stopped talking. I would leave the house in a huff, with a loud door slam.

From then on, I rarely told her where I was going, because I was convinced that she truly did not give a damn. I was feeling sorry for myself and gave up trying to change her. I went about my business of being a teenage boy. I had friends, and sports, and then there was my first girlfriend, Terry. Her family mostly took me in, and they were so kind and loving. I am forever thankful for Terry and that year of true love and first intimacy, and for her wonderful mother, who always treated me warmly.

Ma barely noticed that I wasn't home a lot. She knew I was changing, because I now stood up to her autocratic ways and defended myself from her physically. The first time I grabbed her arm as she tried to hit me, I remember telling her, "You will never be able to hit me again."

She had tried to kick me, and I jumped back and just glared at her, telling her she was useless as a mother and that someone should punish her.

We nearly stopped talking to each other. The apartment was a two-floor configuration, with me sleeping in the attic area, which had a bedroom and a half-bathroom (a sink and a toilet). The stairs were in the hall, and her apartment had a separate entrance door. So I could go past her apartment and go directly upstairs to my own room without setting foot in her apartment. Her bathroom was outside in the hall and that had a shower, so I could even use the shower without seeing her.

I only needed her apartment for the kitchen, and I would go there when she was not home. I'd make many sandwiches and keep them in my upstairs room. Most of the time I ate at Terry's, or I ate out. Ma left money for me on the dining room table if I completed the list of chores she had assigned by leaving me a note.

We talked less and less, and after two years of this, she started to date. I was unable to understand that. I was eighteen and it was too difficult for me, as I felt, wrongly, that she was being disloyal to my father. So I would never meet anyone who came to the apartment to pick her up. They did try to engage me, but I was having none of it. Too bad for me, because I really needed an older male. The dates weren't around for long anyway, and I was not going to get attached to any of them for that reason alone. That's the way it was.

Ma was coming out of her depression and tried to talk to me, but I was totally furious with her for having abandoned me, and I was not going to let her back in. This situation screamed for counseling and therapy, but this was long before anything like that was accepted. We were two suffering people, unable to share our angst and grief.

I think my sister recognized the problem, but Ma refused all professional help, saying she did not have money for that kind of thing. I found this out years later, as my sister, who by then was married with a child, was also mad at Ma for not being there for her and her child.

At least my sister had an adult view of this, because she was ten years older than me and could appreciate, at least to some degree, my mother's situation. I could not at that time. Later, in my twenties, I felt guilty for not understanding Ma's situation, but I also remained angry, as she was the adult and should have known I needed guidance. Many years later, she told me it was because she thought I had a level head and was strong and therefore, I would be okay. Ten years of my issues with substance abuse proved that wrong.

At this point in my story, Ma barked, "Well, I had my own life to contend with, and I was scraping by financially, with a teenage son and a married daughter who was having babies."

"That's it in a nutshell, Ma," I said. "We were both hurting, but neither one of us got any help. But I held you responsible for me, as you were still my mother and should have known how this effected me."

"You turned out all right," she declared.

"Not the point, Ma, I turned out all right because I paid for my own therapy and never gave up on myself. You always were about you, Ma, and rarely did you ask any real questions about how I was doing."

"I didn't know any better."

"That is the truth, Ma, and that's the reason I was able to come to terms with my feelings about you and your lack of parenting. I did not blame you, once I understood you were doing the best you could, given your circumstances."

"Miss Alicia," Thelma interjected, "he was a boy, and you treated him like he was a grown man."

"Thank you, Thelma," I said. "That was what my female therapist said.

"Well, bully for her," Ma snorted.

"See, Thelma?" I said pointedly. "She still doesn't get it."

My Attic, Ray Charles, and the Blues

It was eerily quiet in Ma's apartment during the two years after my father died. My mother never put on the TV or the radio or played any music. The only time I heard her was when someone called on the phone.

I was upstairs in the attic, in my bedroom, almost all the time when I was home. The room had very slanted walls on which I hung my Yankees posters. It had two big windows that faced the street, and I kept them open, even in winter. I bought my first phonograph player, an RCA, and played my 45s and 33s endlessly. The music had a wonderful reverberating sound.

When Ma spoke, it usually was to say, "Turn down that damn music."

I was trying to drown out all the noise in my head, which was one fearful thought after another. I had just turned sixteen, and my view of my future was bleak at best.

We had no money, and my father's life insurance was paltry. My mother worked at the library a few days a week. I had no relatives, except Nanny, to talk to, and the kids at school avoided me. I did not know at the time that they were uncomfortable around me, because they did not know what to say to me. I took it personally and thought they suddenly didn't like me. That deepened my wounds even more. It was very tough times, and I was very alone and scared stiff. I no longer felt like everyone else, and my stomach never stopped hurting.

I got through that spring because I focused on playing baseball, and then it was summer. I still had my summer job in New York City, where I'd worked since age fourteen in the mailroom at my father's former employer, King Features Syndicate. It was over on East 45th Street, a block from the United Nations. At lunchtime, they showed movies in the wonderfully air-conditioned UNICEF Theater. The job also required me to deliver copy to writers in their apartments all over Manhattan and Brooklyn, so I learned the bus and subway system. After work, I would linger at the many music and book stores on my way back to the Port Authority Bus Terminal, which was a difficult place for me now. On this particular day at the music store, I saw an album, Ray Charles, Live at Newport. It looked interesting, as the cover depicted someone wailing on a saxophone. I bought it.

When I played it for the first time, I experienced a feeling that I never had before. It was very powerful, and before the album was finished, I was crying. The song "Georgia on My Mind" made me go to a place that was peaceful and serene, yet sad in some way. The upbeat track "I Got a Woman" made me dance, and I kept tapping to the beat. I was so intrigued by this man, Ray Charles, that I borrowed books about him.

I found out he was a black man from the South who went blind early in his childhood. His mother sent him away to a school for the blind, and he was raised basically without parents. I felt bad for him. His music was a calling to me and shortly afterward, in talking to the people at the record store, I was referred to the blues section. I don't think I ever was the same again. I started going to jazz clubs in New York, and although I was underage, they let me in. Who checks for ID proof at a jazz club?

I saw Miles Davis, John Coltrane, Cannonball Adderley, Peggy Lee, Stan Getz, Nina Simone, Ahmad Jamal, Olatunji, Art Blakey and the Jazz Messengers, the Modern Jazz Quartet, Dave Brubeck Quartet, and Thelonious Monk. I saw Ella Fitzgerald. I learned about Oscar Peterson. The music in my attic was now subdued, and there was no need to drown out the feelings, as this music was talking to them.

I remember my first night at the famous jazz club Birdland on West Fifty-Second Street. The master of ceremonies introduced himself as Symphony Sid, and he said he had a radio show at midnight on the last station on the AM dial. I started listening, and it became a real problem for me to get up and go to school, as I was listening to the show to way past three in the morning. He would interview all the musicians from the world of blues and jazz, and I could not get enough of it. My high school friends were listening to rock 'n' roll, but I considered that daytime music, because the nights, for me, belonged to the blues, jazz, and soul.

I tried to get my friends to go with me to the clubs, but they said their parents would never let them go, so I went on my own. My mother was asleep downstairs as I crept quietly down my stairs, past her apartment and out into the night on most Fridays or Saturdays. I took the bus to Port Authority, and then it was a ten-minute walk to most of the clubs. I'd get the last bus home at two in the morning and stealthily climb the stairs, without Ma ever knowing that I had left. I was finding my own world, full of musicians who spoke to me. It soothed the injuries inside as I learned about loss and pain from a very different perspective. The music healed me in so many ways and yet kept some pain very much in the forefront. I learned about Delta blues and Chicago blues. I listened to early recordings of black men playing guitars in tiny blacks-only clubs. I went to Small's Paradise in Harlem and was one of three white people in the place. The bouncer laughed when he let me in.

"Know where you are going, kid?" he asked.

"Sure do, sir. It's about the feel of the music."

"Good for you, kid. Good for you."

The Adventures Start

Ma was complaining that she didn't enjoy her soaps on TV anymore. She had started to become mildly confused on some days, and she dealt with it by just going to sleep. Thelma kept a close eye on her and said that compared to almost anyone else of Ma's age, she was in very good mental shape.

On this day when I visited, Ma was having a good day and was making my favorite meal, veal cutlet parmesan.

"You know, Sonny Boy," she said as she worked in the kitchen, "I was thinking about all your hitchhiking. I've probably never heard all of your stories, or if you told them to me, I have forgotten most of them."

Thelma was in the kitchen with us, and Ma looked at her and said, "This kid of mine took off, with absolutely nothing, to hitchhike across America when he was twenty-three years old." She looked back at me, saying, "Isn't that right?"

"Well, I had a knapsack and some basics."

"Weren't you afraid you'd be killed?" Thelma asked.

"No, I was a total romantic and had heard all the stories about young men going on the road. It was just my turn to do it."

"Tell Miss Thelma and me how it started," Ma coaxed.

"You mean the first day?"

"Yeah. Go ahead."

I settled myself at the kitchen table and began my tale. "Well, ladies …"

Before I took to the road, my life was full of failure. I had flunked out of college after two years, after having been on academic and social probation for three straight semesters. After returning to Nanny's old apartment, as she was now in Florida, I worked full time in the watchmaking factory and went to school part-time. Then there was the Saturday job selling Bibles door-to-door in the tattered sections of the working poor who were living in Elizabeth, Linden, and Rahway, New Jersey. In my final two years of college, I worked at UPS from four in the morning until noon, cleaning the bathrooms and getting up the truck grease, before going to college in the afternoon and studying until passing out by nine in the evening. I finally got my degree, and then the road was calling. It had been an emotional hell for me the last seven years, and the last three were the worst, so going on a blind adventure looked like heaven to me.

This was in 1965, and all my yearnings to see what was out there had hit a peak. Everything I was reading had some story about the road. The folk singers sang about it. The film makers had a genre called road movies. The beat poets spoke of rambling from place to place. Kerouac's On the Road put me over the top. Bob Dylan told us, "The times they are a-changing." I knew about freight trains, and there was ride sharing, but I wanted to do it the old-school way—just stick out your thumb and go.

America was in the beginning of major change, as we were still reeling from the JFK assassination, and Lyndon Johnson was getting us involved in the war in Vietnam. Racial violence was increasing, and Detroit had seen the riots. It wasn't the safest of times to hit the road, but I said every generation has its issues, and this was mine.

I would learn many lessons on this adventure, some strictly about the art and science of hitchhiking and the others about life itself. My life felt like crap at this point because it was about loss, failure, and nonstop work, and I needed something very different.

I had a small knapsack with a change of clothes, basic toiletries, a straight razor, some Band-Aids, and a comb. The one thing for which I am so thankful was my desire to journal every ride. I had a notebook and two pens. I did not know at the time what I would do with this information, but I thought maybe one day I'd write a book about it. I had seventy-five dollars in my pocket when I headed to California.

I started the journey in New York City's Midtown and tried to get my first ride by the Lincoln Tunnel. No one would even look at me. Then the cops told me to get my ass outta there. I realized this might be more difficult than I had thought. I went a few blocks away from the tunnel on Tenth Avenue and made a primitive sign with my pen and notebook paper that read "USA."

My first ride was in a bread truck. The kid driving it was just going to the other side of the tunnel in New Jersey. The journey had begun.

It took only ten minutes after he dropped me off before I got the next ride—this one from two brothers who were driving their parents' Chrysler to Pittsburgh. They had to stop first in Philadelphia, which was a little out of the way, but I was happy to start my log, and I had already had two rides.

The brothers were open and friendly, and the ride went quickly to Philly. Once there, we stopped in South Philly, and one brother left us in the car. When he came back, he had a terrific-looking girl with him, and she got in the backseat with me.

"This is our sister, Megan," he said.

The four of us took the Pennsylvania Turnpike to Pittsburgh. It was a longer ride that I had expected, taking the entire day, but I got to know this very happy and fun-loving family. Their Pittsburgh parents were celebrating Dad's birthday. As I was to find out, there are many kind, helpful, and thoughtful people in this country who reach out to strangers and help them.

It was near sunset when we arrived, and the brothers would not let me go. I was tired from not much sleep the night before, and Brad, the driver, said he would ask Dad if it was all right for me to stay the night.

I really was torn, as I did not know the protocol for this type of thing, but they were concerned about my hitching after sunset and, quite honestly, so was I. Not only did I join this family for dinner, but they gave me a guest bedroom in their very lovely home. The Johnson family were hard-working and extremely well mannered and kind. I kept saying thank you for everything, and the father finally said, "Just one thank-you will suffice."

I thanked him.

They appeared to be a straightforward, no-nonsense type of family. The dad was a rugged plaid-shirt-wearing, straight-talking guy who had the respect of his family. The mom was more docile and sweet-looking, with her housedress and sneakers. Everyone talked about work and responsibilities. They loved the fact that I was on a cross-country adventure, and the dad told everyone that the trip would be good for me.

In the morning, Brad dropped me off near the entrance to the turnpike, and the next ride came quickly. I was really shocked by how easy it really was. The trucker who picked me up was hauling lawn mowers and machinery. He was headed to Cincinnati. We made it to Columbus and stopped for lunch. I was surprised to see that Ohio did not look much different from New Jersey. Similar gas stations and towns, and the restaurants all looked familiar.

Mack, the trucker, had been a long-haul driver for fifteen years, and he told me so much about the open road and about hitchers in general. He gave me good tips about where to hitch, like from diners and gas stations, rather than from the open road. That made sense. It felt like I had a male parent, which felt odd but very good. He said I probably should get a poncho, in case of rain showers, and carry a small roll of toilet paper. Oh yeah, that was a very good thing to have.

Bathrooms on the road didn't always have paper, and sometimes I didn't even have a bathroom. He also suggested getting a small first-aid kit with iodine. A small sewing kit would be helpful, too. "On the road, you never know when you may need it," he advised, "but it's good to have." I had not even considered that, which shows how green I was when I started the trip.

Mack bought me lunch in Columbus at my first Union 76 truckers stop. I could not believe the size of this huge cafeteria, filled with men in jeans and boots, Their convenience store had everything from magazines to flashlights to camping equipment, as well as food in cans and every type of bad-weather clothing. I bought a plastic poncho and a small traveler's first-aid kit. That made Mack smile.

We got back in the semi and were on the move once again.

Cincinnati was my first disappointing gulp. It was an industrial-looking town with a dilapidated appearance. For some reason, I had always thought of Ohio as prosperous America, but this severely altered that view. Mack said they had an unattractive downtown, and the city was suffering. It was late afternoon when he dropped me off, and I thanked him for all his help. I now had a choice: go northwest to Indianapolis or southwest to Louisville.

I decided to have a cup of coffee and think this out. In the diner, I met a waitress named Louise, who was to become the prototype for my information on the road. Other than the truckers, the waitresses were a highly valuable source of information about the local area and sometimes life itself. After I'd had about three cups of coffee, Louise said that she got off at five, so why didn't I hang around, and we could have a drink or something.

Is this how it is going to be? I thought. Am I going to be dating on this adventure? I asked myself if she was some kind of mass murderer and would bring me home, and then a big monster guy would come in and rob me or beat me to death. Or was she truly just a waitress, a person who wanted a few drinks and some company? I said okay, and we went to a local joint she knew, where we talked.

Louise was my age, maybe a year or two older, and was very direct yet unassuming. She had a quick wit and was sexy in an understated way. Her shiny brown hair and soft green-blue eyes were very appealing. She was working at the diner to get extra money to open her own business with her girlfriend. They worked five days at a salon and were going to open their own in about a year. This woman worked six days a week, and some of those days were fourteen hours long. I was impressed. She was the second person who told me she liked my spirit of adventure and wished that she could do it.

Louise and I shot some pool and drank some beers, which she insisted on paying for. I was not use to that at all. She told me that I would probably need that money. She figured I had enough for half the trip I'd planned. That scared me, because I thought she knew about money more than I did. All I really knew was that I would work or shoot pool or darts, if it got to that point, because that was how I made money in college, in Wilkes-Barre, Pennsylvania.

By this time, Louise said that it was too late for me to hitch, and I was welcome to crash at her place. I no longer was afraid of the killer monster, so I took her up on her invitation. She put me on a sleeper couch, and I slept very soundly. She woke me about four in the morning, and then she put her hand out. I got my bearings and just looked at her. She said nothing but offered her hand again, a little closer. I reached out, and without either of us saying a word, I followed her to her room.

If someone had told me that I would be sleeping with a woman in Cincinnati about forty-two hours after leaving New York, I would have considered it beyond any rational thought. I had a few vague fantasies about maybe meeting women somewhere, but my main objective was the road experience. I never realized that this was part of that experience.

I was internally excited that I was already in western Ohio after two days, that I had met a truly nice family in Pittsburgh and a great long-hauler, and that now I was in bed with a very warm and generous, kind woman. After making love, we fell asleep. She got up before me, and the smell of bacon and coffee woke me up.

Man, do I like this hitchhiking thing, I thought, smiling. Louise was smiling as well as she thanked me for the night. I could not believe my good fortune. We ate breakfast and then she took me back to the diner. We said good-bye, and she told me to stop by on my way back. I chose Indianapolis as my next destination.

As it turned out, I never got back there, though I always wanted to see how she was, and I wondered if she ever got that salon. I'll bet she did.

At this point in my story, Ma told Thelma, "This kid of mine always landed on his feet. People were always kind to him. It's like he had some crazy luck, or maybe it was his father's spirit protecting him. I don't know … I don't know, but he met so many people who fed him, put him up in their homes, and gave him good advice. He was protected from harm."

"Had I really known what I didn't know," I admitted, "I probably never would have gone, but such is life. We learn as we go along."

California's Mexicans

O ver the next weeks, Ma seemed to be holding her own. It was sad, however, to see her slowly lose interest in her appearance, which was her pride for all of her life, especially after she married Geno. He would take her to all the New York hotels for dinner, and they would then go to Broadway. Geno was a trumpet player and for years, he played in the lounges of New York's major hotels with the Eddie Lane Orchestra. Ma would put on an expensive dress and display all her fine jewelry.

Before her world trips, she would boast, "If I am going to Paris, they better be ready to add one more beautiful woman." Ma became a world traveler, and the amount of her luggage would rival Rosalind Russell, or today's Madonna or Lady Gaga.

No lightweight, my mother; she did everything with a flair. She had style and elegance, and she always wanted the spotlight. Not bad for a poor immigrant's daughter who lived behind a picture-framing shop in a two-room apartment. It was the Queen Mary for her and the Concorde, the superfast SST that zoomed across the Atlantic Ocean. Dinner was at the Four Seasons, and dessert could be at the Cafe des Artistes. She had her hair done at the Waldorf, and she shopped on Madison and Fifth Avenues.

Now, she barely bothered to put on lipstick, and if she put on her wig at all, it would be a little crooked, and Thelma and she would spat about it.

On one of my visits, she sat in her easy chair while tinkering with an empty perfume bottle. "So, Sonny Boy," she said, "how's your kids?"

"Fine, Ma. Josh is finishing college, and Aly has just started."

"They are in college already? I must be slipping. The last I remember, Aly was playing soccer."

"They are almost full grown now."

"Well, give them my love."

"I will."

This conversation took a lot out of me, because it was the source of many arguments between us. I wanted my kids to have a grandmother and for them to feel the unconditional love that I got from mine. But my mother was not Nanny.

When my mother would call the house, she would speak to me and ask me how the kids were, instead of asking to speak directly to them. It was not that she didn't love them, but just as she had with me, she could never show it directly. She would say to me that she didn't know what they liked or what they did, and she didn't want to sound like a stranger.

That was the point; she really was a stranger to them—some mysterious woman they knew who globe-trotted and told stories of Rio de Janeiro, Paris, Buenos Aires, Tokyo, and Honolulu. So I would coach her on what to say, but then she would get exasperated and tell me that she was "too old for this grandmother stuff."

Telling her she was their only grandmother fell on deaf ears.

It irked me to see her dote on my sister's grandkids, who were younger than my kids by fifteen years. Ma would play with them and enjoy them. Then one day, I figured it out. As long as they were little kids and listened and didn't ask adult questions, she could be there. It was what she told me one day that rang the bell. She said she really enjoyed me as a child, but then I started to not listen.

I was fine as long as I did what she said, in her way, on her schedule. But once I started to think for myself, I became a problem for her. We went at it like cats and dogs for years. I would ask normal questions, and her answers were authoritative and irrational. Mostly, they were of the "because I said so" variety.

That was good parenting at some point and lousy parenting most of the time. She would never explain her reasons, and that led me to think less of her and demand an explanation. I became too much for her, and once she could no longer hit me, she lost all her authority over me. I would have listened to the reasons why she believed her way was best, if she had only explained them, but truth be told, she did not know why she believed what she did. It was just the way she was raised. Her father was illiterate and an immigrant, unfamiliar with the social norms of America, and Nanny worked locally, sewing in a lace manufacturing shop, while she ran the framing shop. They relied on instinct and the old-country ways in raising my mother.

Ma was unprepared to cope with this new generation of American kids who were doing things very different from the previous generation. These were the baby boomers who became the anti-war movement, the fighters for civil rights and women's rights and gender rights. They were not the do-what-you-are-told-to-do generation.

Ma looked up at me from her chair and asked, "Exactly when did you do all that hitchhiking stuff?"

"What?"

"Don't give me that look, mister. I remember all your stuff very clearly."

"For the record, Ma, I did three hitchhiking trips—one in '65 across America. The second in '69, covering most of the states I didn't see in '65. The third was in '71, in southern Europe and North Africa."

Ma then said something she'd never said before: "I just love hearing your adventures, as they capture perfectly all the balls you had as a young man. Now I think it was really great that you just took off and went to see the world."

"That's not what you said then," I shot back.

"I was your fucking mother. What was I supposed to say?"

"How about, 'be careful, and call me'?"

"Well, I said it now."

"Thank you."

"Now tell Thelma and me about the Mexicans."

"Really?"

"Just tell the nutty story,"

"Si, señora …" I agreed with a grin.

It started with a ride out of San Francisco with a guy who worked in Napa Valley as an electrician. He was going all the way to LA. He smoked way too much, and I kept opening the window, but he never commented on it. We talked about California politics and how crazy he thought the people in LA were—nuts as compared to northern Californians, he'd said. After about one hundred miles, we heard a boom, and smoke started coming out from under the hood. He pulled to the side of the road.

This was a hitchhiker's worst moral dilemma: should I wait with the driver to see if the car could get back on the road, or try to hitch another ride immediately? The last time I had this issue was in Kentucky, when I was traveling with a Georgia peach farmer. We had just stopped at a diner, when he grabbed his upper arm. I knew immediately that he was having a heart attack. I wound up driving the truck to the hospital and spending the night there until his wife showed up the next morning. He survived, and they sent me a crate of peaches for Christmas.

In my current situation, most hikers would leave immediately. That's what I decided to do. But we were on the side of a major highway, California's Highway 1, and hitching was not easy—or legal.

Who came along? A truck full of Mexicans. They stopped to see if they could help. They looked under the hood, and the diagnosis was fatal—a piston rod had shot through the engine, and all the oil was about to drain. The electrician agreed. He would wait for highway patrol, and I jumped in the truck with the Mexicans.

They were a very jovial bunch. They spoke a mixed brand of Spanish and English, which today is referred to as Spanglish. The boys were migrant workers, going to San Diego after having just finished a job. Some of them wanted to go to Tijuana to party. They were passing around a bottle, and when I asked what it was, one of them said, "Señor, es tequila." He told me to lick the top part of my hand, and the guy next to me put salt on it. Then I was told to lick the salt and drink from the community bottle, which I did, and then a lemon wedge appeared, and I was told to bite it. I thought this was really cool.

We stopped at a roadside taco stand, and the boys and I ate a lot of them. Once back in the truck, the guys started singing in Spanish and laughing. They spoke rapidly to each other, what sounded like breaking one another's balls, because the more one guy tried to defend himself, the more the others got louder. I think we were well into the second bottle when I started singing along with them. That bottle or another one went around and around, and that was the last thing I remembered.

When I woke up, I was on a couch. I looked around; I was in a small room behind what seemed like a store. My head had so many questions in it. I was trying to orient myself, when a woman came in from the front and said in Spanish-accented English, "Hello, jou asleep long time."

Did she just say, "Jew sleep long time?" I thought.

I felt my money in my pocket, and my knapsack was right there on the floor. I heard noise from the back room—it was the boys. She gestured that they were playing cards. She walked closer to me and said, "My name es Juanita and jou are in my flower chop."

"Donde?" I asked, wondering where I was.

"Tijuana, señor."

That is when I felt a terrible pain in my head and passed out again.

When I awoke, the boys were still in the back, but the smell of food was overpowering, and I rumbled into the back room. The boys thought I was the funniest thing they had ever seen.

"Mas tequila?" one asked. And they all started laughing again. They invited me to sit down, as they were now eating chili and beans. I ate some of the bread and asked for water. They laughed at that.

"Jou want agua Mexicana?" another asked, and they laughed at that.

The entire experience was well beyond anything that I could have ever imagined. But I was fine. The boys didn't rob me, beat me, kill me, or throw me in a ditch. They, in fact, took care of me. Then they fed me and included me in their nonstop ribbing. The experience solidified my belief in the basic goodness of the majority of people.

I learned, however, to never drink when on a hitch, as you could wake up in another country—at least don't drink tequila from a bottle with Mexicans. I spent the night at Juanita's, and this time, they gave me a rug and blanket on the floor, as the couch was too small. We had huevos rancheros in the morning, and the coffee was divine. The boys offered me a bottle of tequila for the road, but I answered, "No, muchas gracias," and they laughed again. I learned I was only two blocks from the main road that headed back to the States, and I found a family from San Diego, driving a van, to get me back across the border.

Thelma, who had been cutting vegetables as I related this experience, looked at me, shaking her head, and said, "Mr. Ken, I don't believe that story's about you. Don't seem like you would be that dumb, if you don't mind my sayin' so. You lucky you found the right people to take care of you. Gives me the willies thinkin' about it."

"See what I mean, Thelma?" Ma said. "There is a force field protecting this kid. Maybe it's that ghost of his father or something else. But he skirts the edge and always comes out okay. Amazing ... truly amazing."

The Mojave, Ben,
and Little Bird

I just love that story about the Mexicans," Ma said, "and I can laugh at it now because you are safe and sound."

Thelma nodded but said, "Mr. Ken, you was one crazy-ass boy, if you don't mind my saying so."

"Well, ladies, the adventure got even hairier when I headed back East, including the fiasco in the desert."

"Do I know that one?" asked Ma.

"Well, it's really a package deal—all the rides from Los Angeles to Santa Fe."

"I gots time for your storytelling, Mr. Ken," Thelma said, pulling up a chair. "Go on ahead now."

It was time to leave California and head back East. This was going to be a very different ride than the one coming out, because I was going through the hot desert and the southwestern Plains, through some very big states. I got a ride with a salesmen in his midforties. He drove a big ol' Buick with lots of room. He was a straight-looking, shirt-and-tie guy with a short crew cut. Kind of an average, nondescript kind of fellow, the type of guy who never made any waves, a man to make any mother proud.

"Ain't nothin' wrong with that, Mr. Ken," Thelma interjected. She seemed to think this was church, where she should respond with um-hm's and oh yeahs whenever I paused.

I continued …

He said he was going to Oklahoma City and would love someone to talk to. That was one hell of a long hitch, though, and I didn't know if I wanted one ride for that distance. Still, it was a good start, and I could hop off anywhere I chose. This could be a thousand-mile hitch if he turned out to be fun. I wasn't planning to stop in the desert anyway, so off we went.

We went smoothly past Barstow, when the Route 15 sign for Las Vegas caught his eye. Route 15 is the road you take for a direct hit on that neon gambling mecca in the plateau of the mountains. But he passed it and kept going east toward Needles, which is a pit stop in the middle of the Mojave Desert, just before the Arizona border. He said he'd never been in Las Vegas and might take a side tour. I had just had my time of my life with Big Bart in Reno and wanted no part of Las Vegas, not now anyway. He kept talking to himself out loud, and I started to get a sinking feeling that I was in trouble. I make my case for keeping to the plan and getting through the desert.

When we passed the sign for the old state road to Las Vegas, he apparently couldn't take it any longer. He wanted to go to Vegas. "I'm going to go," he said. "You can get another ride at the turnoff."

No matter what I said, he was determined to go to Vegas. I could have gone those hundred miles with him to Vegas, but I knew all kinds of bad things could happen there, and I wanted to see Arizona and New Mexico. So I had to get out.

This was where I learned one of the cardinal rules of hitchhiking: never try to hitch on a highway when cars are going seventy miles per hour. I watch my ride ramble off north on the old two-lane road. I start walking east on Route 66, hoping for a mercy pick up. I was looking for the person who'd say, "I am going to pick up the fool who is hitching on the highway."

No one did.

I spent the night in the Mojave Desert, staring at the stars, which were absolutely breathtaking. I also listened to the increasing traffic whizzing by. You see, most people who know what they are doing go through the desert at night, when the temperature drops thirty degrees or more. Death Valley is not far away from where I was. I figured out why so many people died there. No water. Like me. No water. So I slept in a mixture of soil, rocks, and sand and tiny plants.

In the morning, when the sun came up, there was very little traffic. About eight o'clock or so, local trucks. started cruising by. I was now in full panic mode. I was hungry, thirsty, and itchy from the little ants that bit me in my sleep and were responsible for the rash on both arms and ankles. No longer just a passive thumb sticking out in the air, I went into full-tilt animation. I waved and jumped and flailed my arms.

Hank Peterson, in his 1954 Chevy pickup, saved me. Hank was coming back to Needles from Barstow, and he knew that I was a damn fool in real danger. He knew he had to get me out of there.

He drove me to Needles, where I insisted on buying him lunch. He wouldn't accept it, but he did let me buy him coffee. I hitched easily out of the gas station. Lesson learned. Thank you, Hank.

The next stop was Kingman, Arizona. I arrived there in a VW bus with some college kids who were in a band. They were on summer break. They were a few years younger than me, and they lived in Phoenix. They could take me to Flagstaff before they had to head south. It was a lot different riding with these kids than riding with the Mexicans or anybody else. They were straight American types, no drugs, clean-looking kids with very focused goals. They played in the marching band, got good grades, and might get scholarships for further education. They liked LBJ, as he was a southerner and they told me about Lady Bird Johnson and how she was good for music programs and the arts, in general.

Amazing the facts you pick up on the road. I liked these kids and wished them well. Flagstaff was nothing to speak of, just a dusty little spot in the desert—very hot during the day and just about dead at night. I found a saloon with a pool table, and after getting to know the bartender, I was offered a couch at the house she shared with her brother. She fed me breakfast and even made me a sandwich for the road. This was such a common experience, finding good, down-to-earth people, who were kind and generous.

Arizona was one beautiful place, and the bartender told me I had to absolutely take a side trip north to the Grand Canyon. I figured I had the time.

I hung out at a diner until I found a family who was going to do the one-day trip to the Canyon and back. It was like the ride to Yellowstone—lots of big campers loaded with people, all doing the same thing. The ride was slow, but this was one ride that should have been slow. The red rocks of the Canyon are magma that was formed after the Ice Age cut its way through. Deep waterfalls and multicolored hues were almost indescribable—one picture-postcard view after another. It was a splendid day. The Texas family who took me along with them were humble, not like stereotypical Texans at all.

The father told me that they didn't have this kind of view in Texas, almost as if Texas was supposed to have everything.

I told him we didn't have that view in New York City either.

He laughed. I spent the night on a cot outside their camper, under a little awning that unfolded from its side.

They dropped me off at the same diner where I'd joined them. I was now headed to Albuquerque, New Mexico. I found a couple from Missouri who had taken a trip to California and were headed back. She was a dance teacher, and he was a college professor in St. Louis. The ride through the eastern part of Arizona and the western part of New Mexico has forever stayed with me as the America I read about before it got settled—still rough and majestic and beautiful. Indian country, I thought. I saw many paths that went up the sides of mountains and disappeared into what looked like uninhabitable rock, but the locals said that Indian tribes had lived and flourished there for centuries.

Route 66 is dotted with tiny towns that are so small they just about make the map. A general food store, a gas station, or an inn could be the makeup of these little places, and I loved every one of them. Talk about being isolated. These towns probably have cable connections, cell phones, and satellite dishes now, but then, it still felt like the frontier. I loved the desert and the flowers and cactuses. Sequoias are so beautiful, as they make their stand against the dry, hot climate.

Albuquerque was, to me, a big disappointment. All of a sudden, a huge city rose up out of the sand. In two minutes, there was a double-lane highway with tons of gas stations, billboards, and overhead wires. My first impression was that it was Cincinnati in the sun. It had a cowboy feel to it, but it was Spanish, with too many honky-tonk–looking bars and dilapidated buildings. It was not my fantasy of the great American Southwest. I did not even want to go out and explore. For me to turn down an adventure was new. I had been to so many really interesting places, but this looked more like East St. Louis. So after the Missouri couple dropped me off, I found a cheap rooming house and even spent money on a room, a very rare occurrence on this trip. I had some tacos and went to sleep early.

Everyone who I talked to told me what I was really looking for could be found in Santa Fe and Taos. So the next morning, I was on the road north to Santa Fe. I went to the edge of town and camped at a gas station. An Indian in a good-looking truck said he'd give me a ride. I was so happy to ride with a real Indian. I extended my hand, saying, "My name is Ken."

"Ben," he said as he shook my hand.

Ben? I thought. That's a Jewish name. What the hell is this Indian man doing with a Jewish name? I wanted Sitting Bull or Three Crows. I told him that he was the very first Indian I had ever talked to, and I told him the three facts I knew about Indians. One of the facts was that Indian fathers named their children after the first thing they saw, when they emerged from the birth tepee. He really laughed and said he'd been born in a hospital in Santa Fe. He was named after his mother's father, Ben. He said my historical fact was true, but I was about fifty years behind the times. I then asked him if the other two facts I knew were true: that Indian culture respects and includes its ancestors, and that Indians are great horsemen. He acknowledged both were true.

He did not live in a tepee but had a small house in Santa Fe. He owned a construction business. It was a wonderful ride as he pointed out all the natural features as we passed them. He told me Indians really had it rough with white America, and there was still a strong prejudice and stereotyping of them. He told that me that everyone thought Indians all were drunks. Some were, but it certainly was not the general rule.

When we arrived in Santa Fe, I just could not stop saying wow! Santa Fe was a quaint, artistic city with beauty everywhere—adobe buildings with flowers hanging down long trellises, varied gardens, and multiple statues. He was impressed with my excitement and wonder at all I noticed. He told me I was a unique young man. Then he asked me if it would be all right if he took me home with him for lunch.

I kept saying wow. He just laughed.

Ben took me to his very clean, modest, and orderly home and introduced me to his wife.

"Ken, this is Little Bird."

"Hi, Little Bird, so glad to meet you."

She looked at Ben like he was nuts and said, "Hi, I'm Cheryl."

Then he explained my three facts to Cheryl. We all laughed. It was such a good moment.

Cheryl made us corn, beans, and fried beef with a lettuce and tomato salad. We drank sun tea and had some corn bread. It was lovely, and they both told me where all the best artisans were in Santa Fe. It was another great day.

Ben dropped me off by the town square, which was full of artists showing their works. I spent the entire afternoon walking around, looking at pottery, jewelry, paintings, and handmade leather clothes. This is the Southwest I imagined, I thought. It was beautiful.

I climbed a hill to watch the sun set, feeling at peace with the world.

Ben and Cheryl were probably still laughing.

San Berdo, "No Names, No Bullshit"

Those Indian people was real nice people, Mr. Ken, and I like that he got you good."

"Sure did, Thelma," I agreed. "I have told that story for years and laugh every time."

Ma stopped reading the newspaper and asked, "Was that the trip when you met the showgirl?"

I shook my head. "No, that was on my second trip."

Ma got up to stir the mushrooms she was making for her Italian sauce. She brought the spoon to her mouth and proclaimed, "Needs more garlic."

"A showgirl?" Thelma questioned. "You talkin' bout the ones that be up on the stage with all them sparkly costumes?"

"That's right," I said. "A dancer."

"My Lord, um-um," Thelma said.

"This son of mine, Thelma, has always had no trouble meeting people, especially women." Ma looked over her shoulder at me and said, "Tell her, Hot Shot."

"All right," I said, starting to laugh a bit.

"Oh boy," said Thelma, "this gots to be good."

I chuckled and began, "I was in Las Vegas, walking around downtown's Fremont Street. At that point in time, there were only about six casinos on the Las Vegas Strip—the Thunderbird, the Sands, the Riviera, the Flamingo, and the Tropicana. The new one was Caesar's." I pushed back in my chair, remembering. "I still have the old-time wooden matches they gave out as souvenirs ..."

It was a long walk between the casinos, and taxis were the only way to get around, unless you had your own car. Hitching on the Strip was nearly impossible, as people without cars in Las Vegas looked desperate, and the locals never picked them up. So after walking the Strip, I returned downtown. I really preferred Reno, as Las Vegas in this era was built for big spenders. The lure was the girlie shows and the freebies if you gambled. I had no money for this, and I did not have much interest in the high-roller lifestyle. I played some slot machines and was able to stretch my time out to about two hours.

The food was good and inexpensive, as everything was geared to keeping one gambling. I had no money to really risk anything, so I went to the edge of town and put my thumb out. I was headed to San Francisco.

I waited quite a while for my next ride, which turned out to be the one ride every guy wishes would come true. An honest-to-goodness showgirl, from the Riviera, picked me up in her Thunderbird convertible. She spoke in a Lauren Bacall type of throaty voice, asking where I was headed.

"San Francisco," I answered.

"I'm going to San Berdo."

I had never heard anyone refer to San Bernardino in that way and asked her, "Where's that?"

She said in a very crisp, impatient way, "It's on the way. You want the ride or not?"

I hopped in. I was giddy with joy when she said she was a dancer at the Riviera and had a few days off.

"What's in San Berdo?" I asked.

Keeping her eyes on the road, she said it was her place; she made the trip weekly. As I started my usual friendly question-asking, she stopped me cold. "Listen, good-looking, I work, and I have little time for men or involvements, and don't need nothing but their company from time to time, so no questions, no names, no bullshit, and no rough stuff, and we can have a real good time. Got it?"

"Got it."

It was so unusual for me to not get personal. She did not want to know anything about me, not even my name. I never got hers. I think we made up names for each other. We drove to San Berdo and talked about the world, politics, LBJ, and everything nonpersonal.

At her place, I did see an envelope on her counter with the name Monica Sauralt on it, but I said nothing. Her rules. I saw her pictures in her very clean apartment, and it was obvious that she made good money, as her place was well appointed. We talked about our philosophies about the world and its people. She thought I was kind of softhearted. We spent two days together, cooking veggie burritos and drinking margaritas. We painted one another's bodies with food coloring and took fun baths in her hot tub. She rented videotapes, and we sat on her porch, watching them. We had passionate sex, and she would stoke my hair, like a girlfriend does, and look softly at me. Then the wall would go up. We had an intimate relationship without any grounding. It was exciting, unusual, and a bit off-setting for me. I had so many questions, but she appeared to be a normal person who had very rigid boundaries for herself and was very strong in her self-control.

It was fascinating for me to be with a woman who was so open, physically and philosophically, and yet so closed at the same time. We made snacks of salsa and guacamole and drank Dos Equis beer. She came into my shower and washed my back with a huge soapy glove. We could do anything we wanted with each other, physically. She had a few games she played with me with a mask and drops of chocolate.

At the end of these absolutely joyful, tension-free, and uninhibited play days, she said she had to go back to Vegas. She simply told me that she really enjoyed me.

She gave me a send-off kiss and roared away. It was two days of great fun. I have never met anyone else, anywhere, like her.

When I finished the story, Ma had a big grin on her face and was waiting for Thelma to respond.

Thelma narrowed her eyes as she looked at me and said, "Mr. Ken, that don't sound like no woman I ever knowed."

"Me either, Thelma," I admitted.

Ma's grin widened. "He's a trip, my son—a real trip."

The Brothers' Real
St. Louis Blues

I made Ma get dressed and took her out for lunch, as she needed some fresh air. We passed a big-rig hauler who was cursing out the window and giving some guy in a Honda the finger.

I told Ma that he looked like Lawrence, the racist, over-the-top, big-rig guy who gave me a ride but spewed hate about blacks all the way to St. Louis.

Ma wanted to hear the story.

I verbally went toe-to-toe with this guy for about three hours in southern Illinois while on our way to St. Louis. It was exhausting, as people who hate irrationally are not open to different opinions, and they can suck up all your energy. He railed about the lazy, good-for-nothing "moochers" that just took welfare. I tried to point out that education was the key to social advancement and poverty was its own prison. The results were what he saw on the streets. When one was denied opportunity and the steps for advancement were blocked, then crime and drugs could take over.

When we crossed the Mississippi River into Missouri, it was quickly different, no longer pastoral green. St. Louis was a big city with an urban feel—and not a good one. The Negroes (which was the word for African Americans or blacks at the time) that Lawrence pointed out lived mainly in East St. Louis. We went through a very bad housing area, with many seemingly unemployed people hanging out on street corners. I thought I was back in New York, as it felt the same. Lawrence kept referring to them as shufflers. Downtown St. Louis was better. I saw working people and the activity of city life. They had one hell of an arch that proclaimed it was the "Gateway to the West."

I could not believe that I had traveled that far, to be seeing a sign about the West. It turned out, however, that the West was still a long way from there, but I guess technically anything west of the Mississippi is the West. The Mississippi was one ugly river, all brown from its overswelled banks. It looked like one giant, moving mud puddle.

I said good-bye to Lawrence and went on a search to hear some blues, as I knew St. Louis had a great reputation for playing good blues. I wound up trying to hear the Blues with Lawrence's targets in East St. Louis. I searched out some black guys in downtown who were milling about a shoeshine parlor. After some awkward moments about who I really was, the brothers heard my accent and believed I really was some kind of New York turkey, just trying to hear some good music. I told them that white guys like me just didn't walk into black neighborhoods by themselves without looking for or receiving some kind of trouble. They agreed. Then I said my best line: "But there's no blues in the white neighborhoods."

"I hear that," they said in unison. So the fellas took pity on me and told me to come back around ten thirty, and they'd take me to hear some down-home blues.

There were fancy clubs in the downtown section that played blues, but I did not have that kind of club money. I wanted a more New Orleans type of place, and they understood exactly what I was saying. I found a tavern with a good jukebox. I had a sandwich, read the paper, shot some pool (and won six dollars), and just chilled until I went back to find the fellas. They showed up in a beat-up Chevy, but they were dressed better than they had been that afternoon.

"Lookin' for ladies, I see," I said, getting into the car.

"This cracker's okay," Jerome said to the fellas, and they all laughed.

Later, when I told this part of the story to my friends back in New York, they could not believe that I'd gotten into a car with four black guys I had just met and that I'd gone to East St. Louis to go to a dive bar at night, during those highly tense, racially charged times, and lived to tell the story.

The night was fantastic. These were poor blacks, but they, like me, loved music and women. When we got to James' Joint, it was just as I'd hoped—rundown, packed, hot, and sweaty. It was also smoky, but this was long before the cigarette wars. There was a five-piece combo playing for tips. The piano and the horn were exceptional. Some of the patrons made funny comments to Jerome and the fellas about the white shadow they had with them. We just laughed. Black people are used to being around all-white places, but most whites are not used to being around all-black places, but I was comfortable there, and it showed. I was warned, however, not to hit on the "sistas." I knew that before going in. It was a music-and-pool night, and the pool competition was fierce. I beat four guys in a row before they got Sweet William to put an end to their embarrassment of some honky's whuppin' them in their own building. Sweet William was very good—he moved slowly, like a cat, and shot with perfect touch. I acknowledged my victor and purposefully put my winnings to that point in the tip jar. That guaranteed my safety. They all nodded. We just drank and listened to some great blues.

At the end of the night, I asked Jerome for a ride out of the neighborhood. I was told that I shouldn't go downtown now, and that I could stay with Leroy and Warren, as they had a couch. So after stopping for some late-night soul food, which I pushed around on my plate, I stayed in a very modest second-floor apartment of the brothers Leroy and Warren Dimity.

I reflected on the journey so far. From a separate bedroom with a white family in Pittsburgh, to a warm bed with a woman in Cincinnati, to a hayloft in Terre Haute, to a couch in a black apartment in East St. Louis, this was turning into one hell of an experience. I was loving it.

"Sonny Boy," Ma interrupted, "I don't even know where to begin with you. You talk as if all this is just matter-of-fact normal. You were an idiot. I don't care if you are not prejudiced but others are, and some of them are black. You could have been in real danger in a poor, all-black neighborhood."

I answered, "Well, like someone I love used to say, 'I did not know any better.'"

"Touché."

Big Dot

As I entered the room on my next visit, Thelma was scolding Ma. "Miss Alicia, you keep eating those candies like that, you gonna get real sick."

"How many has she had?" I asked.

"This be her second box."

"Well, Thelma, when we figure out who keeps giving her the chocolates, our problem will stop."

Thelma was agitated. "It ain't like that. She scream at me and call me names when I don't give 'em to her, and by the way, you the one bringin' 'em."

"Whoops," I said, and I leveled my gaze at my mother. "That true, Ma? You cussin' out Thelma?"

Ma grabbed for the nearly empty box that Thelma was holding. "Gimme more," she snapped.

"Raring to go today, huh, Ma?" I said.

"What's it to anyone how much chocolate I eat?" Ma asked. "I look like shit and feel like shit, and the chocolate makes me feel good."

"This is coming from the person who fiercely controlled candy, ice cream, and all sweets when I was young because they were not good for me and would make me fat."

"Wise-ass," Ma sniped.

"Okay, Ma, indulge yourself until your sugar level puts you in a coma." I took the box with its few remaining pieces and placed it on the top shelf of her cabinet.

"Fine with me. I think I'll get as fat as that black woman you knew in the city."

"You remember Dorothy?" I asked.

"Clark Bars," she said smugly.

My eyes widened in surprised. "Wow, that's is right on the button—amazing."

Thelma scrunched up her face and asked, "What that mean—Clark Bars?"

"Tell her," Ma instructed. And so I did, after we all calmed down and sat around the kitchen table ...

I met Dorothy when I was her caseworker. I was working for the New York City Department of Social Services, formerly the Department of Welfare. She was one of the sixteen black single mothers who lived in one of my assigned buildings on the Lower East Side. It was a scary neighborhood in those days—street gangs, lots of drugs, and violence was constant. It seemed that the cops only came if there was a body. I had learned my way around the streets and had a good street reputation with the local gangs—and they loved my motorcycle.

Dorothy had more problems than most of the other girls. She had come to New York from Tennessee to flee her abusive mother's abusive boyfriend. She had never finished high school and had worked as a waitress in a diner before getting pregnant and joining the welfare ranks. By the time I met her, she had three children under five years old. They lived in a one-room apartment with a small kitchenette.

Everyone in the building talked about Dorothy because she never left the apartment. People would buy food for her and care for her children, but the garbage built up because she had difficulty convincing others to take it out. She was addicted to Clark Bars, those peanut-butter-and-chocolate, ultra-sweet bars that came in an orange wrapper. Dorothy ate them by the box—all twenty-four of them.

Big Dot, as she was called, was about 385 pounds. She wore a huge tentlike covering that had to fold over to cover her, with some type of cloth belt to hold it closed, though she rarely used the belt.

On our first meeting, she was sitting on her bed, where she spent about 80 percent of her life, according to my other clients. Her three kids were running around in circles. As the eighteen-month-old neared her, she swooped down with her left hand and pulled the child up and plopped it onto her mammoth left breast—and thought nothing of it. My head was so full of chaos and confusion that I could only watch. There were so many things wrong with this picture that it was hard to think as to what I was going to do first.

Moms Morgan, the building's "mother," helped me get the picture into focus with Dorothy. All the other mothers in the building pitched in to help Dorothy get through her day. They would take her children into their apartments and wash and feed them. The oldest child went to prekindergarten with the other children in the building. They brought home all the necessary school forms for Dorothy to sign.

Dorothy was the welfare case in the welfare building. In the beginning, the other moms always were there when I interviewed Dorothy, as they were fiercely protective of her, fearing any caseworker would take her children away from her. They were there to explain that this house was like an old-fashioned extended family, with aunts, uncles, and grandparents nearby to care for the children. And they were right; Big Dot's children were no different in appearance from any of the other kids in the building.

After I got to know her, and the other moms realized I wasn't going to take the kids away, they then started to tell me how it worked.

"If Dorothy never leaves the apartment," I asked, "how does she meet the men who father these children?"

The girls laughed and said they also wanted to know how she physically accomplished the task, as she was a very, very big girl, and conventional methods might not apply.

The men who fathered the children of the other girls in the building would hear Big Dot bellow that she needed a man, any man, as long as he had equipment big enough to do the job. So they would bring their buddies for Dorothy, having carefully explained that she was a very big girl. The other girls would take the kids during these visits.

Her method was simple. A chair would be placed strategically next to the bed, so that Big Dot could place one leg on it while the other leg stayed on the bed. She would reach down with both arms and hoist all her belly rolls, while the man would stand. Ah! Romance!

One of the men who serviced Big Dot drove a truck that delivered Clark Bars to candy stores. He would bring her a few cases that had "fallen off the truck" every time he visited.

I asked all the girls if anyone was concerned about Big Dot's health and potential for diabetes.

"You do not want to be around when Dorothy is nearing the end of her supply," one told me. "She is worse than a crack addict."

Thelma was still upset with Ma, and at this point in my story, she pointed at Ma and said, ""Just like your mamma, Mr. Ken."

"Ma like Dorothy—very funny," I said, and then continued.

Dorothy became pregnant again, and even though she had all her supports in place and the kids were cared for, the department's guidelines prohibited four children in one room. I did have to intervene, because it was a horror show. Big Dot was at risk for so many medical nightmares that if she had a stroke, the kids would be placed in foster care. So I used all of my resources and found her a big, clean, two-bedroom apartment in Brooklyn.

Try to picture the conversations between Big Dot and me. I tried to convince her that the system would no longer permit her to have four children in one room, as she wondered how she would get her Clark Bars.

I told her that she needed a medical evaluation and treatment, because her obesity, high blood pressure, and sugar levels were probably critical. She probably thought, "Don't this fool know I ain't walked nowhere in a year?"

I told her I had to get her bigger housing; she probably thought, "I can't even cook, and this dumb cracker wants me to feed my own kids."

On and on we went, until I told all the girls that she had to move, and I could do nothing to stop it. In fact, I'd found her a great apartment in Brooklyn, but she had to see it first and approve it, or she would be moved into a welfare hotel. So Big Dot and I, along with two other moms, headed out for Brooklyn. I'm sure this was a funny-looking sight—Big Dot, with her tent robe and a scarf around her head; ninety-eight-pound Eleanor Wilson, with buck teeth and a space between them; Shonda Gillette, a foxy twenty-four-year-old in tight jeans, with her swivel hips; and me, a twenty-four-year-old, long-haired, six-foot white guy, who looked like he should be doing rock-and-roll commercials for Rolling Stone.

These three black women and I headed for the subway. The trek took forever and a day, due to Big Dot's having to stop every twenty-five yards to catch her breath. The cursing was nonstop. The girls wanted me to spring for a cab. The wanted LeRoy to drive us in the Clark Bar truck. They wanted to stop anyone to give us a ride. After a while, we were all laughing that John Lindsay, New York City's then-mayor, should come get us in his limo.

When we eventually made it to Bedford-Stuyvesant in Brooklyn, the street people watched this quartet with curiosity and with amused expressions on their faces. The apartment was on the second floor of a three-family building. The girls thought the building was pretty fancy—it was structurally sound but not fancy. It was in the middle of one of the roughest neighborhoods outside of Harlem.

The apartment had a kitchen with enough room for a big table, a large living room with a bay window, one very large bedroom, and one average-size bedroom. The girls thought it was heaven. They wanted me to get them apartments too. Everyone talked about coming to see Big Dot in her "big-ass place."

Dorothy had to go to the bathroom. After a minute or so, she returned and said that she didn't like the damn place; she wanted to leave.

The girls and I were dumbfounded.

Eleanor told Dot that she was crazy, but Shonda left the room. When she came back, she told us that Dorothy couldn't get into the bathroom. "They have a tiny-ass door to the bathroom."

Sure enough, the bathroom had a smaller-than-usual door, and Big Dot could not get through it. This was one of those moments when comedy and tragedy merged—a cruel biblical-like punishment from the gods when one is about to be set free and then the door closes without warning. There were tears, there were moments of uncontrolled laugher, and there was relief and despair. This pack of assembled warriors had been foiled by the dimensions of an unassuming door.

We trudged our way back to Broome Street. Moms saw us first and immediately knew something was wrong. In our debriefing session, Moms pointed out the success—that Mr. Ken had gotten Dorothy out into the streets for the first time in a year, and that he would find her a place with a bigger door. The story of Big Dot's humiliation later was told by everyone in the entire neighborhood.

Dorothy became ill shortly after that and had trouble breathing. I got her admitted to Beth Israel Hospital and had the children temporarily assigned to others in the building. This was where I made my move. Her breathing problem was directly related to her obesity, and she was at risk for heart attack and stroke. Her cholesterol was astronomical, mostly due to the Clark Bars. I could get her into the hospital's weight-reduction program, but she had to voluntarily sign.

They said she was 255 pounds overweight and would probably be in the hospital for nine months to a year. I tried every technique, appealing to her as a mother and as a woman, but all to no avail. So I used my ace in the hole.

I brought Moms to the hospital. We worked out a strategy beforehand that included a good cop/bad cop routine, where Moms was going to be the bad cop. Moms said, "I ain't afraid to tell this girl she ain't doin' right by her kids with those Clark Bars and screaming fits. And now she can't even get her fat ass in the bathroom."

When Moms was done, Dorothy signed and was transferred to the experimental government-sponsored program for critical obesity. I was drafted into the military shortly after that, but Moms wrote me that Dorothy had lost 175 pounds and was no longer eating Clark Bars. She lived in Brooklyn and said she wanted to see me when I returned to the States. I felt like I had been part of her recovery. But it was Moms' doing.

Ma was now grumpy and muttering that she wanted a piece of chocolate. I turned to Thelma and announced, "Put in the ear plugs. No more candy for Ma."

Ma scowled at me. "Oh, I see. The Gestapo is here."

"Just trying to keep you alive, Ma."

"Do me a favor," she said. "Fuck off."

"Miss Alicia!"

"You, too."

Christmas in Paris

wo days later, I returned to Ma's, and she started right in.

"It's almost Christmas, and I don't have a damn tree."

"What happened to that white one that you keep in a box?" I asked.

"It's probably in the storage bin."

"Want me to put it up?"

"Yeah, it'll add some oomph to this place."

Thelma cleared an area by the window, and I went to get her tree. I was assembling it when I asked her, "Remember Christmas when I called home from Paris?"

"Oh sure, I do. That was a real moment for you and me."

"I am glad you remember it, Ma. It was a very special day, but it did have a bit of a twist to it."

"I don't remember the twist part."

"This sounds good," said Thelma.

Ma was sorting out her jewelry as I finished putting up the white plastic tree, which for some odd reason, she loved. We always had a real tree when I was a kid, so it was offsetting to see her adore this thing. I sat down next to her and began to remind her of the "twist" of that special day …

It was a very unusual set of circumstances that found me on the Champs d'Elysee on Christmas Day. I was by myself, having taken the weekend pass from my US Army base in Heidelberg, Germany. My girlfriend at the time had to stay in Heidelberg to work. My friends wanted a Christmas party on the base, but being Jewish, I ventured to Paris on the train—a very enjoyable ride through the German and French wine valleys. I had stayed previously at a little "pension" (a type of boarding house) on the Left Bank and knew my way around Paris. The Metro was so simple—different-colored dots on the Metro map easily pointed to one's destination. I just pushed the button, and my route lit up—a different color meant a different train.

The trains had rubber wheels, which muffled the sound when the train pulled into the station. I loved riding around Paris by train.

I had arrived the day before and found Paris at its most beautiful. Lovely little white lights were everywhere, and a delicate snow covered this beautiful old city. Paris was quiet the night before, giving to the ritual of Christmas Eve and France being a very Catholic country. I just listened to some jazz in a bistro and retired early. Christmas morning was spectacular—clear and crisp, with the smell of baked goods in the air. The French were very serious about their bread, wine, and bakeries, to say nothing of their zeal for cuisine. Christmas morning was no exception; rolls and croissants were mandatory. I walked through Montparnasse in the Left Bank, where the Sorbonne is located. I strolled past Notre Dame Cathedral, as the bells rang loudly, and I even paused to see if Victor Hugo's Quasimodo was in the bell tower.

Walking along the Seine, I crossed over the bridge past Samaritaine to Paris' main boulevards and headed for the Champs d'Elysee. Once there, the majestic Arc De Triomphe dominated, like the Washington Monument looks over the Mall. It was a wonderful morning, and I had become a little nostalgic for my family back in the States, as I had not seen them in a year and a half. I remembered the presents and childhood toys and the big breakfast on Christmas morning with my sister and parents. I stopped at a breakfast bar in a hotel and read the weekend edition of the International Herald Tribune. Then I continued my journey along Paris' elite avenue.

Then I saw it. Right there in the middle of everything was a sign that advertised USO, "Call home for free."

I never even knew there was a USO or what they did. It stands for United States Overseas, a service organization for military and civilian personnel with proper identification—basically government employees, and soldiers are employees. I went through the door and upstairs, where a very friendly staffer heartily welcomed me. The staff treated me like I was a refugee or something, offering me a full turkey dinner—to be served at four in the afternoon—and yes, a free call to the States. I came back at four, after taking in a French movie. I ate a wonderful turkey dinner and called home and spoke to Ma. My head was spinning all the time. Here I was in Paris, with a full stomach, having just spoken to Ma. And now I was ready to take on the rest of this beautiful Parisian Christmas Day.

As I stepped outside, I started bawling. It was all a little overwhelming. I started walking toward the Arc, clearing my eyes and feeling so fortunate that I was able to experience this day in this magnificent setting. The snow had lined all the tree branches—trees that Napoleon had planted to mark the magnificence of this city. The birds were scurrying for bread scraps, and the tourists were sauntering along the sidewalks. Stopping to take it all in, I didn't really notice, as I usually would, that a man was trying to talk to me.

"Excuse a moi," he repeated.

I refocused and saw a rather average-looking French citizen with a long black wool coat. Again he said, "Excuse a moi."

"Oui?" I responded.

He then opened his coat, and there, on display in the inside lining, were small pornographic magazines, condoms, hash pipes, rolling papers, and a tube of KY jelly. I was flabbergasted. It was like this information was not going into my brain. It was something so unexpected that it shattered my perfect Parisian day.

When I looked at him, the only thing that came out of my mouth was, "On Christmas Day? On Christmas Day?" I walked off, stunned, and only about ten minutes later did I start to laugh as I took my long look at the Arc de Triomphe.

Now every time I see it, I think of that spectacular day and … the creep.

"Oh, that's the twist," said Ma, laughing. Then she leaned back in the easy chair and gave me a mischievous look. "Did you buy anything?"

Clarence, Jesse, and City

On my next visit, Ma again started right in on me.

"Sonny Boy, glad you could find the time to visit your lonely old mother."

"Hello to you too, Ma. I see the victim is alive and in good form today."

"You never come here."

"Ma, I don't want to fight. I come here all the time. You just don't remember it. Your memory is starting to fail you."

"Sure, blame it on me." She then changed the subject. "I watched Deliverance last night. What a scary movie."

"For sure. You remember when I saw it up close and personal?"

"Don't think so."

I made her tea and gave her the scones I had brought.

"Mmm, these are good. Bring more."

"Yes, ma'am. Want to hear about my Deliverance?"

"Shoot."

It was after I returned from the Army, a much more seasoned and experienced person. The Army was great for me, as I had done really well and got to live in and travel all over Europe for two years. The world had gone nuts all around me, with the assassinations of Martin Luther King Jr. and Bobby Kennedy. The political system was under attack, and the nation had just watched the Chicago police riot outside the Democratic National Convention. The war in Vietnam was not going to be won by any standard of measurement, and the streets were filled with protesters for antiwar, civil rights, and women's rights. Now, after the election of Richard Nixon, the youth were on a campaign to no longer be part of what was called the military-industrial complex. Government had become the enemy.

Music was taking over the culture of America, and the land of TV was being invaded by nontraditional TV shows. The government censors were working overtime.

More and more people were smoking marijuana. The cops turned the other way in many cities. I wanted to go back and finish my travels throughout America, as there were states that I had not seen. This time, I was a seasoned veteran who knew what to expect, and having been in Europe, where travel is second nature for young people, I was very ready to get back on the road.

Mostly, I wanted to go to places I hadn't seen on the first hitch, so with notebook and pen, a little bigger knapsack, a rain slicker, and $125, I set off to see the Deep South, the West, and the northern states bordering Canada, and finally, New England.

I was traveling between Roanoke, Virginia, and Knoxville, Tennessee, with a missing-teeth "country cracker" in a Ford pickup. This part of the country was very rural and mountainous. The Appalachian chain was long and arduous to get through. Many of the roads were poorly marked, and once we got off the main road, it was very easy to get lost.

The driver's name was Clarence Culpepper. He kept looking at me like I was from the moon. He referred to me as "City" and said he worked sometimes as a "fixer," which meant he could fix "damn near anythin' that had a motor in it." We had been bouncing along, headed to Knoxville, when he decided to visit his cousin, as it was a short ride up the hill. I knew immediately that this was not good. I had two bad choices: stay with him (then at least I had a ride), or get off in the middle of nowhere, with pickup trucks and cars speeding by. The lesson I learned in the Mojave made it an easy choice; I would stay with him.

We were somewhere near a place called Pulaski, Tennessee, when he said we'd just stop and have a beer and then "git back a-goin'."

I do not pray but this was a time for a prayer. The only thing that kept me focused was the beauty of the mountains. The shacks we passed, however, were scary-looking, with patched-together roofs, beat-up front porches, and car parts and metal contraptions scattered all over the front yards. This was poor-people's country. The hill was a major challenge for his pickup, and after two wrong turns, I wondered if I was ever going to get out of this place. We stopped by some men with missing teeth and torn hats on the way up the hill. They looked at us very menacingly.

Clarence asked them if they knew his cousin, Jesse John, and they pointed to the road we had just passed. We turned around and went about a mile more up the hill to Jesse John's. Clarence was greeted warmly, and Jesse asked, "Whose the feller?"

"This here is City, Jesse, and he's a-traveling with me to Knoxville."

Jesse's wife came out, and she looked more like Jesse than a wife should, I thought, No one knows I am here, and if they tie me up in the barn, no one will ever find me.

Jesse was pissed off at Clarence for not bringing any beer. And I wondered what would be worse: to drink one of Jesse's beers or refuse it. I figured accepting a friendly offer was better than refusing one, so I took one of Jesse's beers. We sat on a broken-down, missing-boards porch, with a few skinny goats running around the front area. There also was a mangy-looking dog with what appeared to be a bad case of fleas. The conversation was painful, because they were poor and uneducated and prejudiced against damn near everyone. I just nodded and did not want to raise one eyebrow, as I kept looking at the ax that was planted in the front tree stump. Jesse did show Clarence his new shotgun and that was about it for me.

Fortunately, we only stayed about a half hour, although it seemed like a whole day. We shook hands, and Jesse said to his wife, "Nice feller, that City," and we rumbled on down the hill and back to the Highway 58. It knew I never wanted to be that rural again.

Clarence drove me to Knoxville, and I was thankful that I was still in one piece. I could not get the scene from Deliverance out of my head. All I needed to hear was a banjo, and I would have passed out.

Right on cue, Ma started strumming her imaginary banjo.

Friendly Birmingham

I took Ma out for lunch at the chain restaurant Ruby Tuesday's, where she liked the salad bar. It was really strange to see Ma wanting to eat in a chain restaurant—that was unheard of when she dined in New York's finest restaurants. She always put down chain restaurants as inferior. When I commented on that, she proclaimed, "It's only a goddamn salad, for Christ's sake, and they do a pretty good job."

When we returned to the apartment, Thelma was folding the laundry. "Mr. Ken," she said in greeting, "Miss Alicia was tellin' me you got yourself arrested in the South."

"Well, it's almost true."

"Where was it? Selma or some god-awful place like that?"

"It was Birmingham. Friendly Birmingham."

"What did you do down there? Those boys is nuttin' to mess with," Thelma said with authority.

"I didn't do anything but look like a white boy from the North."

"That's enough."

"You're telling me."

"What happened, Mr. Ken?"

We all sat down around Ma's table, and I began, "If you are from the North, the South can be a very scary place to be at times. Southerners are very polite people to one another and very gracious, but to strangers, they can be quite the opposite."

This was a difficult time in American race relations, and I was in the Deep South, where the civil rights workers James Cheney, Michael Schwerner, and Andrew Goodman were killed the preceding year in Mississippi. I was in Birmingham, Alabama, on my way to Montgomery and Mobile. Alabama and Mississippi were considered the home and heart of the Ku Klux Klan.

At this time, there was the feeling that everyone who was not local was a potential "outside agitator"—a phrase used to describe people who did not share the southern thinking about segregation—and those agitators were not welcome. Southerners did not need civil rights troublemakers coming down to their towns, telling them how to live. So my New York accent was especially offensive to them.

It would soon take federal troops to open the universities to African Americans. I was on alert most of the time and did not want to do anything to draw the attention of the locals. In my favor was that I was traveling alone.

I was just about outside the Birmingham city limits, hitching south, down the road from a grits place, where I had just had breakfast. A state trooper, wearing one of those intimidating trooper hats and silver reflective sunglasses, like the prison road guard wore in Cool Hand Luke, stopped his police car on the other side of the road, facing me. He just stared. Then he used the handheld radio, slowly backed off the road thirty feet from me, and just sat there. I start sweating immediately. My mind immediately went to chain gangs and fast trials, where innocent people were sent away for long periods of time. After five very long minutes of this torture, another state police car appeared behind me. He parked very close to me, and he also just stared. I was afraid to move or do anything.

INSANITY BEGINS AT HOME

They both got out simultaneously and started to approach. They put their hands on their revolvers and told me to step away from the road, lie face down, spread my legs, and put my hands behind my back.

I did exactly what they told me. They cuffed me, and then they started asking questions,

"Who are you? Why are you on our road? Where are you going?"

I told them I was hitchhiking across America, and my ID was in my pocket. Then I asked them what this was all about.

"We're asking the questions," one told me. "Get up."

My mind was racing, and I was scared to death, afraid they would ask me something racial, because the three white kids who were most recently hanged were "outside agitators from the North."

I told them about being on my cross-country adventure. I even threw in that I was a baseball player, figuring that was worth something in this part of the all-American South. It didn't matter one iota to them.

They told me they were looking for a criminal who fit my description. He'd robbed a gas station.

They took my knapsack, looked in it, and threw my clothes on the ground. The fear and insanity of the moment and the internal panic about the situation I found myself in made me laugh, and I blurted out, "Wouldn't he have a getaway car?"

To which the trooper in the back chuckled. They checked my ID, and then they told me to come with them, as Alabama law forbade hitchhiking on a highway. I was still handcuffed and was put in the back of the state police car. This was a first for me, as I had never been in trouble with the law, but this was the Deep South, and the law might not apply to me. They threw my knapsack and clothes in the trunk. We drove to the grits place. I thought that was odd, but maybe they were hungry. I was sweating profusely and needed a bathroom. Both cops escorted me inside the grits place while still handcuffed.

Everyone inside started laughing when they saw us come in. They were all yucking and whooping it up about how the "good-old boys really scared that Yankee kid."

The look on my face must have earned a few extra yucks.

I had no idea what was going on. I watched the owner of the store and the cops just having a good ol' regular conversation, like nothing unusual was going on. No one paid any attention to me as I stood there feeling stupid, powerless, and confused.

As it turned out, the owner of the grits place was just having fun and was in cahoots with his brother-in-law, the state trooper. He said, "No hard feelings, son." I was told that Wally, the other trooper, would give me a ride to the county line. They took off the shackles.

I asked to use the bathroom first, which got another round of belly laughs. Wally really did take me outside the city limits of Birmingham, where he then opened the trunk for me to get my stuff.

"Sure did appreciate their southern hospitality," I mused.

Thelma wiped her brow with a hankie, as she had started to perspire while remembering her days in the South. It was as if she knew these men personally. "Whew, Mr. Ken, you was lucky those boys was just playin'. That there could have done gone a lot of ways."

"Not for him," Ma said. "He tells these kinds of stories from everywhere he went, and he never got hurt. Ever."

Thelma added, "But those boys in the South makes people disappear, and nobody can do nuthin' about it."

Denver in a Big Tub

Ma was filing her nails with that emery board that I hated—it always sent a shiver up my back. Thelma was helping her. Ma said that she had been thinking about taking a bath, and that brought up the memory of taking baths in Europe.

She began, "We were in Florence, staying at a fancy hotel in one of the piazzas. The bathroom was magnificent, and they had one of best old ornate tubs on legs that I'd ever seen—really beautiful. I would make Geno bring me back every afternoon, so I could soak my arse in it for as long as I wanted. He would get me an afternoon cocktail, and I would just enjoy the good life. Every hotel had their own version of that tub. I liked the French and Italian ones the best because they were so stately and handsome. The German ones were more 'kerplunk' [her word] and functional, just like the people I guess." And then she laughed.

"I remember them, Ma, and I miss them too."

"Yep," she said, "there's nothing like a very warm bubble bath to soak away your troubles."

"I agree. I use the hot tub at the gym after my workouts."

Ma wrinkled her forehead and said, "Didn't you tell me a tub story?"

"A tub story?" I replied.

"Yeah, somewhere on the road," she said indignantly.

"Oh, yeah, that's right. You mean Denver."

"Denver, yeah, that's it. Tell that one."

I said to Thelma, "This one, I never saw coming."

Ma got some homemade applesauce from the cupboard and set it on the table, along with some dark pumpernickel bread—a treat for me.

The Denver story …

I was hitching through the West and hit Denver first. I liked Denver right away. It was a big city and looked it. I could see the impressive Rocky Mountains in the west. I found a Steers Burger restaurant, where I ate the tasty charcoal special-deluxe plate.

I was tired and needed to start to look for the next place to sleep. I went outside, trying to thumb to the University of Denver, as I figured I could crash at a college dorm. A girl driving a clanging station wagon pulled over and asked where I was going.

"Trying to go to the university to find a place to crash."

"Get in. I'll take ya."

Bonnie was about my age, but she looked a bit older. She was kind of skinny but had a very pretty soft face and blue-green eyes. Her long hair hung down her back softly. She was friendly but seemed a tad odd, as her questions didn't seem to follow a logical progression. She had a somewhat inappropriate laugh, which was mainly to herself, but I sensed no real danger with her. We were only about a mile from where she picked me up when we saw two guys hitching. She swooped over and asked them where they were going.

They were locals and were headed only to the west section of Denver. They piled in the car, and I thought it really odd, three hitchers in one car.

Bonnie asked if we'd mind if she stopped to pick up some "necessaries," as it would only take a minute. It was her car, so everyone agreed.

She stopped at a minimart and came out with two six-packs of beer. She didn't say a word as she put them in the trunk.

A few minutes later, as we were again on our way, she said, "Mind if I drop the beer off at my apartment?"

We all started looking at one another. The two in the back snickered and asked Bonnie if she liked to party.

"Sure do," she said.

"In that case," one said, "that's not going to be enough beer." We stopped at the next mart to get two more six-packs.

Bonnie seemed very happy as we rode along, and I found her intriguing. Still, I thought I would get out of the car when she reached her place.

Then she said to me, "We could just stop for a few beers, and I will drive you later."

If it had been just Bonnie and me, I would have said okay without hesitation, but with these other two guys, I had no idea what she was thinking. I didn't even know what I was feeling, as it seemed weird, even though she really had not said anything wrong. It just had a feel to it that she had some kind of plan up her sleeve. I asked if she had a roommate.

"I live with two girls," she answered.

Ha, I thought, picture solved. She's bringing home the bacon.

We arrived at an average-looking three-story house. She pointed to the top floor and said, "That's ours."

I got out of the car and said I'd be going, but Bonnie said, "Nonsense! Just have a beer with us, and I will take you to the U."

I thought this could be a big mistake, but I followed the three of them up the stairs.

Bonnie's apartment was clean, with girlie curtains and fresh flowers. We sat at the kitchen table. She gave me one of her beers and put on some rock music. She said her roommates were in dance class and would be home later.

Bonnie leaned over and whispered in my ear, "I want to show you something."

Here it comes, I thought.

We went into the next room, which was dark, and she flipped the switch to reveal a huge old-fashioned bathtub. On the other side of the tub was a row of record albums and a turntable. There was cabinet with soaps and powders and a counter with towels, all neatly stacked. It looked like the changing room cabana for a pool.

"Neat, right?" she said. "I bet you could use a bath." I was mainly a shower person, but this thing looked inviting, even if the circumstances were weird. She added, "Why don't you just soak for a while, and I'll go back with the fellas?"

"I don't know ..." I halfheartedly protested.

She put on a Beatles record and said, "Go ahead. How many times does a stranger offer you a free bath?" With that. she left the room.

I had thoughts that the minute I took off my clothes, they would all rob me, or some dude would show up, or God knows what. So I just sat there on the stool. The next thing I saw was the two other guys, looking into the room, and they were clearly eyes-wide-open excited about it. They asked her if they could go next, as they thought the tub was "outta sight."

They went back to the kitchen, and I thought it was safe to get undressed and turn on the bath. The tub was so huge that it took a while to fill.

I've been in Denver about one hour, I thought, and I am in a strange girl's bathtub.

As I was in the tub, Bonnie cut through the room, politely said "excuse me," and disappeared into the next room. Two minutes later, she returned wearing a robe that she then dropped to the floor, got in the tub with me, stark naked, and said, "Hope you don't mind."

Before I could react, the two guys appeared, stripped off their clothes, and jumped in with us.

It all happened as if in one choreographed move, and all I could do was laugh.

"Rub-a-dub-dub, three men in a tub," I said.

Nothing sexual went on the for half hour or so that we stayed in the tub. Finally, we all got out, dried off, and got dressed. We went back to the kitchen and drank more beer. Bonnie's roommates never came home, and Bonnie eventually told us it was time to go.

Bonnie dropped the boys off first. She then leaned over and gave me a kiss and said, "You are looking for a place to crash, right? You could crash at my place," and we turned around and went back. I spent the night at Bonnie's, and later, the roommates did show up. One of them asked me, "Did Bonnie do the bath thing? She has a thing about being clean."

Thelma looked at me quizzically as I finished telling the story. "That be a little weird, Mr. Ken."

"At least he got a good bath," Ma said, laughing and serving more applesauce.

Out West, Wyoming, and Waddington

I was in my car on my way to Ma when I started thinking about the American West. I think it was because I had just recently told the Denver story, and last night, I had seen a movie that took place in Wyoming.

I loved the American West from the first minute I saw the Rockies in Denver—just something mystical and magical about them to me. The feeling I got in the mountains was one of serenity and power at the same time. There was also a connection with them to the timelessness one feels in their presence. It's kind of a reminder that we are just here for a speck of time and they will be here forever.

When I arrived at Ma's, I was still feeling nostalgic for the West and told Ma and Thelma about it. They were fussing with Ma's hairpiece, and I said I wanted to tell them about one of the most interesting men I'd met in all my travels: the scout John Waddington.

"I like the western stories the best," Ma said. She added, "The Yankees are playing at one thirty, and I want to watch the game."

"Excellent," I said. It was such a great joy for me to watch Yankee games again with Ma. During the years when we were estranged, I missed those times together the most. She told me Derek Jeter was better than Phil Rizzuto, and she loved watching Jeter play.

"Okay," I agreed. "I'll tell you about the West and the rides leading up to Waddington, and then we'll watch Jeter,"

Hitching out West was the best for me because of the people and the majestic landscapes. I was use to no space at all, coming from New York, and seeing the western states for the first time was truly jaw-dropping."

Hot Tub Bonnie dropped me off in the western section of Denver.

A very pretty blonde wearing a cowboy outfit and hat stopped to pick me up in her Chevy convertible. I told her I was going to Cheyenne.

"Get in," she said, and the next thing I knew, she'd opened her purse and pulled out a Colt .45, saying, "No funny stuff."

I almost had a heart attack. I was not used to being that close to a civilian with a gun. It freaked me out, and I just grabbed the door handle and was out of there in one split second. I was fairly shaken up, and my leg was trembling. After calming down and refocusing, telling myself I was fine, I put my thumb out once again. I kept thinking there really had been no way to see that one coming; it was just part of some of the potential downsides to getting into strangers' cars.

I got my next ride from a trucker who was delivering rail post supplies. He was a rough kind of guy who smoked nonstop and liked life only when he was in his truck, on the road, and "away from all the bullshit"—that was how he put it. He liked my adventurous spirit and gave me two of his cigars when he dropped me off in Cheyenne, Wyoming.

I liked the cowboy town of Cheyenne, with its stables and large pasturelands right at the edge of town. I caught a ride with a couple in a pickup truck who were going to Laramie. He sold insurance out of his office in Laramie, and his wife had come with him for the short ride to Cheyenne, because she had to see a specialist there. They were very easygoing people with a good sense of humor. I sensed there was something dire about her medical appointment. I think they were glad to have me in the truck, so they didn't have to talk about what they'd heard from the specialist in Cheyenne. They pointed out the history of Wyoming to me as we drove through the mountains to Laramie.

They talked about the rough country out here and having to deal with a lot of weather issues, especially the winter winds and snowstorms.

He rattled on about how he had to sell when the weather was good, because people didn't come out to buy insurance when the weather was bad. My one problem with the ride was listening to them sing along with their damn country-dog twang music. There were so many country-cracker music listeners west of New Jersey that I found it irritating. It sounded like the same song, over and over.

From Laramie I got a great ride from George, a horse rancher, all the way to Jackson. He was a big guy in jeans and a white shirt, large cowboy hat, and very large boots. George was a man who never said no to anything in his life. He talked loudly and spoke in bigger-than-life terms, similar to a Texan but without the bragging—just kind of matter-of-fact. He loved the open spaces and said he had a big ranch in Jackson. He worked hard and partied hard. He had been married three times, he said, because he "used them up," whatever that meant. The ride itself was fantastic, with the ever-present mountains and huge valleys and lakes interspersed between wide-open spaces. The sky was big, and the weather seemed to change about ten times a day.

I spent the night at George's ranch in his log cabin-style house. He cooked steak—what else?—and potatoes, and we drank beer. He said I was a "ballsy kid," and he liked that.

"If you ever want to learn how to ranch," he told me, "come back, because I have a job for you."

The next morning he drove me to town and put me on the road that went north to Yellowstone National Park. His last words were, "Remember to come on back, ya hear?"

I rode to Yellowstone with the Stokas family in a huge motor home. It seemed that everyone on the road was driving a motor home. I soon found out why. Yellowstone was huge and was (and still is) a major tourist attraction. People from all over drive there and stay for days. The tourist motels and hotels are usually full, despite being very expensive, I was told. The motor-home crowd loved Yellowstone, where they could see all the majestic sights and sleep for free. The ride was painfully slow but the vista made up for it. I got to see Old Faithful and spent the night with the Stokas family in their motor home, although it was a little close quarters for me. The next morning, I went back on the road to get a ride out of Wyoming and into Montana.

Two old ladies, driving an early-fifties–era Dodge, talked to me at a rest stop. They were going back to Livingston, Montana, and they'd had a hell of a time driving in from there, They asked if I would mind driving them back, and of course they would pay me. Both of them were dressed like old-time schoolteachers, with long print dresses and a tight bun of hair neatly sitting atop their heads.

Are they for real? I wondered. I'd get a free ride to Montana, and even get to drive—not be in the passenger seat, or backseat, or the cargo of a pickup truck—and they would pay me. After they assured me they were for real, I said, "Hop in, ladies. We're off to Montana."

The ride out of Yellowstone into the northwest part of Wyoming was a rough ride—lots of steep hills and sharp turns. If there was bad weather, it would have been really tough, but we had clear sailing.

These two ladies—sisters, I found out—were a feisty duo. Both were widows who had married brothers and were now just "seeing what is to be seen."

I liked that phrase. They told me about their being rural schoolteachers, and Essie, the more talkative one, after retiring, had run a women's clothing and apparel store in Nevada, before relocating to picturesque Paradise Valley.

"Paradise Valley?" I inquired.

"Yes, dear, that is what they call the place where we live, for obvious reasons."

And she was right. It was one of the most beautiful spots in all of America—and I can say that with conviction, as I would see most of it.

The valley is the southern part of the Rocky Mountain chain that goes north and west into Gallatin National Forrest. The valley is lush with meadowlands, and there are foothill paths up the mountains to about ten thousand feet. The creeks that go down the mountains flow into the Yellowstone River. When I was there, rainbows were a daily event. Sunrises and sunsets were truly awe-inspiring.

At night, the stars in Montana were just overwhelming. I never knew the sky was so full and big, with endless streams of lights and swirls. It made me feel like a speck of sand along an endless beach. The ladies and I rolled into Livingston, a small town with one long street and two smaller side streets. People parked their pickups outside or tied up their horses in front Livingston's three restaurants, few stores, or many bars.

I said good-bye to the ladies and thanked them for their generosity. I walked down the street and ambled into a bar that had darts, shuffleboard, many pool tables, and a very big dance floor. It had cowboy pictures everywhere and horsehair bar stools. I started a conversation with the bartender, who said I should come back around nine o'clock, as I'd probably have a good time.

"What does that mean?" I asked.

"Well, fresh meat. I'd kinda go for you myself, but I have an ol' man, but some of my friends might be interested."

I kicked around Livingston for the rest of the early evening, having some five-star chili at the diner and a beer at the rival saloon.

When I returned at nine, a cowboy band was playing some form of rockabilly, with a fiddle and a trumpet to go with it. The bar was filling up, and the bartender remembered me and bought me a beer. I was starting to get a little bit more comfortable with this friendly and generous stuff. About a half hour later, the bartender winked at me and pointed out three very nice-looking young women, indicating they were the ones she'd mentioned.

Montana women, as I found out, were very different from New York women. They were tall and attractive, as well as being very earthy and straight talking—no phoniness or airs about them. I danced with each of them and had a tough time telling them apart. All wore tight jeans and plaid shirts. All had long hair to their shoulders, all smelled delicious, and all talked in a semidrawl—not southern but more country.

We drank beers and laughed together a lot as other men tried to hit on them.

Later on, the bartender called me over and asked, "Which one?"

"Are you their madam or what?" I asked.

She laughed and said, "Course not. I just have a side bet with the other bartender."

"Don't you think it's up to the girls and not me?"

"Listen, fresh meat, these girls see nothing but these cowboys all the time, so a city slicker is a shoo-in."

I liked this Montana already. I wound up going with all the girls to the diner for a late-night cup of coffee and some very bad cheesecake. Man, I am a long way away from Junior's in Brooklyn, I thought.

The girls and I crashed at one of the girls' nearby apartment, over the drugstore. We put her mattress on the floor and all slept like sardines in a can. Somehow, it all seemed natural, as not one of the girls wanted to leave, so by default, we all stayed together. We slept until noon and drew a lot of smirks from the diner owner when we went back there for soup. He just slapped me on the back and gave me the thumbs-up look. I let him think his thoughts and said nothing.

The girls put me on the road west, and I headed for Butte.

I got a very interesting hitch from a fisherman who was going directly to Butte. "I've never known a real fisherman," I told him.

"Dying art," he said.

"I thought there were only commercial fisheries."

"Not out here; they are illegal."

"Then why is it a dying art?"

"No one wants to do it anymore," he said. "Too hard."

He was a tall drink of water and very smart. He said he read all the time, and then he cited quotes that made me feel his junior, even though I was the one with the college education. He talked about Kierkegaard's concept of anxiety and Jung's mandala symbolism, as if this was everyday stuff to him. I was quite impressed. When we arrived to Butte after this very interesting conversation about philosophy and psychology, he said, "You ever been up in the mountains on a horse?"

When I said I hadn't, he told me about a scout he knew who was a guide. This guide, John Waddington, ran a two-day horse ride into the Gallatin National Forest, where he had a cabin for overnights. He would cook a meal for me and make the fire.

Financially, this was a stretch for me, but I was on the adventure of my life, so of course I said okay.

John Waddington greeted me with a powerful handshake. We had a party of four, all saddled up, and went off into the mountains. Waddington was the most informed man I had ever met. He was long and lean, with a wintry, chiseled face with deep furrows on his forehead. He didn't have an overt sense of humor, but his style was reminiscent of a poet as he made his comments about the earth and nature. As we rode, he named all the trees and the type of mushrooms that were growing on them. He identified all the bird calls. He pointed out tracks of deer, wolves, and beavers. He identified the flowers, and then he showed us who lived in what hole in the ground. He had a seamless understanding of everything in the world around us. I shook my head in disbelief about how much there was to know and how little of it I knew. At one point, he stopped and said very quietly that we were not to move or talk.

He pointed to the trees about twenty feet in front of us ... and there was a baby moose.

He told us the mom was not very far away, and if she sensed danger for the baby, she would charge.

She soon appeared, and she was bigger than a dairy cow. The father, with a huge rack of antlers, followed shortly behind.

Waddington said we should slowly back up.

I had ridden horses before but not under this kind of pressure. Where the hell is the reverse? I thought. But Waddington just made a clicking noise and pulled down on the reins, and his horse started backing up very slowly, and everyone else's horse did the same. We got out of there without incident, but I was sweating like crazy. I did, however, get to see my first moose. I loved this trip.

We were horse-sore and tired when we got to the cabin, which looked like the Taj Mahal to me. Waddington made us a hot meal, which consisted of rolled steak, baked potatoes, and green beans, with a lettuce-and-tomato salad. We drank some cold beer. The sounds at night, deep in the Rockies, were wonderful—howlings and grumblings. The stars were so clear and bright that I wanted to touch them. I just sat outside on a rickety aluminum chair with my feet up on a tree stump and felt completely at peace. In the morning, the bird chatter was such a welcome sound.

Waddington made us bacon and eggs and then named all the plants and shrubs surrounding the cabin. We saddled up and rode all day until we got back to Butte. It was one of the very best experiences of my life, and it really taught this city slicker how much there was to learn about and from nature.

Ma had a wry semismile on her face, because what she was about to say would fly in the face of the story I had just told. "I never really went in for that kind of stuff, like roughing it," she said. "Too dirty, and I need a clean bathroom anyway. And my arse would be sore from all that riding. Give me a fancy hotel room with really fine sheets."

"Glad you liked the story, Ma."

"Just in time," Ma said. "Yankees on in five minutes."

It's Always Something

I was at home, playing my guitar, when the phone rang.

"Mr. Ludmer, Gina Mirth from Cedar Crest."

"Oh Jeeezus, I'm afraid to ask—what happened"?

"Sorry to tell you that your mother had a stroke and is back in the hospital."

"Damn ... what's her condition?"

"They don't know yet."

"Okay, on my way, Gina. Thanks."

When I arrived at the hospital, Ma was surrounded by her doctor and a group of medical students. He was telling them that this was a very unusual women, who'd had voluntary knee replacement surgery at age eighty-eight, had a broken hip at ninety-one, and had successfully walked out of the hospital. She then had survived a heart attack and was now here for a stroke.

When the group left, Ma looked at me. One eye was wandering and the other seemed hazy. She reached out with a few fingers. I held her hand and thought I saw a small smile before she fell back asleep.

I found the doctor and we talked.

"We'll know more in a week to ten days, as sometimes these are only temporary," he said to me. I was told that if it didn't improve, we'd have to think of other living arrangements.

With those words, I heard her in my head, telling me, "What did I tell you? It's always something after a hip."

The next days were full of anxiety, as each call to the nursing staff gave me different information.

"She's sleeping a lot and not responding to being talked to."

"She keeps asking where she is."

"She stares most of the time when awake."

"Her temperature is better, and so is her blood pressure."

"She slept almost twenty hours."

"She eats very little."

On the ninth day after the stroke, I stopped at the nurses' station as I usually did on my way to see Ma. Her nurse said, "You probably will not believe this, but she's back."

"What do you mean?"

"Today, she sat up and started talking coherently. Go see for yourself."

I hurried to her room and found Ma sitting up.

"Ah, Sonny Boy, hello."

"How you doing, Ma?"

"Fine. Why do you ask?"

"Why do I ask?" I echoed. "Because you've been here eight days and have spoken only rarely on a few occasions, following your stroke."

"Bullshit," she said adamantly. "I feel fine. I did not have a stroke."

And so the die was now cast for the rest of her days, as she had survived the stroke, but the part of her brain that was affected was the part where new memory is stored. She would not be able to store new memory reliably for any significant period of time. She could recall any memory stored before the stroke with clarity or some confusion, but not anything after the stroke.

Her body had weakened significantly, and her legs were now unstable. She would be bedridden, as rehab was out of the question, due to the fear that she would fall again if she tried to navigate a walker.

She returned to her apartment, this time with full twenty-four-hour nursing care—two more women daily, each doing eight-hour shifts. They prepared her meals and attended to her bathroom needs. She had a wheelchair. My sister and I continued to take turns shopping for her food, and I got her medicines and put them in the pill boxes. I took over her finances and paid all her bills. I took her to her doctors' appointments and out for lunch a couple of times per week. We got a lawyer and set everything legally that needed to be done. She appointed me executor of her estate.

She lived forty-two miles from me, and the ride had become a Zen experience. I would think about my life with her as no longer combatants but as survivors of an epic battle who no longer harbored their resentments. We were road-weary warriors who would now find peace and tranquility with our differences, united by a feeling that despite it all, we still loved one another.

Her conversations were interesting and at times really funny, as she put together bits and pieces of her life in random order, with no ability to differentiate the here-and-now from the past. It led to some marvelous conversations. The amazing thing was that she became the most docile she had ever been in her life. The sharp, biting tongue was a whisper of its former self. For the most part, she was not in any pain, physically or emotionally.

Our pattern from that day on was to continue to have our very long and involved conversations, with both of us telling our stories. She got bored quickly with television as her concentration waned. The radio wasn't any better for her. What she really liked was to tell her stories and to listen to mine. Thelma became a more vital part of this intimate, loving, and at times raucous recollection of our lives, both together and apart.

It was the kindest Ma ever was but, in some ways, the saddest. I never knew her without her sharp, critical voice, her demeaning tone that she used when talking about those of whom she disapproved, which was me a lot of the time. This was like seeing a soldier with a water pistol. She had become pleasant and docile, with only momentary glimpses of her normally feisty self. It was a strange feeling to actually miss the part of her I had hated for so many years.

Nadine and Almost Vietnam

Ma was having one of her better days. She and Thelma were in a lively discussion when I arrived. Thelma was under orders to make the soup *exactly* as Ma instructed, and Ma now barked orders at Thelma from the bed.

"Make sure you cut the carrots lengthwise and thinly. No fat carrot pieces belong in the soup, and the onions should be quartered, not sliced," I heard her demand. Then, after hearing my entrance, she said, "Ah, speak of the devil—here he is."

"And good afternoon to you as well, Ma."

"I was telling Thelma that some of the time your road adventures were outright dangerous, and I was glad that I didn't hear them until many years later. You know, a mother worries."

"That true, Mr. Ken?" Thelma asked. "'Cause most of your stories be fun and stuff."

"Most of the time I was fine," I said, "but there were times when it got a bit dicey."

"Wasn't you scared?"

"Not really, I was out to seek adventure, and go where the road took me."

Ma snorted. "And that road took him everywhere. Tell Thelma about the girl and the Texas Ranger."

"Wow, Ma, good memory. But first I want to know how you are doing."

"Oh, terrific," she said sarcastically. "I skated Walden Pond this morning and then had lunch with Barbara Walters."

"Very nice day indeed," I said, going along. "I take that to mean you are fine."

"I go nowhere and do nothing, but thanks for asking."

"You're a pisser, Ma."

"Tell the story, will you? It's the only entertainment we have."

"Really? Okay, about Nadine …"

I was in Louisiana at a truck stop after a great ride from a long-hauler. I was talking to the waitress, who was interested in my road story, when a somewhat scraggily-dressed young woman sat down two seats from me, and she was obviously listening to our conversation.

"Travelin', are ya?" she asked me.

"Yes."

"Where ya goin'?"

"Dallas."

"Well, aren't you lucky. So am I."

This was one ride I did not jump to accept, as wanted to hear a bit more from her first. She said her name was Nadine, and she was going to Dallas to see her friend and get out of "Loosyana" for a while. She did not appear to be on drugs or drunk, so although I sensed she was a bit odd, due to her thrown-together look and bad teeth, I took the ride anyway.

We started off in her long Chevy sedan, and she began talking about the lousy men in her life. She had to leave her house at age seventeen because her father was a drunk, and would beat her, "among other things."

I didn't ask.

She had a series of boyfriends who beat her because they were "no-good lowlifes." Then she got married, and her husband, the "sonnova beatch," started cheating on her.

I commiserated with her tale of woe, which seemed to go on forever. I thought, why would this woman pick up a strange man, considering her experiences with them? Curiosity got the best of me, so I asked her that very question.

Without blinking an eye, she answered. "It's this way: you need a good man to protect you from a bad one."

I must be the good one, I thought.

"Well, you look like a good man," she said, "and you are not from around here. I have heard that men who are not from around here are better, and so I need the protection of a good man."

So let's see, I thought, she needs me to protect her from a bad man, although we are in a car together, now in Texas. So I'll bite.

"So who is the bad man?" I asked.

"My husband. When he realizes I stole the car, he will figure out I am going to my friend in Dallas."

"So?'

"His brother is a Texas State Trooper. They're probably looking for me now."

I could not believe she actually told me this, but in her mind, I would stand up for her, like some version of the love-story magazine she had read.

We had driven as far as Longview, Texas, when I developed the immediate need for a bathroom. The situation reminded me of my first trip and the pill-popping trucker who kept asking for "greenies" from everyone on his CB—that became my first "emergency bathroom" stop.

When we stopped at the diner, I told her I really couldn't go any further with her.

"Just like the rest of them," she snapped at me and sped off.

"Good-bye, Nadine," I called after her. "May you find a good one."

Ma started making cowboy "whoopee" noises and then said, "See what I mean, Thelma? He always scraped out of trouble and landed squarely on his feet. Just amazing. Tell Thelma about the army. It's the most unbelievable story, and all kinds of very bad things could have happened to him."

"Like going to war and dyin'?" Thelma asked.

"Exactly," Ma said.

I was drafted during the Vietnam escalation, when I was twenty-four—six months from being too old for the draft. I had to leave my job and everything else behind. I reported to Fort Dix, New Jersey, and was scared out of my mind, as all the talk was Vietnam. After two days of processing and getting multiple injections and a complete head shave, a sergeant came into the main room, where 249 other trainees and I were assembled, and he asked the group if anyone had a degree in psychology and could prove it. I had been told by veterans to never volunteer, because it was always something other than what was advertised. Case in point: he'd asked earlier if anyone had a driver's license, and those guys wound up driving wheelbarrows up a hill, picking up everything that didn't grow on it. The US Army had a wicked sense of humor.

I pondered the psychology degree request and thought they probably wanted an experimental lab rat. Yet my college degree was the only thing that separated me from these other draftees, so reactively, I raised my hand.

The sergeant questioned where and when I got my degree and said they would check. Then he took me to a back room, put a large book in front of me, and told me to look at the list—it was a list of social-work jobs. After reading all the descriptions, I told him I was a "91H" psychiatric social worker. I had a degree in psychology, and I was a street social worker in the Lower East Side, so I just put them together.

"The Walson Army Hospital needs one of those," he said. He wrote "91H" on a three-by-five card, circled it in red, and told me, "You'll hear from us."

As it turned out, he'd shown me the Military Occupational Specialty book. I have never found another draftee who had this experience. No draftee ever picks his own job; the army picks it for you.

By the time I finished basic training, I'd lost forty pounds in the relentless heat wave of 1966. I got into the best shape of my life. Final physical test was to run five miles in full fatigue uniform, with helmet and boots, while carrying your M14 rifle. I did it in thirty minutes. On our last night, at ten o'clock, we were put out in the rain to receive our orders for "AIT"—Advanced Individual Training. But this was wartime, so the acronym actually meant Advanced Infantry Training.

Alpha Company was first, and everyone called was going to Vietnam. At two in the morning, we were still in the rain, and they were getting close to calling my company, Victor.

Just then, a private handed the sergeant a note. The sergeant read it and then asked with total disinterest, "Is there a Private Ludmer still here?"

Did he just call my name? Am I hearing things?

My buddy nudged me and said, "That's you, knucklehead."

My hand went up again.

"Fall back in the barracks, trainee. You are not with this group. You will be reassigned in the morning."

And with those words, I never went to war. Had I been in Alpha or Bravo or Tango Company, I would have gone to Vietnam—it was that close. My company went to Fort Riley, Kansas, and then shipped out from Fort Ord, California, to become the 196th Light Infantry Brigade that invaded Cambodia looking for Viet Cong. They lost half their men.

The position at Walson Army Hospital was filled by the time I finished AIT at Fort Devens, Massachusetts, and then the classification system picked me out, and I was sent to Heidelberg, Germany, for my tour of duty. Only specialist draftees (meaning having a specific skill) were in Europe, as regular draftees would have to volunteer for an additional third year to be sent there. As this was full-time war, draftees went to Vietnam. Period. I met only two other two-year draftees in my time in Germany.

I finished my tour after having traveled all over Europe, following the film and jazz festivals. London, Paris, Brussels, and Amsterdam were my weekend haunts. I took vacations in Italy and France. I loved Berlin, even though the wall was still up.

The Army gave me a service accommodation medal for doing my work with prisoners in the stockade. I ran a group therapy session with killers in D block, four floors beneath the ground. They loved getting out of their cells and being able to see one another.

I used my Army experience to get a full free ride to grad school at Columbia, which in turn led to my career as a psychiatric social worker and ultimately, a family therapist ... all because I raised my hand back at Fort Dix.

Herman

Ma was sitting up in her bed, propped by many pillows, when I arrived for this visit.

"Ah, Sonny Boy, so you finally came to see your old mother."

"Ma, I was here Tuesday and got your weekly food and medicines."

"Really? I don't remember that."

She had battled her way back from the broken hip, followed by the heart attack and then, a month ago, the stroke. She'd beaten all the medical odds of recovery and was now back in the apartment, barking orders and ruling the roost.

"So, Ma, how you feeling?"

"Compared to what?" she asked.

"Ah, good, glad to see your edgy self is in good working order."

She ignored my remark and asked, "Know who I saw yesterday?"

"I can't imagine." I knew the next words out of her mouth would lead to a wonderful journey into the now time-altered, miswired confabulation of a mind that once had been crystal clear and vibrant.

"Herman," she said proudly.

"Herman? Where did you see him?"

"In Brooklyn. He was walking down the street past Hilda's house."

"How did he look?"

"He looked fine—a handsome man."

"I would have thought he might be a little thin," I suggested.

"Thin? He was never thin."

"Well, Ma, after being dead for forty years, I thought he might have a weight problem."

"He's not dead, smart-ass. I talked to him yesterday."

"Okay, Ma, but how do you think that's possible? We went to his funeral, near Shea Stadium, forty years ago."

"Really?"

"Yeah, he died early, at fifty-one, from a heart attack."

"Well, I guess I dreamed it." She then directed, "Sonny Boy, give me some of your pretzels."

She was not supposed to eat dried foods, as they would get lodged in her minimally saliva-producing mouth and throat. I reached into the bag and gave her one, along with a glass of iced tea. She bit into it and then glared at me and said, "Could you spare it?"

This was my mother to a tee, sarcastic and funny and somehow always the victim.

I reminded her why she was not supposed to eat dried foods.

"Who said that?"

"Your doctor."

"Well, fuck him. I want a pretzel, and no goddamn doctor is telling me I can't have a goddamn pretzel."

"That's why I gave you one," I responded.

"You are a wonderful son. Now give me another one."

Her calling me a wonderful son, even sarcastically, was totally new. Calling me wonderful had never been possible in our long and contentious relationship.

After she finished her third pretzel, her piercing eyes watching me watch her, she said, "Herman's really dead?"

"Yes, Ma, he's gone."

"But I really believe I was there yesterday, not some goddamn dream."

"Well, you know I tell you the truth."

"Yes, you learned that from me."

"True enough, but not without some ugly lessons."

"Here's where you tell me I had no tact," she grumbled.

"No need to. You already admitted that at your eightieth birthday celebration."

"You remember what I said?"

Her eightieth birthday was a true gala experience, celebrated where she got married, in the Plaza Hotel in New York City. My mother was an elegant woman when dressed to the nines, and she was quite proud that she looked fifteen years younger than her true age. She wore a long silver-blue gown, with her hair coiffed and with a tiara, of course, and looked every bit of the grand dame she was. At her party, she took to the podium and announced that she was a simple woman who had lived an extraordinary life and was lucky enough to have traveled the world. She told her guests that she was never one for a lot of tact, as she was honest to a fault. Then she proclaimed, "From now on, I have earned the right to no longer hold it back, and I won't." To that she lifted her champagne glass and bellowed, "Fuck 'em all," to the roar of the assembled.

"Yeah, I remember, Ma," I told her. "Fuck 'em all."

"Right, fuck 'em all."

I then eased into my first attempt at a reality check with her. "So if he's dead, and you didn't dream it, what was it?"

"I am going crazy."

"No, not crazy," I assured her. "It's the result of your stroke, where you cannot now process new memory for any significant period of time, and you experience old memories as now."

"Really? And how do you know this Mr. Smarty-Pants?"

"We don't have to do this, Ma, if you are going to feel attacked."

Well, excu-u-u-use me."

I've learned over the years to back off when that is her tone. So I waited.

Finally, she said, "You do come here often. Thelma tells me that you come, and shop for my food, and pay my bills, and put my pills in the container, but I can't remember one day to the next. You are probably telling me the truth."

"It's a bitch, Ma. You are with us one moment and then you fade out, get confused, and sometimes get very angry. It's a neurological condition, not craziness."

"What the hell is that wheelchair doing here?" she suddenly demanded to know.

She had not walked since she had her stroke, and her leg muscles had atrophied, so she had a wheelchair. The amazing thing was that in her poststroke condition, she could not process recent information and therefore believed she could still walk. Noted neurologist Oliver Sacks wrote a wonderful book on this type of disorder, about the man who mistook a hat for his wife.

We did not tell Ma that she couldn't walk any longer, because she wouldn't remember it anyway. It was best to leave her self-image intact.

"So you feeling up for a spin?" I asked her.

"Not in that goddamn old-lady thing," she retorted.

"Well, it's only temporary until you regain strength in your legs. The doctor thinks you could fall again, and we don't want another operation."

"I fell?"

"Yes, you have the scar. You tripped on the bedpost and broke your left hip."

"Son of a bitch."

"So in order to get some fresh air, the chair gets you there."

"You driving?"

"You bet."

"Okay, Sonny Boy, where to?"

"You like this cozy Italian place about a mile from here, and they make you a veal cutlet with a salad."

"Who's payin'?"

"I am, Ma."

"Good, let's go."

And so it went. She would bellyache about the wheelchair and all the close physical contact involved with picking her up and getting her into and out of the chair, the car, and restaurant seats. It was exhausting for her and for me. She was probably the world's most independent person and now had to depend on others for everything. She hated it.

When we got back to her apartment, she was tired. Just before she fell asleep, she looked at me and grabbed my arm, saying, "Didn't I tell you that this was never supposed to happen?"

"What's this?" I asked, although I knew exactly what she meant.

"Me, like this." She waved her hands outwardly to indicate all of her condition.

"That's true."

"I always told you that if I ever got like this, you were to take me out back and shoot me."

"That is what you said," I agreed.

"Well, waddya waiting for?"

"Ma, there were many times that I would have gladly obliged, but I don't want to do it now. Because I truly love you, and taking care of you is something I choose to do."

"But what about me?" she pleaded.

"It's always been about you, Ma, from the day you told me you had no more to give me, to the day you remarried and told me there was no room for me, to all your demands and criticisms and selfishness to where you can't even appreciate all that is being done for you. It is my turn, and you will just have to suck it up and live, being helped by your family."

"We'll see about that."

"Good night, Ma. Love you."

"Leave me alone."

"Nice, Ma, you can't even say good-bye?"

"If you don't go, I'll get the goddamn wooden spoon."

It was time to get outta there.

Bucking Sundays

On my next visit, there was no recollection on her part of the conversation about taking her out back. She merely said, "Well, look who's here—my long-lost son."

I ignored the dig. "Hi, Ma. I brought you some chocolates."

"What kind?"

"Milk chocolate, mixed—some have cherries in them."

"Atta boy! Pass 'em over."

We had our usual catching-up conversation, where she told me about the incompetence of everyone who was attending to her, except Thelma, and she gave out the usual shots at my sister.

"She shops for her own food with my credit card," Ma complained.

"How do you know that?"

"I ask for the bill."

"Ma, stop that stuff. It's not worth it."

"Listen to you, Mr. Bucking Sundays."

This was truly wonderful—she had remembered the exact phrase I had used for Sunday when I was eight years old. "That's funny now, but it wasn't then," I told her.

"Bucking Sundays" was fraught with tension, laughs, and tears. It started with an announcement from my mother: "You will be going to church with your sister, starting this Sunday."

"Why?"

"Because it will be good for you."

She already had a repertoire of things that were good for me, and I didn't like any one of them. It either tasted bad, like Listerine or cough medicine, or it was that enema bottle that my German mother relished, as if it was a cure for any ailment. I don't know what it is about Germans and colonics, but they really swear by them. Even up the lake, where there was no running water or inside bathroom, my grandmother would drag out that damn enema bottle at the first sign of a sniffle.

So anyway, on that Sunday, I was off with my sister to church.

My freethinker mother didn't go, and my Jewish father would not even talk about why I had to go; he just said it was because Ma wanted us to go. Church was a big building across the street from my grammar school. It was only a three-block walk, and when we got there, I knew a lot of the kids. They were all sitting in huge rows with their mothers and fathers. We sat down and tried to not look different, but Al Whitten said, "Where's your mother and father?"

"They're sleeping," I said.

My sister then jabbed her elbow into my ribs and told me to shut the hell up, because this was church.

A good-looking man in a long robe came out on a stage-like thing, and stepped up to a podium. He talked to us about being nice. I got a little sleepy, as it was a bit boring. But then we were told to stand and take out our hymnals. I ask my sister what that was. She picked up a book, and we turned to a certain page. Then an awful-sounding organ started to play and we were to sing along. In the history of these Protestant people, some guy must have thought this was a good idea, but let me tell you, it was the biggest turnoff possible. They were singing in some other language, with words like thee and thine and whilst, and the songs had no melody or beat. I looked at my sister as if they were all crazy, and she said that I would get used to it. Fat chance.

We sat down again in our seats, which they called pews—that seemed like a funny word for a seat. Then the organ started up again, and a plate of money was passed to me.

I remember thinking that was neat and that church was getting better. I reached in and took a few dollars and happily passed the plate to my sister.

"Put that money back, you idiot," she hissed. "You give money; you don't take it."

"You have to pay for this? Why?"

"Shut up."

Six months of this ritual had me totally numb. It was like school but worse, because I couldn't talk or laugh. Mr. Poole, the minister, was a nice man, but he was not funny, and his stories all sounded the same. From what I could figure out, church was a place that said if you believed in what they told you and lived a "good life," you would go to this place called heaven when you died, and you would live forever. I found that a bit of a contradiction. You died, but you lived forever. No matter whom I asked where this heaven place was, no one could tell me the answer. They always pointed up. I already knew that couldn't be right. We lived on this planet that spun around the sun, so on any given day, pointing up changed. There was also one more big dilemma for me. These Protestants believed in Jesus, the Son of God, who had a real mother named Mary. So he had a mother but no real father. I had heard of Mary, because when my Catholic grandfather would swear, it always started out with "Jesus, Mary, and Joseph."

Joseph wasn't in this church. They also didn't have any saints, like my friends who went to the very scary and huge Saint Michael's— they had lots of saints who watched over them. But Catholics really scared me, because the nuns wore strange, long black clothes with cardboard across the foreheads, and they also had to go to church on Saturday as well as Sunday. Joey De G. use to tell me he had to confess his sins.

I asked him, "What sins?" He was only ten years old. He told me it was his thoughts. I thought, Holy moley, these Catholics patrol your thoughts.

He then said he had to say Hail Marys after his confession. The only Hail Mary I knew was a last-gasp pass at the end of the football game. He said he had to say about ten of them to show God he was sincere about his confession.

Whew, at least we didn't have any of that where I went. We just had Jesus. That also confused me. The Jews had Moses and David and Solomon and Isaac, and their book is called a Torah. But the Catholics had Jesus, and we had Jesus, but we were different. The explanation never made a lot of sense. They both were Christians, but they believed different things—but they were really the same.

My father explained this paradox the best. He said there were three types of Jews: Orthodox, Conservative, and Reformed. They fought like cats and dogs about which was the right way to be, and they never agreed, but they all became Jews whenever an Arab entered the room.

Got it—we believed in the same God, but the rules were different. We were right, and they were wrong, and most important, we were not them. Now I understood why all the wars in the world were fought about religion. it is kind of silly when you think about it. We all die anyway. So these church charades went on, and then my mother said, "We are moving to Forty-Ninth Street by the boulevard. You will get a bigger room."

I loved the apartment on Forty-Ninth Street. It was six houses off the boulevard that overlooked the entire New York skyline. Walking to school every day and seeing that vista always impressed me, and it made me want to go to New York. It was like a calling, a seductive whisper of hope and change and the unknown, all just a short bus ride away.

When we were at our Forty-Ninth Street apartment, another maternal pronouncement came on our first Friday there. "You know you still have to go to church."

"I know," I said, "and there's one on Forty-Seventh Street that I pass going to school."

"No, no, you go back to Twenty-Ninth Street," Ma insisted.

"Ma-a-a! But they have one right here."

"No, the one on Forty-Seventh is not your church," she continued. "Twenty-Ninth Street is your church."

I thought, My church? That's not my church. That's the one you send me to. I don't believe a word they say in there.

No amount of arguing would work. The real reason was Nanny, who lived three blocks from the Twenty-Ninth Street church. We always went to her house after church, and this also gave my parents some time alone without the kids.

There was two ways to go to church. Walk one block and take the bus, which wound itself around Union City until it dropped us off one block from church—that took forever. Or walk four blocks to Bergenline Avenue and take the trolley. I fought long and hard for the trolley option, but my sister never wanted to do the walk. She was a teenager, and they get always get everything backward. So there was chronic pleading and fighting every Sunday, until one time I actually left her and took the trolley myself. She, of course, turned me in, and that option was forever lost.

Then it happened. My sister turned seventeen, and we could now take the family car to church. It was a '49 Chevy with a stick shift. My sister was always nervous and could never get calm enough to work the clutch and gas pedal properly. She was always popping the clutch, causing a violent bucking within the car, and then it would stall. If she did this while on any incline, it was even worse. That introduced the emergency break into the clutch, gas pedal, gear-shifting nightmare.

With me laughing and getting back at her for all her terroristic treatment toward me, the ride to church became known as "Bucking Sundays." A double-entendre phrase, which when said in my house, brought an ever-so-slight smile to my father's face, until my mother gave him "the look."

Cousin Edward

Ma was looking at old family photos on the day I next visited, and she was in a nostalgic mood. She kept bringing up old family history stories. Then she said directly, "Listen, as a shrink, do you think therapy could have helped your cousin Edward?"

"Absolutely," I said. "He was a classic anorexic, and family therapy would have highlighted what his parents were doing to him. His own anxiety could have been brought into the light. We could have redirected his anger more appropriately so that his resistance to his parents would not hurt him."

"Wow, that was a mouthful. Sorry I asked."

"Excuse the shrink-speak," I said. "I still have many feelings left over from that exposure."

"You always liked Edward."

I nodded, but in truth, I always felt sorry for my cousin Edward, as he had it pretty rough. We were only six months apart in age. We grew up together in what obviously was a pretty nutty family. His father, Charlie, my mother's older brother, was a blank spot in my growing-up years, as I knew there was something wrong with him, but I did not know what it was back then. He never finished high school and never learned to read. The family hid this piece of information, and my mother only whispered it to me when I forced the conversation. When he was about fifteen years old, he dove into a pool from a high dive while the pool was being refilled. It had only about five feet of water at that time. He split his head open and was put in the hospital. The family said he was never the same after that. (I don't think he was in very good shape before he dove into the pool.) Anyway, Uncle Charlie was a master of smoke and mirrors when one asked him anything he could not answer.

He got a job in the Blickman's factory, where he read blueprints. I do not know how he managed the rest of the job, but he worked there for years, to his credit. I learned to not ask him questions, and by the time we were nine, Edward had stopped talking about him.

Uncle Charlie married Marie, whom I always liked, a fireball of an Italian with a raucous extended family. They were loud and always screaming, but they served fantastic meals. Uncle Charlie belonged to an Italian American social club on the corner. It was a mob-run place, and Uncle Charlie was the weekend bartender. Edward and I were allowed in because we were kids and no threat to anyone. I liked the place because they always had free bottles of soda and pretzels.

It was in this establishment that Uncle Charlie said a very prophetic thing to me. "Remember this: one day, probably long after I am gone, there will be a racetrack in the Meadowlands, and we will run it."

He said this about 1952, and twenty-four years later, the racetrack opened alongside Giants Stadium in the swampland that was the meadowlands to locals.

Charlie and Marie were usually a source of argument in my house, because my father could not stand the way Marie bossed Charlie around. My mother would tell him that it was none of his business. We stayed one week with them at their mosquito-ridden swamp hut, down the shore, and it confirmed that down the shore was not a good place to be.

Cousin Edward grew up in a small apartment with his mother and father. His parents' relationship was rocky at best, with Germanic, nonverbal Uncle Charlie and fiery, nonstop Marie. Edward was very thin and the constant comparisons to me were painful and awkward for both of us. My mother, being who she was, always pointed out how healthy I looked compared to Edward.

Edward had a food thing. He only ate chicken-noodle sandwiches made with white bread and would drink only milk. His mother would make Lipton's chicken noodle soup, scoop out the noodles, put them on white bread, and fold the edges over. He even took these to school. He refused all vegetables, 90 percent of all cereals, except Cheerios, and all meats. Today, he would have been treated for a severe eating disorder, and as a family therapist, I would have honed in on his relationship with his parents.

Back then, it was just "weird Edward," and everyone except me went along. I sat at the table with him when his mother would monitor his food intake. She would make him a hot dog and tell him he could not go out until he ate it. When she turned around, he would take a piece and quickly hide it in the radiator. It always worked. At night he would go back to the kitchen and throw out the evidence. He never even ate ice cream, even when out playing with me. He did have one huge vice: he would eat French-fried potatoes from the White Castle with tons of salt. He swore me to secrecy to not tell his parents about his eating them.

It wasn't often that I got to eat with Cousin Edward, Marie, and Charlie, as my mother always insisted I be home for dinner. There were some Saturdays, however, when Edward and I played at the Roosevelt Stadium near his house, and I got to eat dinner with them.

Saturday night dinner at Marie and Charlie's was a tense, loud environment. Uncle Charlie had a few drinks in him and just wanted to eat and go lie down on the couch. Marie, who worked all week and cleaned and cooked on Saturday, wanted to go out.

At dinner they would yell at one another and at the same time, tell Edward to eat—eating disorder genus right there. He did say that they did this every night. He refused to eat after they refused to stop fighting. He was proud and fought his defiant war in his own way, and the sad thing was that his parents never figured it out. This severely impinged on his health and social activities. He wanted to play football for Union Hill High School but did not weigh enough. The coach told his mother, "He would break in half out there."

Edward developed rickets, as his bones were weak and brittle. He never received any formal treatment, nor did his parents receive any counseling for themselves or him. He shared only a little of the dynamics of his family life, because he was embarrassed. He also knew it was not healthy to not eat.

Edward suffered for his disorder all his life, although he did learn to eat a few more things. He got a job as a letter carrier for the post office, and that had great benefits and job security, until his shoulder gave out under the weight of the mailbag, and he had to go on disability after multiple operations. I visited him as a grown man with two kids and was happy to see his kids were of normal size and flourishing. He said only one thing to me about his ordeal, and it was that he thought his parents were both stubborn. He learned the lesson, and the table he set was full of warmth and laughs. He did laugh and told me that he now ate Campbell's chicken noodle soup, because the noodles were bigger.

Ma continued to show me more pictures and actually found one of her entire family. She looked up at me and inquired, "You saw Edward?"

"Yeah, at his home in the mountains of northwest Jersey."

"I am happy to hear that he came out okay."

We continued to peruse the family photos.

"Well, to be honest, Ma, it's nice to hear that now, but you never helped him when you told him how skinny he was all the time."

"I was trying to show him that he could be like you if he ate."

I was incredulous and started to pace around. "Really? You never had a thought that it was a psychological/emotional problem that made him not want to eat?"

"No. No one thought that way then."

I looked directly in her eyes. "So he was what, in your mind?"

"Lazy. He didn't want to chew, and those noodles proved it."

"Well, Ma, it's a disorder that requires treatment, and you can die from it."

The conversation was getting tense, and Ma started shuffling the pictures.

She put her head down and stated, "I didn't know. No one did," and finished with, "He was just weird."

I pressed on. "Well, I feel for him. He suffered a lot, missed out on a lot, and the problem was with his parents."

"Sure blame the parents," Ma scoffed. "It's always their fault."

"Not blame, Ma. It's about responsibility. Did they never think that they were causing him emotional difficulty when they fought at the table every night and then simultaneously told him to eat?"

"I guess they didn't."

"Ma, stop with the shuffling." I kept going. "That's my point, and he suffered."

Ma said back snarkily, "Yeah, and I'm hungry."

"Jeezus, Ma! Well, how 'bout a noodle sandwich?"

"Knock it off."

The Jews Are Coming

When I opened Ma's apartment door, Thelma indicated Ma was asleep in the living room. Seeing Ma draped in my father's old afghan blanket caused me to gasp. The sight of her immediately brought back a flood of memories of my father taking his late afternoon nap in the living room, with that blanket draped over him. I hadn't seen that blanket anywhere for years. My job back then, at dinnertime, was to gently wake him, as he was never to be startled due to his heart condition.

I sat on Ma's sofa and just watched her—she looked so peaceful. I thought how strange life is as we repeat its cycles. I approached Ma the same way as I had approached my father—gently, stroking her arm and speaking softly.

She opened her eyes easily and smiled. "My boy," she said, "it's good to see you."

We then had some tea with Thelma, and I knew I had to talk to Ma about an issue that had been on my mind for weeks now.

We talked about recent news events, and then I said, "Ma, I have a question for you."

"Shoot, they are free today."

"Can you tell me what it is with you and the Jews?"

"What?"

"You and the Jews. You really don't like them."

"What is this? You lookin' for a fight?"

"No, just a talk. All my life I have heard you make comments against Jews, but you really do not have prejudice against anybody else."

"Are you nuts? Did you forget that I married a Jew?"

"That's what makes it so fascinating. You marry an Orthodox Jew in 1932 at age eighteen. Not many Gentiles were doing that. It was very strong of you to stand up to potential criticism from the Christians around you. As for your potential Orthodox Jewish in-laws, you had to know they would not come to the wedding. Then you spent your life bashing them, because they didn't come."

Ma sighed. "It's no secret that they roughed me up pretty good, but I had nothing against them."

"Then why all the comments about Aunt Helen, who use to do 'all that Goody Two-Shoes Jew work at that Temple'?"

"It was true. She was not a good Jew. She just did that to keep face with all those money people."

"Ma, that is a very prejudiced statement. It implies you know her motives and who is a deserving Jew and who isn't."

Ma shook her finger at me. "Bullshit! Aunt Helen was a phony, and she did those Jew things just so Sam's business would look good."

"You could say the same thing about Post 18 for sponsoring my Little League team, or any plumber, electrician, or lawn service who put their name on the back of any kid team's jacket."

Her face became sterner and her voice rose as she said, "Look, I stood up to marry your father, and they denied my existence and then your sister's and cut your father off as well. It was only when you came along that they even knew I was alive."

"I understand that is an Orthodox belief. Right or wrong, it is what they are taught and believe. Who are we to judge?"

She opened her hands, palms up, and stated, "Well, in my opinion, that's too Jewish."

"Oh Je-e-e-sus, I heard you say that all my growing-up years, and it took forever for me to get over it."

"It's true."

"No, Ma, it's not. It's just your opinion, based on your hurt and anger."

"Oh, Mr. Fucking Therapist is in the room."

I shot back, "Do you say that about Christians? Are they 'too Catholic' for going to confession? Are they 'too Protestant' for singing psalms in the choir? Are they 'too Jehovah's Witness' for going door to door? Are they 'too Islamic' for praying five times a day?"

Ma moderated her voice. "I don't have much religion in me, but I don't understand one that let's people pretend that others are dead because they don't believe as they do."

"Okay, you don't understand, but I would point out that there are many paradoxes in religion. Christians believe in turning the other cheek, yet more wars have been fought in the name of their Christianity than anything else. The Arabs cannot stop fighting among themselves, with centuries of sectarian wars between Shiites and Sunnis. Look at the Asian countries wars because of tribal religious differences."

She leaned in and used her listen-to-me voice. "It's not all Jews. It's just the ones who think they are the chosen ones."

"It's a false argument, Ma. Each religion believes they have the inside track to God and therefore look at others in a lesser way."

She sits back. "Maybe."

"When I was in grad school, Ma, they taught us that America classifies its poor as worthy or unworthy. The worthy ones get 'benefits,' and the unworthy ones get 'handouts.' One system was beneficent, and the other was authoritarian and discriminating. Like today's Democratic and Republican differences. The United States looks down at places like India because of how they treat the poor, yet it completely overlooks how blacks were treated generically in this country for 250 years. They were treated like the unworthy poor, yet the Appalachian whites do not have the same prejudice against them, although they were at the same uneducated poverty level."

Thelma interjected, "That's so right, Mr. Ken. You tell her."

Ma threw up her hands. "I don't know about that stuff, but I do know that those Jews stick together and when one says go left, they go left."

I took the bait. "That is total hogwash. Have you ever been in a room of Jews having a discussion? No one agrees with anyone else. Wait a minute—you've had Italian friends all your life. Don't you think they are kind of clannish and stick together? What about Olga? Wasn't she Hungarian and would listen only to her Hungarian friends? Sticking together is an immigrant social survival kind of thing. It preserves your culture and keeps you connected to your traditions and beliefs. The Jews are no different from the Germans, Italians, Irish, and now Spanish, who all lived in bounded communities before they acculturated."

Ma was undaunted and heating up again. "That's it, Sonny Boy, all true, except the goddamn Jews hated acculturation, and that is why they kicked me in the ass. They thought your father sold out."

"To them, he did. It wasn't about you; it was what he did. To them, the tradition is to not intermarry. Period. If you do, you're out. All they knew about you was that you would not have a Jewish child. End of story. Their familial line stopped with that marriage. They only came back because I could restore the familial name by marrying a Jewish girl."

She had a disgusted look on her face. "By that time, I wanted nothing to do with his family."

"And that cost me, as I received no cultural or religious training from one-half of my family, because you punished him for his family, and he chose to hide it."

Her tone became mocking. "Ah, poor Sonny Boy, never became a Jew."

I become indignant. "No, Ma, I am. It's my birthright, and my father's mistake was not believing enough in himself to make it without giving up his religion, family, and culture. He had a brother who would have helped him make money in the embroidery business."

"Your father wanted to be his own man."

I raised my voice. "He was, and we all paid the price for that. He could have done many things and kept his family, but he thought being invisible as a Jew was the way to go. But this is America and New York and not Prussia. It cost him, it cost you, and it cost his kids."

She said very firmly, "He did the best he could, and he was better off without them."

"You are so wrong. That is your anger talking. Everyone needs a family for support and the passing of traditional family values. It's the glue in the mix."

"Oh yeah, well, every time I saw the Jews coming, I would cringe and just hope they'd go back to Brooklyn."

I felt beaten by this argument and said, "Too bad, Ma. You blamed them for their beliefs and never learned to respect them. It's no different today. The Orthodox still want the old ways, and the Reformers want the new. The newest class of immigrants band together until they learn the language and culture, and the beat goes on."

Ma put up her hand to silence me. "Enough of this crap. Where's my lunch?"

"One bagel, with chopped liver and onion, coming up, pickle on the side."

"Very funny, wiseass."

"One more thing, and then I'll stop."

"Make it fast. I'm starving."

"You know after Daddy died, I kept looking for someone in his family to reach out to me and offer some guidance. No one did. Then when I was thirty, I read an article in the paper about Murray Ludmer, who was my father's first cousin."

"Wasn't he a big-shot lawyer or something?"

"Yes, and I called him. He was delighted to hear that I was just graduated from Columbia, and he invited me to his Passover family dinner in New Jersey. I had finally found who I was looking for. He was tall, bright, and successful, with a booming law practice. It was such a gift for me to meet an intelligent, sophisticated male family member. He had a wonderful wife and two grown kids, and he lived in a spacious home in Wood-Ridge. He reached out to me right away and said he would offer advice on how to build my practice, and we set up an appointment for two weeks later in the city to have lunch and get to know one another."

"Sounds great. I never knew you met him."

"He had a heart attack and died the very next week, and it was over before it began. I was devastated and felt it was an omen—that it was something that just wasn't ever going to be for me. I was right, and it has been an ache in me that never seems to fully go away."

"I'm sorry, Sonny Boy, but don't fret. You made it anyway."

"Yeah, I guess so."

"Now what about my lunch?"

Age 1

with great grandmother Omah

Age 5

Family 1945

155

with dad

Barbara Nanny Ma Omah

Family

Father 1942

Ma's kid

with Clem Labine Age 12

Wooden Spoon Queen

Parents 1932

Terry

high school years

E5 1968

Heidelberg apt

Outpatient
Psychiatry
Heidelberg

Der Hund

Paris 1967

Mt. Tamalpais 1969

San Fransisco 1969

Montana 1969

Village years with
Toady and Cathy

Greenwich Village 1970

with Janice 1970

Columbia Years

with Ken Ferris 1970

California

with Randy Fuengirola Feria

Ma and Geno

Age 35

with Ma 1986

Jill, Aly, Josh

Ma at 80 with Geno

Josh and Aly

Jill and Mia

with Josh and Aly

with Jill Patagonia

Heidelberg 2013

Sorrento

Istanbul

Argentina

Matches

Looking for Horns in Tulsa

When I arrived the next time, Thelma was making brownies and still thinking about the showgirl story I'd told her a while ago. "That for real, Mr. Ken? That showgirl no-name thing?"

"Absolutely, Thelma, 100 percent. I also met a lot of women while traveling the States, and they were very different from one another. I even met one who had never seen a Jew before."

"Lucky her," Ma said sarcastically.

"Stop it, Ma. You just never let it go."

"Where this woman from?" asked Thelma.

"Oklahoma. Let me tell you about the horns ..."

I got a hitch with a rancher named Hanks, and we made it to Oklahoma City. It was once a frontier town and had no big downtown, to speak of. It had some city elements, but it was vaguely similar to Los Angeles, all spread out. I found a shop that rented bicycles, as I just wanted to use my legs, and this city looked difficult to walk around in.

I took the two-hour rental—no deposit, no leaving a driver's license or fifty dollars, like in New York. When I talked to the proprietor about it, he simply said matter-of-factly, "People don't steal bikes around here," and he added, "Where would you go with it anyway, that I could not find you, if I wanted to?"

Amazing, I thought. New York life is really jaded when it comes to this simple stuff. I had a Chinese Laundromat guy who did my shirts for years. When I lost my ticket, he made me wait five days because that was the policy, yet he said it was "nothing personal."

I took the bike, peddled around, and found a little park with ducks in a pond—moms and kids and ice cream. I realized after talking to a few people that unless one lived and worked here, there was not much to see or do. But I enjoyed just being there, as it was relaxed and comfortable.

I found Oklahoma to have the most beautiful contrast in colors. The red dirt is everywhere, and it is deep and awe-inspiring. It was summer when I was there, and the combinations of red, blue, purple, and yellow flowers with the deep-green grasses made for a beautiful soft vista. As to the people, they appeared hard working, with leathered faces, and they spoke like straight-shooters. The people I spoke with, for the most part, did not like big cities, and by my standard, Oklahoma City was not a big city, but it was very big to them.

"City folk all a-livin' ona top of one another," the general-store man, Leonard, said to me. He had been running this small store that sold a variety of foods and general merchandise for over forty years. He had his opinions. "Damn Indians drink too much and tear things up on Saturday, after they get their government checks."

I told him that sounded like every cowboy I had ever met.

He explained that cowboys were different. "They work every day, real hard, and need to kick up their heels a bit. These Indians just sit around and sit around."

After bashing the Indians, he said he was a good Christian man, and God would forgive him for talking that way, but he also added that God didn't have to live with "these damn Indians" like he did.

I almost told him that his God probably made those Indians, but I held back from saying it.

My next ride came when I was not looking for one. A woman came into the store when Leonard was still bashing the Indians.

"Oh, there you go again," she said to him. "You wouldn't be talking that way if your Millie had not run off with that young stud Indian boy."

"Nuttin' to do wit' it," he said.

She turned to me, and after she eyed my knapsack, she politely asked, "Where you from, young man?"

"New York, and I am going back East, ma'am."

"Well, I need a drink first, and then I'll take you for as far as Tulsa, if you are going there."

"Sounds good to me."

I dropped off my bike and piled into her Chevy pickup, and we headed for a roadside saloon with a jukebox and a pool table, just like the other sixty thousand bars in America. Emma Sue W. was thirty-eight and divorced. She was quite sassy, with overly red lipstick and a curvy figure. She looked to be in good shape, but her hands looked more like a cowboy's than a woman's. She said she ran a small animal farm in Tulsa, Oklahoma, and had been to the big city to visit her grandmother and her older sister. She was on her way back to Tulsa, where she had two kids of her own—her younger brother's wife was looking after them while she was away. She had long, kind of wild red hair and jewelry that did not go with the jeans and cowgirl hat she wore. Her blouse was a bit more open than it should have been.

She told me I talked funny and fast and asked if I could shoot pool.

"Yes, ma'am, I am considered a good pool shooter."

"We'll see," she said, her eyes widening.

After three or four beers, I had beaten her at pool, as well as everyone else in the bar. They wanted to start doing shots, but I told her that it was time for me to go.

She said, "Only because I am driving."

We left and got into the truck. Emma Sue grabbed me behind the neck and gave me one big-time kiss. It got hot and heavy, as Emma Sue was a woman who went for what she wanted. We had started fumbling around, right there in the parking lot, when she suddenly stopped and started up the engine. She drove about ten minutes, without saying anything, although her breathing was heavy. She pulled over by a creek, and we got out and watched the sun set on a blanket she had spread out. While moving her hand to unbutton my shirt, she stopped and looked at me, "What the hell is that thing hanging around your neck?"

"It's a mezuzah," I answered,

"A what?"

"It's like a cross that Christians wear."

"You're not a Christian?"

"No, ma'am. I am Jewish." No need to tell her the half part.

"Now you stop right now. My name is Emma Sue, not ma'am, and that's how you will call me. And holy Jesus, I have never met a Jew person before."

I informed her of the proper etiquette—that she could call me Jewish, or refer to me as a Jew.

"I have heard that you people are money stealers and cannot be trusted."

"Well, thank you for your honesty, but Jews earn a lot of money because they are educated, are considered smart, and work very hard."

"You mean to tell me that you are a Jew, even though you look like every Protestant that I have ever seen, and you shoot pool better than any of those boys back there?"

"Emma Sue, that is true."

"Let me see that thing around your neck."

I showed it to her. "Back home, everyone has one, and we put them at the entrance to our homes," I explained. "It is like putting Saint Christopher on your car dashboard,"

"What are these funny-looking letters?"

"That is Hebrew."

"My, my."

She went on to tell me about every stereotype she had ever heard about Jews—sneaky, steal from poor people, smell funny, cannot be trusted, and cheap, cheap, cheap.

I was incredulous, so I had to ask, "Did you know that Jews wear those funny little circle yarmulke hats to cover up their small horns?"

No, she said, she had had not heard that—and then she rubbed her hand through my hair. It was as if she thought it might really be true, and then she saw the astonished look on my face, and she laughed. "You are putting me on."

I knew then how far I was from New York. This woman was thirty-eight and had never met a Jew. Or if she had, she did know they were Jewish. I kept thinking, Why would they even have prejudice out here against Jews? She had never seen one, and yet she knew they were people she could not trust—and they trusted everyone out here. I was blown away.

Emma Sue quickly said I was different, which I am not, and tried to change the subject to get us back on track. When that did not work, she admitted, "I have absolutely ruined this moment, so let's get goin'."

Once again, we got into her truck and headed to Tulsa. After a while, she said she was sorry for the things she'd said about Jews. "You're a very fine young man," she said, "and if all the Jews are like you, then I will have to change my opinion."

I thought she was sincere.

I took one last shot. "Jews are like everyone else, Emma Sue. Some of them, you will like, and others you may not. No different from being in a whole room full of Catholics or Protestants or Muslims."

I told her that the one thing I objected to was prejudice, and I went on to defend all the target groups. When I got done with my diatribe, she quietly apologized for hurting my feelings.

Apology accepted.

She told me she was going to show me that her heart was in the right place, and when we got to Tulsa, she would make dinner for me.

"Why, thank you, Emma Sue. That would be greatly appreciated."

I liked saying Emma Sue every chance I got. Not many New York women use a middle name. But out here, Billy Ray, and Joe Don, and Bobby Mack were common names, as were Peggy Lynn, and Loretta Mae, and I guess, Emma Sue.

Emma Sue's farm was delightful, quaint, and very well maintained. She raised chickens, rabbits, minks, and chinchillas. There were also dogs and cats everywhere. She made us a fine dinner, with candlelight and wine. She called her brother's wife and said she would pick up the kids the next morning, as she was entertaining.

We hadn't talked at all about anything after dinner, but I guess I looked like a sure thing to her—like most men. After dinner, we went into her lovely log cabin living room, and she put on whatever rock ballads she had—when we were in the truck, I'd said I'd heard enough twangy country music in the past three weeks to fill a lifetime.

She excused herself and came back later wearing a very sultry silk robe. She sat down next to me and said in a 1940s movie-starlet voice, "You like?" She was a very well-endowed woman, and she meant business. Nothing like an older woman taking the lead and telling me exactly what she wanted. It was a very sweet night. We slept upstairs in a loft section she had built off her living room. I remember feeling the breeze through the open window as she fell asleep, nestled next to me. I could smell the animals and the flowers—delightful. It brought back "the lake."

In the morning, Emma Sue made sausages and eggs and strong coffee. I had a great shower, and she my washed clothes and hung them on the line. I thought this was great. She dropped me off on Route 66 and said she had learned something from me, and she would do better in the future. That was very sweet of her, and I thanked her. She kissed me good-bye and was off to pick up her kids.

Thelma's brownies were almost done, and the aroma filled the air. "You sure find 'em, Mr. Ken," Thelma said.

Ma shook her head and said, "He found them everywhere, all colors and types."

"Wasn't that bad, Ma."

"Yes, it was. I thought for years that you would never be able to settle down, because you seemed to need an endless supply."

"Ma, I was single, and it was the sixties. Everyone I knew did not want to be married or tied down to family life."

"Yes, you were the free generation," she remarked, "a little bit like it was in the twenties for me."

"So you knew?"

Ma continued while her brow wrinkled a bit. "No, dammit, I was too young. By the time I knew what the hell it was all about, I had a child, and it was the '30s Depression."

"So you missed it?"

"Sure did," she said. "I always felt I was too young for what I chose."

I queried, "Is that why you always told me to wait until I was thirty before getting married?"

"Probably."

"Well, I listened."

She looked to Thelma and stated, "I think that was the only thing he ever listened to me about."

Smelling the freshly baked brownies, I walked over to Thelma and said, "At least I listened."

Thelma proudly stated, "C'mon, y'all. It's brownies time."

We all sat at the table, polishing off Thelma's brownies and enjoying just being there with one another.

Carnival in Rio

Ma was in a fun mood the next time I visited. After we had a light lunch of her homemade chicken salad, which she had Thelma make according to her microspecific instructions, she asked, "Did you ever have those Caipirinhas when you were in Rio?"

"Yes, by the pitcher," I answered.

She smiled as she remembered. "Jesus, they were good."

I replied, "But they can knock you off your ass."

"Well, Mr. Gonzo, I remember that story of you in Rio."

"I remember that you, Ma, had told me to go there."

"You two certainly do get around," Thelma interjected. "You both was in Rio?"

I nodded. "Yes, Ma went with Geno and raved about it, so when I got my chance, I took it."

"Is it as good as Mardi Gras in New Orleans?" Thelma asked.

Ma said, "I was not there during Carnival, but from what I saw, it was just about Carnival every day to those Brazilians. They never stop moving, always dancing and singing, even on the beach. They continually eat and drink; they are a fun people."

"I agree; you can have New Orleans," I said. "The Carnival there is minor compared to the real deal in Rio de Janeiro. Let me tell you about my Carnival in Rio. ..."

I had Brazilian friends who would not stop badgering me about coming to see them and the real feria—the authentic, mama lucca of big-time parties. So I took the eleven-hour flight to stay with them for a week of nonstop revelry. What happened to me there is one of the very best experiences I ever had, which included a bit of drama, of course. I had originally met my friends Paolo and Nerida in New York, as they were friends of a mutual friend in my summer rental house in East Hampton. We hit it off immediately, and they invited me to stay with them in Rio de Janeiro.

A few words of explanation first: the big parties in Carnival do not take place on the street. To the Brazilians, that is the poor people's parade. Although all of Rio joins in the street festival, the real deal takes place in the private soccer clubs. My buddy and his wife were avid soccer fans, like most South Americans, and they were fiercely devoted to their national team. During the week I spent with them in their open-air, top-floor, beautiful apartment, I went to see a match between Brazil and Argentina, their sworn enemy. The stadium held 110,000 people. I had never heard that level of singing and noise. When I was stationed in Europe, I saw a match between Germany and England, but that paled in comparison.

My fiercely devoted soccer-fan host couple explained how it worked. They were members of one of Brazil's biggest soccer clubs. The clubs compete against each other for bragging rights and a big trophy. As with American golf clubs, it is considered a privilege to join. The club also competes with the other clubs during Carnival to put on the biggest and best ball. Their club was very popular; it had a long waiting list for membership, and the Masquerade Ball was considered the event of the year.

Costumes were required—the best ones showed a lot of skin, with elaborate adornments and plumage. An outrageous hat was a must.

Elaborate jewelry on headdresses, painted faces, and glistening bodies were the standard. Being nearly nude was common, and others would be dressed for a ball. Paolo's wife, Nerida, said I should go as a Roman god—a stripped-down Roman god. My costume consisted of a bikini bottom, sandals with crisscrossing leather straps that went up to my knees, and a gold floral wreath on my head. My entire body was sprayed with gold glitter. Nerida hung jewelry around my neck and put about ten bracelets on my arms. And she made up my eyes with black and dark green shadow.

When we all were dressed in our costume best, we headed off to their soccer club. It was a huge two-story brick building with six-foot-high walls surrounding the entire property. Inside, there was a monstrous ballroom where the party was to take place. The rear exit led to formal gardens and sitting areas. It was a magnificent building, decorated with flowers everywhere, as well as strung-up lights and feria lanterns. Ribbons hung from the rafters. It was quite elegant, colorful, and inviting. The costumes were even more elaborate than I expected.

At ten o'clock, the samba band began, and they continued nonstop until sunrise. The band was on a huge stage, and when they were exhausted, their stage retracted, and a second stage emerged with an entirely new band. I never saw that anywhere else, ever. The music had to be nonstop—that was the tradition. The thunderous beat to the amplified music enveloped everyone.

While dancing, the Brazilians passed in a whirl of color and sights. Naked bodies rubbed up against one another, and hands and arms were everywhere. After a while, I just lost myself in the music and the intense feeling. Drinks were nonstop, including the Caipirinha, a rum-based lethal concoction that will make every inhibition cease.

I had danced for over three hours and had many Caipirinhas, so I retired to the gardens to rest and get some air. A Brazilian beauty in a skimpy, topless costume sat next to me. We talked for a while and then returned together to dance. My friends saw us together and toasted us.

By the end of the evening, I had blisters on my feet and could barely walk. The last I remember, I was walking to the gardens to sit down.

I must have passed out and rolled off the bench into the garden area with the plants, because that was where I woke up. It was morning, and the place was empty and locked up. My friends had left, thinking I was with that Brazilian woman. When the staff closed the door to the garden, they apparently did not see me. There I was, in the garden of a locked soccer club, wearing only a bikini bottom and with gold glitter spray now smudged all over my body. I had no money, no identification, and did not even know the address of my friend Paolo.

I climbed up the trellis of the flower wall and hoisted myself onto a tree that went over the wall. I lowered myself to the outside sidewalk below—but then wondered what to do. Unfortunately, it was then that I decided that walking around would only get me in trouble, so I sat on the steps of the club and waited for it to reopen. I was a funny-looking sight to passersby. About an hour later, the cleaning staff arrived, and they let me in.

I managed to get through the language barrier with one of the workers and indicated that my friend was a member. Would he please look up Paolo's number and call him for me? I pantomimed what had happened to me. To my amazement, this worked, and I spoke to Paolo, who could not stop laughing. It was a bit daunting to be that naked and broke and lost—and in a foreign country where I did not speak the language, all at the same time.

"Paolo picked me up within twenty minutes. We later laughed every time we thought about it, but I have a suggestion for any future revelers in Rio's Carnival: don't leave to go to the ball without your address and cab fare stuffed in your bikini."

Ma smiled and gestured with her hands, as if to say unbelievable. "Now Thelma, who does that happen to that doesn't wind up beaten up or in jail?"

"I guess Mr. Ken," Thelma answered. "He one lucky man."

"When I was in Rio," Ma added, "we stayed in Copacabana, at a ritzy hotel, got all dressed up and took cabs everywhere, and never had to worry about being naked on the street."

"All true." I smiled and added, "But who had more fun?"

Gays Everywhere

I was feeling good when, on my next visit, I entered Ma's bedroom and said playfully, "Hey, Queen, what's shakin'?"

"The only queen here is long gone," Ma answered.

"Really? Why's that?"

She pointed to herself. "Look, Sonny Boy. Take a good look."

I complimented her, "I see you, the grande dame, and a beautiful apartment."

"Bullshit. I saw myself in the mirror. It's a horror show."

"Ma, you're ninety-two and a half, and you look terrific."

She smirked. "Nice try, Mr. Smooth-Talker, but my hair is thin, ratty, and ugly, and my face looks like it fell off. I have more ugly liver spots than a leopard, and my tits are these pathetic droopy air bags."

Thelma admonished her, "Miss Alicia, you hush up now."

"It's the fuckin' truth, and you two are foolin' nobody with this flimsy charade of compliments." She looked directly at me as she said, "And you—you are more of a queen than me, Mr. Greenwich-Fucking-Village."

"What? Where is this coming from?"

She waved her finger at me. "No matter how many girls you slept with, there was always that question about you."

"And what question would that be, oh, mother of mine?"

She made her I got you face and stated firmly, "Well, I remember when all of your hometown thought you had switched sides and were batting for the other team."

I smiled disbelievingly. "Really? You know damn well they were just a bunch of homophobes who associated everything in the Village with being gay."

She used a lawyer's voice, as if interrogating me in the courtroom. "Did you not have gay friends who you hugged in public?"

"Yes."

"Well, I guess they wondered what you did with them in private."

"And you? What did you think?"

Ma sat back as if remembering. "There were times when you wore those tight leather pants with all that jewelry and your long hair. I thought you looked more like a girl than a boy."

"It was the sixties, Ma. My whole generation wore crazy, colorful clothes, and everyone had long hair. It was a statement against Johnson and Nixon and America's war machine and not about our sexuality."

"Well, you asked."

"Was you a gay boy, Mr. Ken?" Thelma asked matter-of-factly.

"I'm not gay, Thelma, although I do very good spot-on imitation. My gay friends tell me it's my true self screaming to come out. But gays always think everyone else is gay, and if you are not, you at least secretly want to be, or are in denial that you really are gay. But alas, I'm not gay."

Ma spoke in her derisive tone. "Who does that imitation thing? Very homo."

"Ma, that is 1950s language. No one calls people 'homo' anymore."

"Homo-schmomo, it's in you!"

"Thelma, maybe you have an objective ear," I suggested. "You tell us what you think. Let me tell you how this started. ..."

I lived in the West Village, an area noted for housing Irish poets, the New York arts scene, pottery shops, and folk and jazz music bars.

There were writers, actors, dancers, and theater companies. There also were many playwrights, film people, and sculptors. It was a place where free expression was and still is accepted. It also had a very large gay community; Christopher Street was its center. The Stonewall riots, which launched the gay rights movement, were in my neighborhood.

I lived with my girlfriend, Karen, who owned a tiny, nervous, white Maltese dog named Bunky, who peed on the rug incessantly. I would take Bunky out for the last walk each evening. It might be one in the morning as I walked along Washington Street, one block from the Hudson River, and waited for ol' Bunky to do her business. There coincidentally were empty meat-market tractor trailers parked across the street, and they were used by the gay community for meeting, exchanging body fluids, and assorted other activities. There also was a late-night transvestite population that walked these streets, trying to pick up men in cars, usually those from New Jersey.

One night as I was walking Bunky, I met Bob, who also had a nervous little dog that peed a lot. He lived nearby on Greenwich Street. While talking to Bob as the dogs did their sniff thing, a car pulled up, and an obviously gay man looked at us. As it turned out, he was from my old town in New Jersey, and he was on the prowl. After he said hello, and we exchanged a few comments about nothing, he said, "I know you, and I can't believe you're gay also."

I had a girl-chasing reputation in high school and played football and baseball—activities not associated at the time with being gay. I also hung out with the "in crowd," and no one ever thought of me as gay.

I looked the guy square in the eye and told him I was not gay, but within a few months, rumors had spread all over my hometown: that I had moved to the Village (true) and was seen walking a little faggy white dog (true); I had very long hair (true); and I was dressed very colorfully while talking to a very gay man at one in the morning (true). I couldn't say anything at the time that would not sound ridiculous. If I were gay, I would admit it.

Bob and I continue talking, and he invited me and Karen to one of his parties. "A lot of different people will be there," he said, "plus some great food, music, and wine." We went, and we loved it. There were fun people who sang and danced and told fantastic stories, some with wild affectations. We invited some people back to our place, and friendships were born.

I also found out that on Thursday nights, there was a killer card game at Bob's, so I went to that. Bob knew I was straight, but many of his friends didn't. They sang to me, got my drinks, brought me food, and generally flirted with me. I thought it was a fun, so I played along. On my fourth poker night there, one of my patients came in, dressed up in a full gown with high heels and a red wig.

He started screaming, "I knew you were gay! I knew it!"

"I'm just playing cards with my friends," I said.

"You have a lot of pretty friends," my patient said to me.

At that point I questioned if playing cards at Bob's would be good for my new career, with all the confidentiality issues that therapy brings.

These friends of mine were very warm and caring and demonstrative with their feelings. Hugs were common. A hug from a gay person, even in public, should mean nothing different than one from a straight friend—except when it's done in Sheridan Square in front of a few high school friends, who had come to the Village to see if the rumors about me were true. After that day, the rumors went wild.

I looked over at Thelma, who had a quizzical look and pursed lips.

"Thelma, in general, I've had more fun at parties and gatherings with a gay crowd than with a straight one," I said. "I mean, who cannot laugh when a twenty-seven-year-old flaming black queen prances out in a tutu, with a boa, long cigarette holder, and eye glitter, and belts out 'People'?"

Ma blurted out, "Normal people don't do that."

"So, Ma, I guess I'm not normal, because we went to cross-dressing parties, and Karen even put on a strip show as a male dancer. It was a lot of fun. I have always enjoyed gay people and consider myself a fun person, and a true defender of everyone's rights. And if that makes me gay in your eyes, then I am gay."

"I don't think he gay, Miss Alicia," Thelma offered. "He just wild."

Ma folded her arms and said in her judge voice, "It's in there somewhere."

Wiggling my fingers effeminately, I asked Ma, "Want thum juith, Ma?"

"Homo."

The Columbia Years

O h, here he is," Ma greeted me as I walked into the room.
"And good afternoon to you, Ms. Perky," I responded.
"Watch it, Hotshot, I'm feelin' my old self today."

That usually meant I should be ready to duck, because the zingers were loaded, and it just was a matter of who would be the target.

Ma was reading the New York Times, something she rarely did, so I commented on it.

"You left it here the other day," she said. "And don't give me that surprised look."

"Well, you usually read the Post."

"Oh, I see. Not smart enough for you?"

"Just saying, Ma."

Ma pointed at me and looked to Thelma. "Thelma, Mr. Smart-Guy, here, did take me on a very interesting tour of his smart-ass university."

"That so?"

"Yes," she continued. "I had never been to an Ivy League campus, and it was wonderful. All those fancy big buildings, and the cafeteria was gorgeous and as big as an auditorium."

"I was very happy to take you there," I said, "as it was a special place of recovery for me. I had climbed out of the 'failed college boy' role and could now walk around with my head up, and I wanted to show you where I was now."

Ma had a twinkle in her eye. "He brought me to their library, and it was as big as a football field. Never saw so many books."

"Not that big, but impressive nonetheless," I said.

Ma lamented, "I remember wishing I'd been lucky enough to go to college, but being poor as a pauper, the idea never really came to anything."

I added, "It was good to see the proud look on your face when I showed the security guard my ID card."

I started thinking back to those years ...

But those years were full of uncertainty as well as creativity and craziness. I had zero money. I was living on the money that the Veteran's Administration sent me as part of my GI benefits, which totaled $110 a month. I was living in a rent-controlled apartment on West Eleventh Street in the West Village for $52.90 a month. With Con Edison and New York Telephone taking up another $25 monthly, it left me with about $30 for everything else. That was a dollar a day for food. So I got jobs working around my schedule of two full days of classes and three days of work (for credit, not pay) at a supervised field placement. I was placed on the Lower East Side and worked for the Federal Mobilization for Youth program and then the Henry Street Settlement House. My second year was in an outpatient psychiatric clinic.

I got various jobs in Village restaurants and bars. I cooked hamburgers at the Corner Bistro; waited tables at Shaun's on Seventh Avenue, next to the big-time Riviera Tavern; on Sundays, David taught me to cook omelets at his David's Pot Belly on Christopher Street. And I tended bar at White Horse Tavern on Hudson Street. The White Horse was one of the most popular of the Village bars, and many famous musicians came in there to sing on their off nights. Richie Havens and John Sebastian, among others, were regulars. We would close the door about one in the morning, and everyone would pile into the back room to listen and sing along. It also was home to actors and playwrights and writers. It was a local bar that usually was packed and quite raucous, due to its Irish-writers-and-storytellers-bar reputation. I will never forget my first night "behind the stick" (bartending) at the Horse.

Toward the end of that night, a woman about fifty years old at the end of the bar started singing. I ignored it. She asked for more drinks, and the more she drank, the louder she got. Some of the other patrons looked at her with scorn.

At one point, it got to me, and I told her to be quiet, as she was getting too loud. A few of the other younger red-haired patrons said, "If she wants to sing, she can sing as loud and as long as she wants."

"Well, as long as it doesn't bother anyone else," I agreed.

"If it bothers them, throw them the fuck out," a patron answered.

The woman berated me, asking to no one in particular, "Who the hell is this young piece of crap?"

I saw she had support and chose to leave her alone.

At some point, she left, and a few of the young men around her said, "We won't forget this."

I had no idea who they were, so I ignored it. When I closed up and was walking down Eleventh Street to go home, a few of those guys were sitting on a stoop. I heard one say, "There he is."

They formed a circle around me, and within seconds, there must have been ten of them. "Do you know who we are?" one asked.

"No."

"We are the Hanleys, and that was our mother who you told to shut up. We are here to teach you some manners." Just as they stepped closer, I saw a guy I knew named Mike. He ran the moving company up on Hudson Street.

I called out to him, "Mike, can you help me here?"

He came right over and said, "I know this guy. What happened here?"

The Hanleys told Mike of my indiscretion with their mother.

He said to them, "He's a good guy. I know he won't do that again. He didn't know."

They grumbled but retreated, saying, "That's a warning, asshole," as they walked away.

As it turned out, Mike's last name was Hanley too. He was the oldest brother and carried a huge reputation. He saved me an ass-kicking. I eventually became friends with the family after some awkward nights, as I learned to let Mae Hanley sing all she wanted. I did reproach the bar owners for not giving me a heads-up on the Hanley family mom. They just laughed and said, "This is an Irish bar in an Irish neighborhood. You should have known."

I got to know all the other restaurant and bar owners. They were part of a huge informal network of people who provided refuge in their villas to traveling Village friends in idyllic locations as far away as Portugal and Spain.

My Columbia years were a time of frantic energy between school, placement, and working, while acting, modeling, and doing everything else that was happening for me in the Village in my upside-down world between 1969 and 1972. One of the most difficult events of my life took place during those years, after I returned from Germany. I was strongly against our involvement in the Vietnam War, and at that time, the racist George Wallace was running to be the president of the USA. He was to speak in New York City at Madison Square Garden.

I joined a relatively moderate protest group assembled on Seventh Avenue, one block south of the Garden. We were nonviolent and only had signs that stated our objection to an openly racist man running for the highest office in the United States. The police kept us penned in and far out of earshot as Wallace's motorcade pulled up to the Garden.

After Wallace made his entrance, the police took down the barricades. The crowd then stood around and talked about whether we were going to wait until his speech was over.

At this point, a whole squadron of police on horseback assembled across Seventh Avenue, one block to our north. The protesters were puzzled by this massive force of police for such a relatively small gathering. We thought was there something else going on that we did not know about.

Then, seemingly right out the movie Dr. Zhivago, the cops on horseback charged the crowd, and as they came by, they wildly swung their billy clubs.

It was an absolutely surreal moment. We were a constitutionally assembled group of protesters, carrying only placards, being run down by the New York City police in order to support a racist governor of Alabama. It made no sense whatsoever. Why did they not have trouble with this man who screamed, "Segregation now, and segregation forever?"

That day has lived with me as one of the most baffling events ever. When we protested at the Moratorium in Washington the next year, and those police charged, I understood, because that was a much more volatile crowd. The potential for political embarrassment was greater in Washington, DC, and that was about the Vietnam War. Nixon wouldn't have it, and he and Attorney General John Mitchell sent in the horses. This is what my America was turning into.

By the following September, I was enrolled at Columbia. My first classes were in the Andrew Carnegie mansion at Ninety-Second Street and Fifth Avenue. I bought a motorcycle with my last dollars, because I could not afford a car, and the subway was inconvenient and unreliable.

The building was testament to the magnate who built it. With twelve-foot doors and one-foot moldings, and paintings that could have hung in the Metropolitan Museum, it was an unreal setting for class. I walked around there with my mouth open for weeks. It also had an inner courtyard with statues and formal flower displays that served as a sitting area to study.

An interesting point is that Ma's father, Pop-Pop, worked on the frames of the paintings that hung in the mansion. His boss, Mr. Kelleher, who owned the framing business, had been commissioned by Carnegie to frame many of the works that hung there. As I went to class I wondered, which one is Pop-Pop's? He built the frames in the building, because they were too big to transport easily in those days.

I would sit in class and just think to myself, wow, Pop-Pop met Andrew Carnegie.

My next two years were at the main campus on Morningside Heights on West 116th Street. That felt so incredible. I was on full scholarship at a very prestigious graduate social work school. Many of the legends in the field of social work were my professors, and we used their books for our class work. I would go to Low Library or eat lunch in John Jay Hall. It was a feeling that I was surrounded by knowledge and scholars, and measuring up was always the challenge.

I would ask myself over and over, how'd I get here? I never was a great student until I arrived there. I had worked hard in the US Army, and I think that was what did it. I also did well on the graduate entrance exams, which was a first for me. I did well at Columbia because of one fundamental difference between every class I ever attended before then and the expectation that Columbia had of its students. Before, teachers had asked me to give back what I read by taking various tests—either essay of multiple choice or sometimes tricky true/false questions—to see if I knew the material. At Columbia, it was expected that I knew the material before I went to class, and in class, the discussion was on what I thought of the material. They wanted me to form an educated opinion. My own. It had to be well presented, by knowing what the hell I was talking about. That lit me up, and I applied myself, because I really felt my professors wanted me to learn, not quiz me about if I'd learned.

During my last year there, quite an historic event occurred, due to the political times in which we lived. It all converged when Mark Rudd and others took over the school's Administration Building in protest of Columbia's connection to Dow Chemical and the making of napalm, which was being used in Vietnam. Columbia was accused of being part of the research for the Military Industrial Complex. They also questioned Columbia's connection to South Africa and apartheid.

The fact that Columbia owned many building along Columbus Avenue led to their reputation as a slumlord, and all these factors cumulatively led to the takeover on the main campus. It received national media coverage, and the university actually shut down before we were ever able to take finals. My transcript for the 1971 spring semester has only "P," for pass. There were lines of police at the university, and I had to show my ID every fifty yards. It was chaos on campus and in the USA.

My money was at a critically low period during my last year, and I did not have enough money for food. Columbia paid for my classes, but I had to buy my books, and they were very expensive. I went to the Grand Street Settlement House and told them of my situation. It was very humbling to have to beg for money, because I was now twenty-eight years old and had been working steadily since I was fourteen. Although I was working, it wasn't enough to pay all of my bills. They gave me $1,000—such a kind gesture. I made it last for ten months, as I only bought food with it.

When I finally graduated in 1971, I was twenty-nine years old, poor as a welfare client, and had to make a decision. I could stay in the Village world of nightlife, with many friends, good people, and great adventures. I could maybe do more acting or modeling; maybe go back to doing more with television. Or I could use my connections to open up a restaurant. I knew big-time restaurateurs who made tons of money and had managers doing their dirty work and mailing them checks in the Caribbean or Mediterranean. I knew writers who finally made it with a screenplay or a script. My head was spinning. I could continue with my degree and get a straight job as a therapist in the mental health field.

I really did not know what to do. So I worked at the bar full time for a few weeks and put together enough money to do what I loved the best. I would fly to Portugal and hitchhike around. I would bring my pen and journal. I would decide there what I wanted to do. Europe, here I come. Again.

Columbia changed me, and I am forever thankful to them for giving me that scholarship. It was my biggest life gift ever. I also have to thank the US Army for what it taught me about life and what I learned about myself. I found out I had some natural talents and that I had to learn more about how to use them.

Nanny Alice

Ma was playing cards with Thelma when I arrived. They were eating some very red ripe cherries. I greeted them, and then Thelma informed me, "She been pretty good, Mr. Ken. Her granddaughters were here yesterday."

"Really? Which ones?"

"Lauren and Julie were here," Thelma answered.

"What did they call her?" I asked.

"What do that mean, Mr. Ken?"

"By what specific name did they refer to her?"

"Alicia, I think," Thelma said.

"That's my name, wiseass," Ma retorted, giving me the evil look. This was a touchy subject, as it had a lot of family history behind it. I was momentarily sorry that I brought it up, as it was one of those festering issues for me. I guess I was looking to at least have my say.

"Thelma, do you think it's odd to have a grandmother referred to as 'Alicia' by her grandchildren?"

"Well, I thought it a little funny that they didn't call her Grandma or Nanny or something like that."

"That still bothers you, doesn't it, Mr. Sensitive?" said Ma.

"Yes, it does, not so much for your made-up name but for the lack of desire to be a grandmother."

"I told your sister I was too young to be a damn grandmother," Ma retorted. "For God's sake, I was forty-three years old."

"That's how old I was," said Thelma, "when I became a grandmother."

"Well, the Queen, here," I began, "almost went out of her mind when her daughter referred to her as 'Nanny Alice' when she presented her with her newborn granddaughter."

"Nanny Alice?" Thelma replied. "I like it."

Ma gave me the armed-and-ready look. "Don't start, mister."

"Not afraid of you anymore, Ma," I told her. "The days of beatings, silence, threats, name-calling, and punishments are long gone. And to be fair, you should take some of your own medicine."

"Is this about your kids?" she asked.

"You know it is."

Thelma got up and started to leave the room.

"No, you stay, Thelma, please," I said. "I want an outsider's opinion."

"Is this court now in session?" chirped Ma.

"Yes, it is. Thelma, granted, Ma was young for a grandmother, but it's because she had my sister when she was nineteen. My sister was twenty-four when she had Lauren, and that made Ma forty-three."

"That not so young. We have grannies in their thirties where I am from," Thelma said proudly.

"I am not black," Ma said, her face deadpan.

"Ma, Jesus Christ."

"It's true. Black people have kids younger," Ma stated with both arms folded.

"Can we move on?" I asked. "When my sister called her 'Nanny Alice,' Ma went nuts and told her to never call her that again—ever. She wanted no reference to Nanny, grandmother, grandma or grand anything. She would now be referred to simply as 'Alicia.'"

"Well, that is her name," Thelma argued.

"No, her name is Alice. Alicia sounded fancier to her, and everyone knows grandkids needed fancy-named grandmothers."

"Are you done?" Ma snapped.

"No, I am just getting started. My sister had four kids, and they all learned to call her Alicia. Then my son was born when my sister's youngest was nineteen. I approached my then seventy-one-year-old mother and asked if she was old enough to be called Grandma. You know what she said?"

"What?" Thelma asked.

"It would confuse her other grandchildren."

"I never said that," Ma protested, barely audible.

"You certainly did."

"No way."

I went on, "But that is not what gets my goat. It's what she said after that."

"What did I say?"

"You said, 'Don't have too much expectation for me babysitting or doing a lot of those grandmother things, because I am too old.' For my sister, she was too young to be a grandmother, and for me, she was too old."

Thelma chastised Ma, "Miss Alicia, you said that? Mm-mm."

"The worst part was that she saw my kids only when convenient for her, in between her world travels. Her great-grandchildren, who were younger than my kids, were doted on, because they could all be assembled in one spot, and she could make her usual grand-dame entrance and then whisk away."

"I always loved your kids," Ma insisted.

"That is true, you did, but I was mad that they never got a grandmother, as Manny and his family were gone, even when I was a kid."

"Your kids stayed with me once or twice," Ma said.

"True, but at my house, and the kids still remember it because it was so rare. So my sister's kids, to this day, still call their grandmother

Alicia. I never use that name, nor would I ever allow my kids call her that."

"Feel better now?" Ma asked.

"No, Ma, it is just one of those feelings that is hard to get over. All parents want the best for their kids, and I could not provide them with much extended family, due to the craziness you brought to it. It all fell to you to offer something, but grandma was just not your thing."

"So shoot me."

"Too easy, and I don't want to shoot you now. I wanted you to be a mother and then I wanted you to be a grandmother. Is that so much to ask?"

"Well, you turned out okay, and so did your kids, so stop bellyaching, and get me something to eat."

"Okay, how about some nails?"

"Mr. Ken!" Thelma scolded.

"Sorry. Give me a minute."

"Hold it, Mr. Pitiful. You think I was the only one difficult here? Thelma, my son here," Ma said, pointing her finger, "was a real challenge, a real piece of work, and I spent many nights worried sick about him."

"Mr. Ken's a real fine son, if you ask me."

"That's now, granted, but when he was loose and running around the Village, thinking he was a beatnik and then a hippie, it drove me crazy. He was smoking pot all the time, and then he thought he would go into the movie business and acted like a French movie star!"

"What?" I asked.

"Don't 'what' me, monsieur. Who was that skinny French actor you idolized? The one with the Gauloises—that French cigarette—hanging from his lip?"

"Jean-Paul Belmondo," I proudly answered. (Belmondo was a role model for me, as he was a star in the French New Wave cinema verité.)

"That's right," Ma continued. "I thought you had lost it for sure. Then, Thelma, he thought he was Jack Kerouac and took off on his crazy-ass adventures. I never knew if I would ever see him again."

"Ma, it wasn't that bad."

"Oh yes, it was. Then he bought himself a motorcycle and raced around Manhattan while stoned out of his mind."

"Well, that was not my finest moment," I admitted, "but it was screaming fun."

"Mr. Ken, you did all that?" Thelma asked.

"Yes, Thelma, it was different then. We were young and pushing all the boundaries during those anti-war years. We tried everything new, and Timothy Leary was big at the time. I don't regret it."

"This sound normal to you?" Ma asked Thelma, and then she glared at me. "You were crazy and did crazy things." Ma's eyes went back to Thelma as Ma said, "He acts all mature and grown up now, but don't let that fool you. He had a wild streak in him that took years and years for him to outgrow. All the time, he never listened to a word I said."

"That's true. You had your say enough with me when I was young, and I got to believe your messages that I was never good enough, because that was all you ever told me. Constant criticism and belittling was my diet. So yes, I stopped listening to you, because I found that people in the world liked me and thought I was funny and was plenty good enough."

Ma shot back, "Yeah, all those homos and weirdos in the Village that you called friends."

"They were educated people with a different value system than yours, and attacking them now still proves you just don't get it."

"Get what?"

'That you are narrow-minded and judgmental, critical and demeaning of things you don't understand."

"Well excu-u-use me," she mocked.

"When I failed out of college and was broke and had to work two full-time jobs just to pay my bills, you said, 'Serves you right,' and offered no help whatsoever. Not only were you judgmental, but you were punitive, and I knew right then I could never ask you for anything again. And I never did."

"Made you a stronger man because you learned your lesson."

"You could look at the lesson I learned from many perspectives, including the one where you learn you can't rely on your own family, or specifically the only one who is left. We should probably just leave it at that."

"Oh, so you can't take it? Want more proof? What about all those out-of-your-mind nights you went to that rock-and-roll place in the East Village?"

"Ma, those were some of the best nights ever. It was the Fillmore East, the epicenter of hippie rock-and-roll music of the sixties. I saw every top band. These were the Woodstock years. Are you kidding? I saw Janis Joplin, Richie Havens, Jimi Hendrix, the Doors, the Rolling Stones, Joe Cocker, the Who, Frank Zappa, the Grateful Dead, Al Kooper, Butterfield Blues Band, Buddy Guy, BB King, and Ravi Shankar. I could go on forever. The music was my generation's fuel."

"The fuel was drugs. Who you kidding?"

"Okay, they went together, but I was not out of my mind; I was totally involved. The bands would give free concerts in Central Park every Friday afternoon, and tens of thousands would attend. These were social and political events. We were trying to end the war in Vietnam, and we succeeded."

"All right, calm down. Now where's my goddamn lunch?"

"Okay, whew." I took a deep breath and then another one while attempting to quiet myself. I looked directly at her now, with a smile on my face, and said, "Especially for you, dear Mother, I have one, spaced-out, weirdo, Village homo, veggie burger coming up."

She gave the glare. "You are a regular riot."

Nelly and New York Slow

I brought Ma some Italian cheeses from Balducci's in the Village on my next visit.

"I can smell that bag from here," she said excitedly. "Bring it over."

She loved fresh cheese and told Thelma to cut some up. I then produced the fresh bread from the bag, and she was like a little kid, saying, "Oh boy, good eats." Ma had dined in the finest restaurants in Paris, Rome, New York, London, and Hong Kong, to name a few, so a food compliment from her meant something. "Balducci's, right?"

"Absolutely."

"Mr. Ken, what's Balducci's?" Thelma asked.

"It's the best fresh Italian deli in New York," I responded. Then I produced the olives and tomatoes and prosciutto.

Ma said, "I'll forgive him for all the dumb stuff he did if he keeps bringin' the goodies."

"Oh, you will, will you? And what dumb stuff are you referring to?"

"All that Village stuff, hitchhiking everywhere, late nights, motorcycles, fast livin', damn near killing yourself a zillion times, not to mention what I don't know about. He was livin' crazy, Thelma."

"I was young and had a good life appetite," I said.

"Thelma, my second husband, Geno, used to say to me that he wished he was Ken when he was young, living a young man's dream."

"Geno said that?"

"He said it all the time."

"Ma, all he said to me was, 'Don't forget to wear rubbers.'"

"Right, we didn't need to hear about babies."

"You and me both." And I continued, "Well, Thelma, I can tell you that not everyone thought I was fast."

"That so?"

"Let me tell you both about Kansas City and Nelly."

We all sat at Ma's bedside, eating our Italian delights, and I began …

It was late afternoon when Martha, a wonderful lesbian woman I had the pleasure of meeting, dropped me off in downtown Kansas City. Martha had read me like a book, picking up on my New York accent and guessing I was a college kid on my first real adventure. She gave me some places to go while in Kansas City. I wandered around but did not form a clear opinion of the place. It was like a collection of many other cities put together. It was flat. It had an okay downtown, smaller than St. Louis, and it was very clean. I had the Wilbur Harrison song in my head about "Going to Kansas City," and I wanted to see what Twelfth Street and Vaughn looked like.

I could not believe there was a song about this intersection. But when I heard the song again and really listened to the lyrics, I understood better. It's a shady part of town, and the ladies there are for sale.

Kansas City is known for making great steak, but steak was expensive, and I was on a bare-bones budget. I decided to head to my best on-the-road earning machine—a tavern with a pool table.

I found Sonny's Grille, a beat-up-looking place that had many tables—always a good omen—and many ranchers looking to talk loud and play pool.

These guys were talkers and not shooters. I had played much better competition in St. Louis. The guys I beat there could beat these guys. In order to not get them pissed off at me, I told them up front that I was good player and that they probably would lose. I said that purposely. Being ranchers and drinking alcohol only raised their competitive spirit. After playing for about an hour, I wanted to stop, but they were taking their turns, trying to beat me. It worked perfectly and when I had the steak money, I told them that was enough.

I went to Arthur Bryant's and had a sirloin with mushrooms and onions. I think I can still remember the taste; it was that good. I also had a great big baked potato and a side salad. I had not eaten that much since I left New York. I paid for the meal with the rancher's singles and still had two left over, so I headed to the Jungle Club, one of Martha's suggestions.

The Jungle Club was one wild and crazy joint. The entrance was something that you might expect King Kong to walk through—huge fake trees with vines everywhere. A fake waterfall and a fake pool guided you into a huge dancehall, with three bars and an entire section of pool and darts in the back. The band would start at nine in the evening, but now it was just the jukebox. I knew that this was going to be a good night—it was one of those premonitions based on a good feeling about this wide-open, weird-looking club.

The girls started arriving in twos and threes. Most were dressed in jeans with checkered shirts. Some had short skirts with bandanas around their necks, and a few wore small cowboy hats.

I decided to go to one of the couches in the pool table area and watch the level of skill. The players shot well. The live music would begin about half an hour later, and then a very cute and perky young woman sat down next to me on the couch.

I was immediately captivated by her green eyes and soft, light brown hair.

"You not from around here, are you?" she asked me.

"Does it show that much?"

"Sure does."

She said her name was Nelly. After about five minutes of chitchat, she said, "If you are not going to ask me to dance, then I am going to have to give it to one of these local boys."

Did I just hear that correctly? I thought. If "giving it" meant what it meant back in the Village, then she was making a direct proposition. "Either dance with me, or I am leaving with someone else tonight" is what I thought she meant. So I stammered a bit and said, "Well, we can dance, but I came here to shoot some pool."

"I love a man who knows how to use his stick."

Okay, message was clear. Either she was insane or hormone hot crazy, or both. As we danced, she started in with the little moans. I thought it was way too early for this late-night stuff, and I knew I had to get away from this firecracker. We finished the dance and I excused myself to go the men's room. While there, I tried to think this one out. If I have her all over me, I will not shoot well. If I tell her to take a hike, I will miss out on whatever she has in store for me. So I came up with my game plan, which was to dance with someone else. That most likely would stop her in her tracks, and I could see later on if she still was around.

I then walked near the bar area and asked a young woman to dance. Near the end of the song, Nelly walked on to the dance floor, whispered something to the woman I was dancing with, and walked away. The dance was over, and my dance partner said a brief thank-you and took off. What the hell did she say to that woman? I thought. I probably do not want to know, because she is a bit scary and maybe dangerous.

I went back to the pool tables and signed up to play. I didn't see Nelly and figured she had staked out someone else. I was on a roll from having played earlier and felt relaxed against this better competition. By the third table, Nelly was now waving fingers demurely at me. I nodded.

I sat down. and Nelly sat down next to me—and she was completely different. Now, she was calm and a little more distant than she had been earlier.

"You are a very good pool player," she said. "What else can you do well?"

Here we go again. I thought. So I said, "I can ride a fast motorcycle and make a pretty good cocktail."

"Is that so? How good of a kisser are you?"

I was getting a little embarrassed by the direct forward shots this woman was taking. I like a woman who is not afraid to lead, but that usually came after I had done a lot of the talking. So I said, "You are a very attractive woman, and I would be glad to spend some time with you, but quite honestly, you're scaring me a little."

"Just where you from?" she asked.

"New York City."

"You sure don't act like a big-city guy, except for your pool playing. Anyone of these local boys would have had me outside by now, and you are all timid or something."

"Let's make a deal. You sit with me, and I'll play another round of pool, and we can talk." I cannot believe I just said that. I sounded like most of the women I had ever met. I was putting the brakes on this really attractive woman because I wanted to play pool and was a little scared. I tried to regain my bearings to see if I really wanted to be with her. She was either focused on what she wanted or was a psycho heat wave who could wind up out of control.

"Deal."

That's all she said. She morphed into a normal person, who clapped and cheered for me and gave out information about herself.

I shot very well on the second round and made eight dollars before I retired. Nelly then asked me to ask her to dance. I felt good about that, because she picked up on how I rolled.

I asked, "Miss Nelly, would you like to dance?"

"Why, thank you, Mr. New York Slow," she said, and she smiled at me in such a way that made me feel like a real country bumpkin.

No one who ever knew me would call me slow or shy or nonadventurous, but here was that farm girl from Missouri, basically making fun of me for being "old school." It was really a mind-turner.

We left the Jungle Club to go to a place she said we could dance slow and have a nightcap, which we did. Later, when we left that place, she just started to drive, without saying a word about where we were going next.

I figured at this point, I should just go along and enjoy it.

I asked her where we were going.

She said, "We did the first part your way. Now we do it my way. Fair is fair." She drove to a farm not far outside of Kansas City. There was a substantial farmhouse at the end of a long drive, but we went past it. "Folks live there," she said.

Another long road led to a smaller house, and she pulled up in front. "Home," she said, pointing to it.

Her house was a combination of hippie blue-light, Day-Glo madness, and farm-style soft and natural, which was quite appealing. She put me on a hide-covered couch and put some bluesy rock-sounding music on the stereo. She said she'd be right back and returned about five minutes later, wearing a series of long veils. She started to dance and twirl. She was graceful and sensuous. She whirled into the next room and came back with two small glasses of what tasted like Drambuie.

She whirled and stripped and teased and played, and on her next return, she had a joint, which we smoked. Then she offered her hand, and I followed her into a room that was decorated like a cave. The ceilings were lowered by hanging light-cotton, multicolored blankets, and her lamps were muted purple and orange.

I really liked her style. She was not inhibited in any way and was lots of fun—a unique woman. I asked why the psycho came on in the bar.

"No sense playing games," she said. "Women can do what men do, period."

She was absolutely correct, and the next ten years would bear that out, as women shed servitude and freed themselves sexually. She was an absolute delight, and we romped around her cave until early morning.

She got me up to see the sunrise, which was magnificent, and then we fell back asleep. She served fruit and yogurt for breakfast, and I said I was going to take a detour and head north. Nelly put me on the road to Des Moines and said that she was glad that I finally let myself go and that I should really enjoy life more. Enjoy life more? Any more fun and I'd make it into the Hedonist Hall of Fame.

Ma and Thelma had eaten most of the cheese plate while I was talking, which I realized only when the story ended.

"That for real, Mr. Ken?" Thelma asked.

"Absolutely, Thelma. This little farm girl was way ahead of me. She was direct and dead-on honest. In the coming years, I got to appreciate her more and more. She had no double standard, and it was good for me to change my view of what women could and could not do without sacrificing their integrity or reputation."

Ma said in her disapproving voice, "She sounds loose as a goose to me."

"I know exactly where I got my original view" I said, "from the moral high-ground person herself."

"Bullshit. Good is good, bad is bad, and loose is loose."

"Thank heaven we have finally found the one person who knows good from bad. You should have been a judge, Ma."

"Not a bad idea. I am just like Howard Cosell. I tell it like it is."

"On that note, I will step down from your appointed throne."

"Go ahead make fun, but I am right and always will be."

Jimmy D

Ma was mad when I arrived and was railing about all the violence on television.

"Everyone shooting one another and all the robberies and rapes. It's disgusting. The world is going down the crapper. I am glad I won't see much more of it."

"Yeah, it's pretty rough out there these days," I agreed.

She continued, "Goddamn politicians do nothing about it, and we just get more and more guns, and the bodies are piling up. Not safe to go anywhere nowadays. I am sure glad you are no longer going to those violent crazy people's houses."

"Believe it or not, Ma, I miss it sometimes. It was real life, played out on the spot, and I did help many people not make their lives a lot worse."

She made her critical face and pointed out, "You didn't save everyone, did you?"

"No one can do that, Ma."

"Thelma, Mr. Help Everyone, here, had a job where he went into violent and crazy people's homes and put himself in terrible danger."

I sat down next to her. "Ma, I was a trained professional, like many others, just doing my job."

"Mr. Ken, that sounds like God will remember you."

"I don't know if he got the memo."

Ma's brow furrowed. "What was the name of the man you felt so bad for? The one you used to see in prison?"

"Jimmy D. He's the one who had a heart of gold but lived in a world where the odds were heavily stacked against him, like lots of others."

"What happened to him, Mr. Ken?"

"This is a sad story, Thelma, not my usual kind of stuff."

Ma ordered, "Tell it, Florence"—a sarcastic reference to the British social reformer and founder of modern nursing, Florence Nightingale, who helped everyone—"and she'll see what a crazy job you had."

I had seen street people all my life. I'd worked with gangs in the Lower East Side and helped those who lived in the low-income projects. But I had left the city and was now working in Elizabeth, New Jersey, a multiethnic working-class town that had its share of street people. My job setting was a mental health center, and I was chief of Psychiatric Emergency Services. It meant I evaluated everyone brought in to the emergency room by the police, rescue squad, or by ambulance. I triaged them to determine where they needed to go: inpatient psychiatric, outpatient referral, state hospital, or just spend the day or night and go home. Part of this job was also to provide emergency field evaluation, which meant I went to them to determine, on the spot, what should happen. This part of the job required me to initially train the police in mental health awareness and increase their sensitivity to everyday human problems. They hated it—and me.

This field evaluation was much more dangerous, as it included the public at large in an uncontrolled environment, such as people up on roofs threatening to jump, or someone holed up in a house making threats. It could be anyone acting dangerously in a public setting.

Before mental-health triage training and psychiatric awareness training began, these folks without any screening had fallen into the hands of the police, who were only too happy to club them or shoot them. Many an epileptic having a seizure in public in the old days would have been billy clubbed. Alcoholics in DTs were a favorite police target, but now they had to stand back and at least give me a chance to talk them down without anyone getting hurt. With jumpers, it was always the bystanders who were the problem. As many horrified onlookers with hands over their mouths would watch, traumatized by the person on the ledge, there was always someone who would yell, "Jump!" In my way of thinking, that was the person the cops should have billy clubbed.

A phone call came in that a man was holed up in a house, threatening to kill himself or his kids, or anyone who got in the way. I took the psychiatric nurse with me in the emergency vehicle, and we met the police captain, who said we better get this done quickly, as he couldn't hold back the cops much longer, and the mayor was tired of this game anyway. The house was a beat-up, two-story A-frame with a seedy lawn. Toys, bottles, and various odds and ends were scattered about on it. The cops said his name was Jimmy. I went up the stairs and entered the hallway. The downstairs front door was open, so I climbed almost to the top of the second flight of stairs, calling out my name and saying that I was not a cop. "I'm here to prevent violence to anyone."

"Fuck you!" came from behind the door.

Good, I thought. At least he's talking and responding. I asked if anyone was hurt or needed medical attention.

"Not yet."

Excellent. "What do you want?" I asked.

"I want a fucking life."

This is real good, I thought. "Me too!" I shot back.

"You? You have a life."

"Yeah, but I put it on the line, talking to people holed up in a room with kids inside, and I don't know if they are crazy or not."

On this day, that particular phrase disarmed him. He opened up the door and said, "I'm not crazy. I'm pissed off. I've had it." And on and on he ranted. I asked if I could see the kids, and he eventually invited me in. The kids were in the bedroom, huddled together. They were scared but looked well cared for. Jimmy was a good-looking man with clean clothing, and his house looked no different from others in that neighborhood. I had no concern of neglect. The children, although frightened, were well nourished, so there was no concern of nutritional neglect.

"So Jimmy, here's my problem," I said. "I have armed cops downstairs who will shoot you if they think you are a danger to the kids. They will shoot you if they think you are a danger to them."

"I know, fucking cops. You don't have to tell me about them."

"You haven't done anything wrong yet, but the only way they will go away is if you come with me, to the hospital, with the kids, and we evaluate them, and you and me just talk this out. No charges, no one gets hurt or jailed or shot."

He said to me, "I kinda like you, and not for nothing—you've got one fucked-up job."

"I know."

Jimmy and his two kids and I sat and talked about life for a while. He calmed down, but he was still in danger of exploding.

"Jimmy, we have to go now before the cops shoot you and maybe me"

"Why would they shoot you?"

"Because they are cops, and that's what they do, and they don't like me on their turf."

I had to promise him that he wouldn't lose the kids and finally, he agreed to come with me.

I made sure he was unarmed, and he even agreed to a pat down—I told him it was necessary because the safety of the children was the number-one priority. I radioed outside that we were coming out, unarmed, and that he would go voluntarily to the hospital. Some of the cops didn't like it, because no one would get hit, and they had just stood around doing nothing. They liked action.

Jimmy's story was a working-class tale of violence, childhood abuse, and alcoholism by both parents. It included drugs and battles with his father, the police, and rival neighborhood kids. Then there was his violent, unstable wife, a high school dropout who became a go-go dancer. They married when he was twenty-one and she was eighteen. Neither one finished school, and both had limited skills. He worked with a carpentry subcontractor and made decent money when he worked. But his wife was still an active addict and stole the household money to buy drugs.

I convinced him he needed to come see me at the Mental Health Center so we could find solutions to his overwhelming problems. He went home that afternoon with the kids after everyone was cleared.

As unusual as it was, he came back to see me weekly. People like Jimmy do not believe in counseling or therapy. They see it as a sign of weakness, but my hook with him was his kids. I convinced him all they had was him, and he needed to be able to help them to not repeat his life. He came to like and trust me. We talked for months, and he fought his inner demons that demanded violent retribution for the ills cast upon him.

He struggled with impulse control and alcohol binges. For a while, we had his wife in detox, the kids in Head Start, and he was working steadily. I guess the thought that he could have a normal life started to creep into his head, but that, unfortunately, was the bitter pill he had to swallow, because he could not have a normal life.

His wife relapsed, stole the rent and food money, and spent it shooting up drugs on a day when Jimmy was drunk. In a drunken haze, he tracked down, shot, and killed the drug dealer. He was given twenty years to life in state prison. I continued to see him after sentencing.

He was calm in prison, as he knew so many people. He would cry for his kids, who were placed with his older sister. He said he looked forward to our visits and wished he had not been drunk on that day he shot the pusher. He thanked me for my help in getting his kids placed, because that "no good wife of mine would really fuck them up."

Then he put his hand on my arm and asked me, "What's wrong with you, man? You spend your time trying to help people like me, and they fuck up and go to jail anyway."

"It's a fucked-up job, I know, but Jimmy, somebody has to do it, and quite honestly, not everyone shoots the pusher."

Jimmy replied, "That's who the cops should be shooting, if you ask me."

After I finished Jimmy's story, Thelma looked warmly at me and said, "You a good man, Mr. Ken, but your mama is right—that be one crazy-ass job."

Swami Satchidananda

When I entered Ma's apartment, she was in a heated argument with the building supervisor. I heard her say, "That's what every lazy person says—'it's not my job.'"

"But Mrs. B., the outside windows are not housekeeping. That's maintenance."

"Bullshit. Then you get them to do it, because my goddamn windows are filthy. Oh, there's my son. You tell him why you won't do my windows like you are supposed to."

The supervisor said, "Mr. Ludmer, please, tell your mom that we only do inside work, like hallways and meeting rooms. Outside is grounds maintenance, and they contract window washing every spring and fall to a power-washing firm."

"Hear that, Ma? You are yelling at the wrong guy."

"Well, get me the right guy to yell at."

"What's the problem?" I asked both of them.

"Goddamn windows are filmy, and I cannot see out of them."

Thelma was also frustrated with Ma and told me, "She be gripin' at them windows for days now, so I called this man here to see if he could help."

"Thank you, Thelma. I'll take it from here."

The supervisor was glad to leave.

Ma was in one of her moods that showed her impatience and haughtiness. If she wanted something done, it should be done now and exactly the way she wanted.

I called Maintenance, and they confirmed window washing would be in three weeks.

Ma threw up her hands in exasperation. "Three weeks? The lazy sons of bitches should be fired."

"I will relay your wishes to them, and I am sure that will be very helpful. You know, Ma, you really need to be more Zen about these things. They have schedules to follow."

"Oh, listen to Mr. Spirituality, the guru."

"No, really, Ma, you have to cool it. The world does not revolve around you."

Her nose flared, and she used her Germanic forceful tone. "I pay for service, and I want it."

"Tell you what, Ma. I will call the swami, and he will grant your wish, and the windows will magically become clean."

"You are the one who believes in that crap, not me."

"Are you kidding? The Zen thing has helped me become calmer and more focused, and it is certainly not crap."

Ma uttered disapprovingly, "Ever since you saw that swami guy, I have heard you blather away about inner this and inner that. It's hogwash smoke and mirrors, if you ask me."

My tone stiffened. "You weren't there, and it still is the single most impressive experience I have ever had. Nothing comes close."

"What did you see, Mr. Ken?"

"It was see and feel, a total mind/body experience—truly amazing. Thelma, I witnessed the power of a swami and what a human body is capable of doing." I've always believed I cannot lie to my body, because it does not lie to me. It always knows more than I do, and once I learned to listen to it, I became healthier.

In my work as a therapist, I have seen all types of abused bodies, spirits, and souls—these are people who have eaten, drank, smoked, or worked too much, or loved too little, or have not stopped to take their inventory until it is much too late. I am thankful to Ram Dass, the enlightened ex-Harvard professor Richard Alpert, and the Swami Satchidananda for putting me on a path to inner life, some thirty-seven years ago. Since that time, I have done my yoga religiously, a little odd at the gym, all these years, but all gyms are now starting to have yoga and Pilates classes.

It all began back in the sixties, when everyone was searching for enlightenment because of all the horror that was going on around us, like war, poverty, and racism (like today). As John Lennon taught us, there was lots of bad karma going around.

The acid trips helped open the brain to other senses and experiences. The cultural journey was to find the balance and harmony to match the inner feeling of wholeness and good. Questions abounded as how to find this path. India seemed to have a leg up on other cultures, with their monks and stories of tremendous inner power. I read The Tibetan Book of the Dead with enthusiasm, and Ram Dass' Be Here Now seemed right to the point. I ate better, became a nonviolent person, slept in all states of consciousness, and tried to find a way to live that was Western and Eastern at the same time.

It came to a head on one of those days when I experienced something that changed me forever. That day happened in 1969, when I was a graduate student at Columbia. I started reading about Zen Buddhism, which was a long way from my roots in existentialism with Sartre, Camus, Simone de Beauvoir, et al. In addition. I thought the Theatre of the Absurd with Strindberg and Pirandello made more sense than the formal religions, which all had terribly violent histories.

This Zen thing, however, got to me. Inner enlightenment—what an interesting idea. Finding truth and harmony had always been on my list, but this nonmaterial stuff was fascinating. I knew a little about Zen when I saw a bulletin that Swami Satchidinanda, who was a Hindu teacher and not a Buddhist, was coming to Saint John the Divine's synod house right on the Columbia campus. He was the founder of Integral Yoga and performed for the masses at the Woodstock Peace and Music Festival a few years earlier. I went to check him out, as I was curious about all inner forms of enlightenment. The Synod House of the church was a two-story structure, with pews downstairs and a balcony around the periphery of the second floor.

The place was packed for the event. On the stage was a huge pillow, with a microphone placed in front of it. Candles were everywhere. There was an electric feeling in the audience—these people seem to know what was coming. I'm just passing through, I thought. It was early in the afternoon. No one was doing any drugs, a somewhat unique experience back in those days. Usually a crowd that big would provide a contact high. I knew this was a different crowd—it was a church, for God's sake, and grad students did follow laws.

In walked the swami, dressed in a long flowing robe and no shoes. He had a had a huge white beard and very long hair. His darkish skin was a vibrant yellowish-red, and with the yellow robe, he looked very majestic. He sat down, crossed his legs, and started to talk about spiritual life and enlightenment and the truth. Somehow, the words seemed real, coming from him. As he spoke, people went into a type of meditative trance and looked very much at peace. He spoke of a path and the steps to get there. The room became more relaxed as he spoke softly into the microphone. He told us of the rituals to become a monk and their trials to attain Nirvana. He spoke of the monks in the upper regions of the Himalayas, who attained the final stage by performing a specific ritual—having to dry a series of wet blankets with only their inner body heat. The wet blankets were put around their shoulders while they were naked and sitting in the very cold caves of the mountains.

Swami said he sensed the intellectual resistance from a nonbeliever. He paused and told the audience that he was going to do something very different, as he sensed the mixed spirit in the room.

With that, he asked everyone to please sit quietly while he meditated.

What happened next, I cannot explain, even though I experienced it firsthand with about fifteen hundred other people. Swami sat quietly and then said some Hindi passages. Then, emanating from him in waves, came a heat force that felt like something one would feel by sitting in front of a heat lamp. The rows nearest him experienced it first, and there were gasps. Then it went to all sections of the room, and finally, it reached the balcony where I was sitting—and it took my breath away.

Picture a rock being dropped in still water and the waves that follow. The heat that Swami produced was incredible. He had turned up the heat in the room by at least ten degrees. Then suddenly, it stopped. He continued to speak of the power of inner peace. Whoa! No gimmicks, no nothing, I thought. This man had sent a heat wave from his body that was felt over one hundred feet away and up one floor. He demonstrated the power of his knowledge.

It's hard to go back to a normal life when someone shows something like that. I spent a good portion of the next forty-seven years trying to duplicate what he did. The best I can do now is raise and lower my body temperature a bit, as well as my blood pressure. After that, I still need help. I have developed a deep and lifelong respect for people who dedicate themselves to this quest for inner enlightenment. They are peaceful people who only want knowledge, not material things or gain. It still fascinates me when I remember that experience.

Ma didn't say anything. She didn't know how to refute what I had just said.

Thelma tried to rescue me. "Mr. Ken, I heard about peoples like that, and I wished I would have been there, like a Jesus miracle."

"Some things we never can explain, but just being witness to it can change us forever."

Ma now chimed in, "Hallelujah, hallelujah. Well, call him and tell him to shoot some soap and water on my windows."

"I will, only if you promise to stop yelling at people, Ma."

Monsieur Le Jango

We were all in Ma's living room, sipping a little wine that I had brought.

Ma seemed to like her wine more and more these days, and believe it or not, she was developing a sense of humor, as she laughed a lot more.

She said, "I wish I was back in Vienna and having this wine there. I loved the quiet elegance of that city. But you know those Austrians."

"What does that mean, Ma?"

"It's so strange to sit in such a beautiful place and have to look at little men with red faces who are wearing short leather pants with suspenders."

I replied, "Yeah I guess that is a sight, and it is different."

"Mr. Ken, what was the most different place you was at?"

"I don't know, Thelma. Depends on what you mean by different."

"Like everything strange—foods and stuff like that."

Ma laughed and stated, "He was in Morocco with camels and Arabs."

"Ma, is that bad or something?"

"She asked for different. That's different."

"That's for sure," I agreed, and I started to chuckle as I thought about it.

Thelma smiled. "I know that chuckle. He about to tell another one of his shake-your-head stories."

"You will shake your head with this one."

"Go on now, Mr. Ken. This better be good. I'm waitin' to shake."

I was in Spain and was going to Marrakech to see a friend, a Moroccan man who had studied film at NYU but now had returned home. The flight over the Mediterranean and down the Moroccan coast took just a little over an hour. I had many fantasies about exotic Casablanca, with thoughts of Bogart and Ingrid Bergman in Rick's Cafe, and a completely different culture. I was excited when I took a bus from the airport to downtown. The more I rode along, the more the vision in my head faded and was replaced by a city that was in great disrepair. Casablanca was unappealing, with graffiti everywhere. The streets were dirty, with blowing garbage and animal feces. It was not at all visually enjoyable.

The Islamic women were covered in their burkas, and the men seemed to look at me with disdain. I did not know if I was paranoid, but I trusted my feelings. This place did not feel safe. I went to a café where I saw that some Europeans were talking, and I asked them if they had stayed in Casablanca.

"Unfortunately, yes, this place is unsafe. There are many thieves, and its uncared for and not the city it was twenty years ago."

I had not planned to stay in Casablanca, as my destination was Marrakech. I asked them about it, and they said, "An entirely different world there. You will be happy there."

I walked to the central transportation station and got a ticket for Marrakech. The ticket stated it was the Marrakech Express, and it left at midnight. Midnight? I spent the day walking around and finding enjoyment only with the markets and the tea shops.

At night, I stayed close to the transportation hub, as there were no bars or entertainment places that I could find. At the time, I did not know that drinking alcohol was against their religion. All I had was a paperback book to keep me entertained. The Marrakech Express could not come fast enough to suit me. Detroit looks better than this place, I thought, even after the riots.

I finally was about to board what I thought would be a train—but it was a bus. I made sure it was going to Marrakech. The driver assured me, in French, that it would arrive seven in the morning in Marrakech. I got on the bus. Everyone was dressed in Islamic attire. The bags were packed onto the roof, and off we went into the darkness for the all-night-long ride to Marrakech.

About two hours into the ride, the bus made a horrible noise. It stopped and we were told to get off. We piled out into this eerily dark yet beautiful land, just a bit north of the Sahara Desert. The Moroccans calmly took out their pipes filled with ganja, a soft dark hashish, and started passing the pipe around to everyone—except the women. They smoked this stuff in a long pipe with a metal screen and sometimes added Turkish tobacco to enhance the flavor. Two puffs on it, and I was completely paralyzed. It all seemed so normal to them. No one was yelling or worried. Then I had this thought that it was two in the morning, and I was standing on uneven ground in the middle of Morocco, stoned out of my mind, with a group of Moroccans, going to a godforsaken unknown place, while looking at more stars than I'd ever seen in Montana—and I really didn't care. We piled back on the bus and were on our way again, but this sort of stop happened two more times.

By the third time out of the bus, I was speaking my college French to a twentysomething man, whose French sounded worse than mine. I don't know if it was my trained New York ear, but I blurted out in English, "What part of the city are you from?"

He grinned and said, "Bronxville."

"I'm from Greenwich Village."

I learned his name was Dave, and he was working for the Peace Corps and lived in a compound in the Kasbah in the old city. Is this cool or what? I told Dave about my friend Mohammed and the café in Marrakech that he ran. He knew him and said he was a great friend to Americans. We talked most of the rest of the way; Dave was really very cool guy. He told me there were two Marrakeches. The old city, where he lived, was primitive and Muslim. The new Marrakech was European and modern, and French was spoken.

We arrived in the old city at a wide plaza, where people were setting up their booths for trading and shopping for the day. I saw booths with trinkets, rugs, blankets, glass bottles, woven fabrics of all types, genie-looking lamps, and food I didn't recognize. I heard thunderous music everywhere, as well as chimes, bells, flute-like instruments, and drums. I saw tiny storefronts crammed next to one another. I loved it. It felt safe and exciting. The booth owners competed like warriors for every dollar they could get.

Dave and I ate some meat soup and had some natural tea leaves in a glass cup. Bronxville Dave said I could stay with him at the compound, but it was a half-mile walk through the Kasbah. He told me stay close.

The Kasbah was a series of winding dirt streets with many narrow passageways, leading to different sections with houses on both sides. There was no electricity, and each block had a pipe sticking out of a wall, with a spigot for running water. People filled their pails with water and brought it to their houses for cooking, cleaning, washing, and toilet needs. I remember doing that up the lake with Nanny. A Moroccan toilet was a hole in the ground, conveniently placed in a corner of a tiled room. One poured the water down the hole when finished with the toilet. No one had to tell me not to drink the water.

The compound was deluxe, Moroccan style, which meant it had its own courtyard behind a high wall. It had two stories, with a kitchen, which meant an open brick-like structure, where you burned wood to heat up a large metal plate—the stove. There was an ice box, but ice was a problem here, and most things, like dairy, perished very quickly. Dairy items had to be purchased daily at the market.

My bedroom was a bare room with a wooden bed. The bed had strap meshing, where I was to throw down blankets and sleep, luxury style. The room had open windows but no screens. It reminded me of the inner courtyards of most West Village brownstones. The main room downstairs was tiled beautifully and had straw and mesh chairs and a big wooden table. Woven fabrics hung on the white walls. Four other people lived in this compound with Dave.

I took a version of a shower—I heated the water, poured it into a watering can, and had a go at it. After a little practice this was refined into dipping a cloth into the warm water and applying soap. Washing hair was more intricate, but you get the picture.

Dave and I headed off to meet Mohammed. We found his store just off the main plaza. He was still the same very warm, soft-spoken, polite man I remembered, and he made us feel very relaxed and accepted in his presence. Knowing he'd studied film at NYU, I asked him how did he wound up with a cafe/pipe store in Marrakech.

"This is home," he said. "I did not like the competitive pace of life in New York City. My father started this business, and I have a girlfriend here."

Mohammed planned a party for us that night with a friend who owned the only disco in the Kasbah. He said to come back about nine, and they would entertain us. Dave showed me around the plaza. There were little kids dancing barefoot on pieces of broken glass for money. That is something you do not see every day, and I put some money in the hat that the father had placed near the kids. I thought, that has to be brutal if that's the way you have to earn the money.

There were cows, donkeys, chickens, and goats milling around in between the people. We had to watch our step, as it was like New York when the transportation was horse-drawn carriages. The square was full of life, which included every kind of hustle. This is a flea market gone berserk, I thought. I love it.

Dave and I ate more meat soup with delicious puffed bread, using a small shovel-type utensil that worked very well. This meal was delicious and was followed by fresh-leaf tea in a glass, with a honey-spearmint mix. I loved the big brass kettle they used to pour the water. The contrast from Casablanca to Marrakech was dramatic. This was an old city, but it was well cared for, as men with branch brooms continually swept up.

We hung out, and I met a few of Dave's friends who would be coming to our party. We went back to the compound, where he introduced me to the other residents.

They were all very serious in their desire to help this community. The women were teachers, and Roy was a nurse. Dave was the community liaison officer, and he worked directly with the locals in getting programs for education and health off the ground.

I had dinner with them and thanked Dave for offering me his hospitality. He said, "We entertain travelers all the time. The room is yours for as long as you want it. One rule—help out."

You never needed to tell me that.

Dave and I went downtown at nine to meet Mohammed and his friend Harish, who owned the disco. The place was one floor down from street level.

"The Disco" was a converted 1940s Wurlitzer, which could play record albums. There was enough smoke in the place to kill any microbe we might have picked up on the way in.

They served dry wheat crackers and tea and some dried meats. The disco was packed, and every fifteen minutes, the locals went upstairs to "meet" ganja—the same one I had "met" in the desert the previous night. After hitting the ganja pipe, this place felt like Studio 54. The club was packed with European women who were out "slumming." We danced the night away.

Somewhere along the way, I lost Dave. At two thirty, I realized I was alone and very, very ganja-impaired.

I headed off by myself in the Kasbah to find the compound, but my finely tuned sense of direction had been altered by the ganja and next to no sleep the night before. Was it two lefts and a right? Two rights and a left? I wandered around for about ninety minutes, getting increasingly more paranoid and nervous. No one knew I was here. My passport was in my knapsack back at Dave's, and I did not even know his last name. I'd thought the experience in the desert the night before was a bit weird, but this foray was light-years ahead. The streets had no lights; the only light was from the half moon. I was working to keep down the panic. I just keep hoping I would not run into a pack of thieves.

Then I got lucky. I smelled something familiar and then recognized the pathway that led back into the main square where the disco was located. Almost two hours had passed, but I was happy to be in the same spot where I'd started.

I fell asleep, alone in the square, curled up in a rug by the tea shop. The next thing I knew, the square was alive with early morning activity, but I stayed on the rug until the owner showed up. I started to walk around and decided to lower my visibility by dressing more like the locals. I tried on a few items and finally settled on a jellaba, a long woven robe with a hood, something like Moses would wear. This jellaba was tan with vertical black and white stripes. I still was wearing my boots, as they were easier to wear than to carry.

I found Mohammed, and he gave me explicit directions to Dave's. He said he liked my outfit and called me an honorary Arab. After some morning tea, and armed with the written directions, I was once again off to the Kasbah.

On the corner of the square was a Moroccan version of a cinema that was showing an Italian "Spaghetti western" knock-off, with French subtitles. Its title was Monsieur Le Jango. I laughed when I looked at the billboard, because it was a tall Clint Eastwood-type character wearing a jellaba, very similar to the one I had just bought. He was also wearing boots. He had reddish-brown longish hair and a strong jaw. The guy looked like me—or maybe I looked like that guy.

About two blocks into the Kasbah, I noticed a swarm of little kids had started to follow me. They were muttering and giggling, and as they got closer, one yelled out, "Monsieur Le Jango!"

I stopped to look around, and they came running. I thought, What the hell. I am him. And the kids went nuts. One kid had a pencil and a pad of note paper. I started signing autographs as Monsieur Le Jango, and the kids were beside themselves. The parents approvingly nodded—a real movie star, right here in the Kasbah.

I looked up and there was Bronxville Dave, smiling from ear to ear while shaking his head. He had been watching this whole thing go down, and he said, "Man, you are in Marrakech only twenty-four hours, and you are already signing autographs."

It was a truly priceless moment.

The Queen's Skeleton

So how's the Queen today?" I said quite jovially, when I saw Ma sitting in her bed with her arms folded and a somewhat dour look on her face.

"She grumpy today, Mr. Ken," Thelma answered.

Ma scowled. "I want to get out of this place. It feels like Hoboken."

"Whoa, that bad?" I inquired.

"No air in here, and my backside hurts."

"What that Hoboken mean?" Thelma asked.

I turned to Thelma, who was making cherry pie. "Hoboken was where she was born, and the comment refers to the very small, cramped quarters where she grew up with her brother and parents, behind her father's picture-framing store in Hoboken. It had only two rooms."

Ma waved me off. "What the hell would you know about it? You grew up in five- and six-room apartments."

"That's true, but I had no air also."

Ma started in, "Very funny, Mr. Big House. Didn't hurt you any, did it? You turned out pretty damn good for having no air."

"Thelma asked about Hoboken, and I was just trying to tell her what you meant."

Ma pointed her finger at me and lectured, "When I am gone, you can tell anybody you want about me, but right now, I do my own talking, got it?"

"Got it. Man, you are in your old form today."

"How old am I?"

"You are almost ninety-two and still the Queen."

She mocked me as she feigned nodding off. "Some fuckin' queen!"

"Miss Alicia, that's very bad language," Thelma scolded.

"I don't give a good goddamn. I have to get out of this rat hole."

"Ma, this place is a palace, but if you want to get out, we'll go out."

Thelma asked, "Why she called the Queen, Mr. Ken?"

"Tell her, oh Queen. I don't want to speak out of turn."

Doing her best eye roll, Ma stated, "My son is referring to the name his sister gave me after I started to travel."

"Because …?"

"Because they thought I traveled like a queen."

"You didn't?"

"Not really."

"Ma, you had five suitcases and a trunk whenever you went anywhere."

Now quite indignant, she explained, "That's because I went nowhere as a kid and was dirt poor and had two parents who never finished junior high school. I was cold and hungry all the time."

"Whoa."

"Don't whoa me, Mr. Big Bucks. It's true, and I hated that smelly little place we lived in. I could never bring anyone there because I was too ashamed. My father was illiterate; so was my brother. My mother tried, but she had no education, and my grandmother never went to school. She spoke only German."

I nodded. "Humble beginnings is what you used to say."

She continued, "Well, I finished school and made sure my kids got educated, and when it was my turn to travel, I did it right."

"You sure did."

"And goddamn it, I earned it," she said and then tightly pursed her mouth.

"Correction, Ma. Your kids paid for their own education. Thelma, the Queen, here, is the only person I know who sailed the Queen Mary to London, just so she could fly the supersonic Concorde home."

"That true, Miss Alicia?"

Ma smiled broadly. "And I loved every minute of it."

"It took her poor parents weeks in the hull of a freighter to get here, so she certainly improved on that one, didn't she?"

Thelma showed us the pie and looked to Ma. "My, my, you had the life. No wonder they call you that."

"Well, it was terrible in Hoboken and no better in the godforsaken bungalow that they rented up in Mombasha Lake."

"Wasn't fit for a queen, was it, Ma?"

"Fit for peasants, that hovel."

"But good enough to send me there every summer! Don't get me wrong, Thelma. I loved it there, because of my Nanny and because I was a young boy."

"Better you than me," Ma said in her condescending voice.

"The Queen's skeleton is bared," I announced.

"That's right. It was going to be top of the line for me, no second best."

I matched her tone. "Nothing too good for the Queen."

"Fuckin-A right. Now get me the hell out of here!"

"The Queen's chariot awaits," I said as I pointed to the wheelchair.

"In that?"

"Beats my having to carry you."

"Some fuckin' queen. Queens have thrones, and this fucking flimsy wheeled contraption is no goddamn throne."

"Make up your mind, oh Queen. Lie here and curse the damn thing, or use it and get the hell outta here."

She then proclaimed, "All right, let's go, and I hope you remember this on the day when they are putting your ass in one."

"The thought warms me greatly, oh Queen."

And after the uncomfortably close contact (for her) of getting her out of the bed and into the wheelchair, she said in her most derisive tone, "And change that cologne or whatever that is that you are wearing. It smells like grilled cheese."

"You don't like my eau de walrus?"

"Very funny wiseass. Just drive the damn chair."

"Avec plaisir, at your service."

She looked at Thelma. "And have that cherry pie ready when I get back."

And off we went to get the Queen some air and some good food.

Judith

Ma was sitting up in her bed and reading, something she did less and less these days. I gave her the bag of croissants I had brought.

"Thank you, Sonny Boy. You continue to amaze me. Why the hell are you being so good to me?"

"I don't know, Ma. Maybe mental illness?"

"Very funny."

"You know, ladies," I said as I looked at Ma and Thelma, "I have been thinking about our days together, and the more I talk about these adventures, the more I miss them. I was so young and carefree and could go wherever the wind took me. It was so great for me to see the America I had fantasized about and meet all those different people."

Thelma sighed. "You sure did have you a good time, Mr. Ken."

Ma chimed in, "Yeah, he met 'em all and went everywhere, and you know what, Thelma? He sent me postcards all the time. They are here somewhere in a box."

"Hey, Ma, remember the one I sent you from Reno?"

"No."

"The gambler?"

"Oh, that other man you talk about all the time."

"Big Bart."

"Right. Big Bart."

"That was part of a week that started in Montana with the horse ride, and went to Utah's Salt Lake City, and wound up in Reno, Nevada."

"Look at his face light up when he think about that," said Thelma.

"Let me tell you about that week, one of my best," and I began …

After Montana, I could not believe that anything in this area could be better than what I had just seen. I felt my trip was already a success. In a matter of twelve hours, I had tried to rope an unbroken stallion in a corral in Butte, then worked as a ranch hand putting up wooden fencing along a pasture, and helped install a door on a barn. I had eaten a late lunch in a field over a campfire, and at the end of the day, I'd ridden a horse to town with two authentic cowboys. That was not an average day for a city guy. With a very happy and thankful frame of mind, I headed south to Utah.

From Butte, it was back on the road, along with two ranch hands— jeans-and-plaid-shirt-wearing, wild-type young bucks—who picked me up in their old, rattling, beat-up Ford truck. They were going down to Idaho Falls, Idaho, which was in the southeast part of the state. That was not too far from Salt Lake City, which was my next big destination.

They kept telling me that Salt Lake was way too civilized a place and that a man could not have much fun there.

They were happy to be drinking their beer from cans that they picked up at bars along the way. The amazing thing was that it did not seem to affect them. They informed me that it was all in the pacing, just enough to keep your edge, and "you gotta keep eating." They stopped for chili dogs and cheese fries at every eats place we came to. The combination of the smelly old truck and the nonstop beer- and -chili-dog-induced farting kept me glued to the window the entire ride. I was very happy to wave good-bye to these two gas mains. I took the next ride from a businessman named Jonathan in a very snazzy Chrysler.

He made sales of mountain hiking equipment from catalogs, which he kept neatly in boxes in the backseat. Jonathan was a Mormon from Salt Lake City. He wore a shiny gray business suit and small wire-rimmed glasses that made him look meek. The heavily wetted, thinning hair made him kind of a Don Knotts-looking man. He told me how wonderful it was there in Salt Lake.

"Real nice, decent people, with a good work ethic, and a rigorous love of the Lord."

Oh boy! This sinning, half Jew from New York stayed well under his religious radar. Talk like that just made me nervous and uncomfortable. I kept changing the topic to baseball and New York, and he kept talking about the good life in Salt Lake. At one point, he did ask why I was going to the good city of Salt Lake?

"I am cross-country hitching, and Salt Lake is next. I have never been to Utah, and I wanted to see what a big city out there looks like."

"Well, it's got a lot of big buildings downtown, insurance mainly, and lots of good, clean entertainment."

I thought the ranchers were probably right. I couldn't stay completely quiet on the subject, so I asked him if Utah was a state that didn't allow alcohol and late-night stuff.

"Oh no, son, we have beer (3.2 percent alcohol), and the bars stay open late, all the way until one a.m."

"That late?"

"Yessiree."

I usually went out about midnight back in the Village, so I wasn't expecting a lot here. He did do me one favor, which I thought was good of him. We detoured to go see the Bonneville Salt Flats out by the Salt Lake. It was the flattest piece of land I had seen since I left Kansas. He told me all about the land speed records that were set there. I thanked him for the detour. That was sure a whole lot of salt.

We made it to Salt Lake City in the late morning. This was one of those rides that felt like I was still a teenager in my parents' car—no air to breathe.

Salt Lake wasn't a place for anybody else who didn't live there. It was a very big and superclean city, and everyone was pleasant and polite. What was wrong with that? I believed it was reflected in their very narrowly focused conversations and opinions. It was a very different lifestyle, and it either was your cup of tea or not. It felt similar to visiting the Amish in Pennsylvania or the Hassidim in Williamsburg, Brooklyn. I felt like an outsider.

This was the Mormon capital of the world, and other than Brigham Young, the big polygamist, everyone else seemed on the straight and narrow. However, I did spend a very enjoyable day in the Western Museum. They had displays of frontier-era guns and tools and a sparkling photo exhibit of the Old West lifestyle, showing the hard life that the pioneers endured. The women in the pictures all looked old, yet they had young children. It seemed harsh and unflinching, considering the weather out there in the winter. It was not for me.

The multiple cups of coffee in various little diner places filled in some of the time gaps. I had a good burger in a café. The friendliness was getting to me. Big smiles and such pleasantness seemed somehow phony, and I just could not believe that they meant it. I kept thinking, probably unfairly, that they were all graduates from the Dale Carnegie course on winning friends and influencing people. In New York, when someone is that friendly, you are probably being hustled.

At night I went to a bar that featured the Wizards, with a guy named Lefty Logan on guitar. This music was not acid rock, nor was it punk rock, but it was the "loosest place around," according to the bartender. My sense was this was like the young Christian church band that had to clean up its language before they were allowed to play. This place was one step lower than that, but it felt very different from every other place I had been in, all across the States. Even the bars seemed mannerly and too quiet.

I danced with some local girls named Bonnie and Melinda, who were very friendly and wanted to have polite conversation. It was enjoyable, but I kept thinking that I'd better watch my language, and that made me feel even more uncomfortable. Most of girls left by ten thirty, and the bartender said some "straggler women" might come in around eleven thirty. I did not even ask him what that meant, nor did I really want to know, as the term was enough for me. So I talked to some of the guys, shot pool, played shuffleboard, and wound up at a midnight card game at one of the guys' houses. It felt like any night in a college dorm—chaos everywhere and no one notices. The game went late, but I had crashed on a couch, and by seven o'clock, I was outside, headed back downtown for breakfast.

I found a good diner, very minimally decorated with some prominent American flags, that served the early morning office crowd.

"Good morning, young man, and how are you today?" said a very mom-looking waitress.

"Why, I am just fine," I answered, forcing a smile.

"That's wonderful. Now what may I get you?"

One thing about the West: they give you one huge breakfast for a reasonable price. The waitress so was nice and polite that I got that feeling again, that the friendliness didn't seem real. It was like I was waiting for the other shoe to drop, and the "real" person would tell me to go fly a kite. The New York version: the guy behind the counter wearing a food-stained T-shirt scuffs his way over and stands in front of you, scowling, and then just looks at you. After you tell him your order, he says nothing and skulks away.

After breakfast, I was back on the road. I had seen enough and wanted out of here. I was waiting at an intersection when a brand-new, long, shiny 1965 Chevy Impala convertible, with an attractive young woman in a curled-up cowboy hat stopped at the light, right in my path. She peered over the top of her sunglasses at me, looked away for a few seconds, and then looked back and asked where I was going.

"I was looking to get out of Salt Lake."

"You are going the wrong way."

"I know. I'm just about to cross the street."

"Oops, sorry," she said as she realized she was blocking the crossing path. She adjusted her sunglasses, like Susan Sarandon did in the road movie Thelma and Louise, and each of us tried to quickly size up the situation. Her face was very cute, with a straight nose and small dimples. She had rich soft, flowing hair.

I broke first and offered, "Well, I was really heading west."

She smiled and said, "Oh."

I searched for the perfect response, something that Paul Newman would say. I thought this was one nice car and a ride from this woman would be a bonus, but she was just waiting for the light.

She saved me further anxiety and asked if I was in a hurry.

I wanted to get the out of town, but this woman was really good looking. I flashed the biggest grin I could muster, just like Paul Newman, and said, "Well ... that depends."

She mumbled something to herself and finally said, "So ... why don't you just hop in, then?"

I hopped in.

"My name is Judith, and I'm a Mormon."

"Hi, Judith. I'm Ken, and I'm Jewish."

Funny start to a conversation, but I guessed that out here, you gave your religion before you gave your last name. We just rode around, going nowhere in particular. It was eight thirty in the morning, not a usual time for dating. I complimented her on the car, and she said her ex-husband had given it to her for not testifying that he slept with an underage high school girl.

That seemed way too personal information to tell a virtual stranger in such a short period of time. That particular indiscretion by her ex-husband, in Salt Lake, was equal to a double homicide in the East. These people were Mormon. Sex was not their thing; choir was.

I told her that I was sorry to hear that.,

She nodded and smiled warmly. Judith kept glancing over at me and seemed a bit awkward or embarrassed, as she appeared to be blushing. I sensed that she liked what she saw but was having some difficulty with it. After about ten minutes of small talk, she said she was just riding and trying to clear her head on which direction her life was going to take. Maybe I was a nice diversion for her. She then offered, "Wouldn't a picnic be nice?"

"Okay," I said before I even thought about it. I immediately starting asking myself, Am I totally nuts or what? I am trying to get the hell out of Salt Lake, and I just said yes to going on a picnic. A picnic. Have I completely lost it?

Judith may have sensed my dilemma, and she asked, "Have you ever been on a picnic before?"

I wondered what she must have thought of New York life, but I assured her I was familiar with the basics of a picnic. I kept looking at her and loved the quiet, centered presence she had. I was not sure how to process all her direct talk about deeply personal issues with a perfect stranger, but she seemed dead-on honest. She had a slight sparkle in her bright bluish-green eyes. I convinced myself that the picnic idea might turn out okay, and I finally said to myself, What the hell? Just go with this thing.

We went shopping. At the Henderson's, we bought bread, cheese, fruit, nuts, and some chicken salad, and when the State store opened at ten, we added the wine. We headed south for a half-hour drive and got to a little stream that was nestled picturesquely at the bottom of a small mountain. We spread out her little pink-and-green blanket that she had in the trunk, and we set up our picnic. We spoke easily about politics, President Johnson, and the scary buildup to the war in Vietnam, and we both agreed that the country had really changed since the assassination of JFK. She was against all war on religious reasons, and I told her I was participating in teach-ins at universities, which warned against getting involved in a land war in Asia.

As the crisp clean air of the open fields wafted over us, she softly told me that she had married her high school sweetheart, and it broke her heart when he slept with that student. She was on her own now and had to decide if she was going to leave Utah. It didn't matter who was in the wrong; a failed marriage in Salt Lake was a negative stigma.

"Really? But you weren't the one who cheated."

"Doesn't matter," she said again. "I am still a divorced woman."

"That's not right," I said.

I felt so bad for her, as it was evident that her life was shattered. She was very kind in the way she spoke about others and children. Paradoxically, she seemed fragile yet strong.

She explained further that she was much better now and was learning to find her own way. The shock was over, and she had decisions to make. We had a very enjoyable, nicely paced picnic, and the wine tasted so clean and delicate in this vast fresh-air setting. At one point she rested her head next to my thigh and looked up at me with what I thought was a very deep, probing gaze. I just reached down, smiled, and stroked her long, soft hair. It was a moment of connection, and it felt very good.

She told me I was the nicest-looking man and giggled a bit. And she said that I had a unique, funny sense of humor too. That felt good.

I told her she was very attractive, and her honesty was very appealing. I sensed how good a person she was and let her know that. Later, we were walking in the stream, laughing and throwing some rocks into the water, when she suddenly stopped, looked up at me, and said, "Would please do something for me?"

"Okay. What?"

"Make love with me now, here, by the creek."

I was really taken off guard. I fumbled for words, as everything quickly went on tilt in my head. "Are you sure you want to do that?"

She looked at me and whispered, "Um hum."

This was what every young man would love to hear, having a beautiful young woman who just said it straight out. But my reaction was more to her situation, and I told her, "Judith, you are hurt and confused, and you might not like yourself later."

"No, it's not that, I want to. Please." She then reached up and put her hands behind my neck and gave me a soft, yet passionate kiss. I looked at her eyes, and they had glazed over. She then put her lips to my ear and said, "Please."

"You sure?"

She answered with a more intense kiss. Her kisses were delicious, and my engine had started.

We walked to a more secluded grassy area, and she led the way, holding my hand. It took a few minutes to get there, and she never flinched. She kept pulling me along. I told myself that she must really want to do this. We resumed kissing, and the clothes flew off. When we got to it, she was very ready.

We made love like we had been doing it for years together. She was straightforward, with no embarrassment or hesitation—natural and comfortable. No sign of that earlier awkwardness, as it was replaced with ease and passion. Later, when we were lying on our backs and looking at the bright deep-blue sky with fast-moving clouds, she told me that I was her second man, and she had always fantasized about doing something like this, spontaneous and joyful.

She said that it felt wonderful.

I was so happy to hear her say that.

I never knew women had those kinds of fantasies, as I thought only guys thought that way.

She looked at me a little cautiously and asked me if I thought any less of her for taking the lead.

I told her she was the most refreshing woman, and I applauded her strength for acting on what she wanted, when others might have held back. I knew that everything she was telling me was true. This was a first for her, and she was following an inner plan, and it all worked fine for her. I was the lucky recipient of the right time in the right place.

We spent the entire afternoon, eating, drinking, talking, laughing, and making love. When this wonderful, romantic afternoon was winding down and the sun was fading, we headed back to Salt Lake.

At about six o'clock we said our good-byes, and we both felt it was an exceptional day. She dropped me off downtown, where she had picked me up, this time across the street, facing west.

Judith's last words to me were, "Thank you. You were wonderful."

My usual ease with words was missing, and I bumbled out something like, "You too." I kicked myself for that comment; it fell way short of the mark.

I watched her turn around and head back to downtown. It was rush hour, Salt Lake City style, and no one was stopping.

Twenty minutes later, her '65 Chevy convertible stopped in front of me.

"My place?" she asked.

This time I gladly hopped in. We both started laughing, and she leaned over, gave me a kiss, and said, "Let's have more fun. I was riding to my house when I said, 'I don't want him to go,' and so I turned the car around and was hoping and praying that you would still be here."

"Salt Lake has a no exit policy for me, I guess. I am so glad you showed up."

Judith's was a moderate-size ranch-style house with a fully landscaped, colorful front yard. It was very welcoming. Inside it was spacious and felt just like her, warm and comfortable. There was a big old stuffed couch with brightly colored fabrics and blankets everywhere. The plants were my favorites—Swedish ivy and big ferns. She had pictures of her with children on her hall wall, as well as some family pictures. None showed her ex-husband, as those pictures were obviously removed. She had a well-stocked floor-to-ceiling bookcase, and I recognized many of the titles. I loved seeing her American section, including the classics from Emerson, Thoreau, and Longfellow. Her home was light, and the feeling was that someone had paid attention to detail. Wooden floors with contrasting-color throw rugs made it look very balanced.

We made dinner together and opened another bottle of wine. After a very enjoyable slow dinner with candlelight and the sounds of Brubeck playing in the background, we read Wallace Stevens and Emily Dickinson poems from her very fine collection of poetry. We danced to soft ballads and fed one another cupcakes that we had so carefully baked. We lay together outside in her hammock and talked about how big the western sky is, and how good it felt to just hold one another. She made late-night coffee, and we watched Shane. We were sated and went to sleep in her enormous bed in a beautiful shabby-chic kind of room at the end of the house.

We slept peacefully, and I loved how this woman smelled. She had a soft lavender aroma that I found intoxicating. Her skin was moist and smooth. Her curves were all in proportion, and I found two lovely dimple spots on her lower back that I loved to kiss. When we awoke in the morning, she looked over at me and said, "Wow, a man that likes to snuggle."

"Don't tell anyone."

The day started off with a laugh—those are the best days. I insisted on making an omelet.

"You cook?"

"Sure do. I have a German mom who insisted that I learn how to cook, shop, sew, do laundry, and care for plants and animals, as well as learn to be clean and efficient, while getting an education, so that when it comes time for me to pick a woman, I won't pick one whose job it is to take care of me. I'll pick her for a different reason, as I can take care of myself."

(Right on cue, Ma, who was attempting to pat herself on her back, stated, "Ha ha, you tell 'em, Sonny Boy. What a great mom." Thelma chuckled.)

Judith stated, "That's impressive."

"No, it's just German. They are all like that."

We ate the omelet and decided to spend the day in the mountains. We found another eye-popping vista with deep caverns and multicolored fields of flowers. I was quite impressed with the physical beauty of Utah. We had picnic number two and made love in an open field; it was magnificent. I could not believe this was the same hesitating woman I had met yesterday morning, as she was now dancing freely in the wind, running around a field with not a stitch on. We started to kid one another about who was the most insatiable. The longer we spent together, the more her face changed. It was becoming rounder as the tension lines from her ordeal faded, at least temporarily. The day flew by as we talked about our lives up to that point. She said she loved my adventurous spirit, and I loved her calm, balanced way.

We were from different ends of the lifestyle continuum, as I was surrounded in New York by many people, changing all the time, with flux as a norm. She had a small circle of stable friends and family, which were enveloped in the Mormon community.

She wanted to hear about my living in Greenwich Village among artists, writers, and poets. I told her of the cafe society that existed in the big coffeehouses, such as the Figaro and the Feenjon, with their numerous poetry readings. It was commonplace in the Village to be sharing a beer at the Lion's Den or the White Horse Saloon with actors, musicians, or columnists from the Village Voice. I was a folk music lover and told her about Washington Square Park on Sunday, with Pete Seeger and all the banjo and guitar players. It was a time of turmoil, and I told her Bob Dylan was the man of the day in New York. I loved his poetic messages.

The times truly were "a-changing." Talking about all this did make me a little homesick, but I was enjoying this woman and this time here in spacious Utah.

Judith told me she grew up in Denver, until she moved to Salt Lake to be in a more Mormon community. She loved it in Salt Lake and had thought that she would be raising a family there.

Her family values were about honesty, service, and commitment, and that was why it was so devastating when her husband violated two of her core values. I felt for her, as she had suffered immensely, and for her to suffer further humiliation seemed unfair and wrong. Her parents were in town and also her older married sister. They offered her comfort, but people talk, and it hurt.

We returned to her house, had a nap, and made yet another tasty meal together, as I grilled some pork chops with shallots and mushrooms. Afterward, she took me downtown to their only folk-styled coffeehouse, and it was surprisingly familiar. This place had the same motif as New York City's Le Figaro, only the newspapers plastered on the walls were different.

There was a middle-aged man on stage, strumming a guitar and singing well-known folk ballads, from Woody Guthrie to the Weavers. We talked with some people she recognized, and they did give me the stink eye a little, because she had never been seen with anyone before. I felt flattered that she would show me publicly, and I told her so.

"I am not going to stay beaten in a shell any longer, and they better get used to it."

That made me feel so good for her to speak that way. I hoped it would be true.

We spent the night wrapped closely in one another's arms, as my male protective gene must have become activated. I wanted her to feel warm, safe, and secure, and at least for this night, she could let her guard down and feel special and cared for. It must have worked, because she told me in the morning that she hadn't slept that deeply for months. I was so happy for her.

I cooked breakfast and then offered her a warm Hatha Yoga massage.

"Oh, goody," said this now gleeful, childlike person as she raced to the bed. We put on soft music, lit the incense and candles, and did the whole relaxation routine from head to toe.

The real joy for me was seeing the change in her over the two days, as she was now so relaxed and seemingly carefree. It felt good to bring joy to someone who had pain, and she was the most appreciative and responsive partner. We made love one more time. By this time, we both had a little difficulty walking without some after-passion pains.

The drive back downtown was a bit sad, as we knew we had to say good-bye for real. She dropped me off, facing west, at the same spot, and we kissed one last time.

I told her to have a life filled with love, as she deserved only the best. "Don't settle for less," I said.

"Don't you mind my tears," she said. "They are from joy. Thank you for being you."

I felt myself well up also, and we wiped away each other's tears. I got out of the car, and she drove away, honking the horn. It took some time to compose myself.

I think I will really get out of Salt Lake this time, I thought. Good-bye, sweet Judith.

"That was one sweet story about Judith, Mr. Ken, but I thought you was tellin' a gamblin' story," said Thelma, who was now getting some cream for Ma's arms.

"That comes next," I said.

Big Bart

I was now headed to Nevada and ultimately, California. This was to be one long ride, and I had two choices: go straight and head to Reno and San Francisco, or go south to Las Vegas and Los Angeles. I opted to go straight ahead. I put out my thumb and said to myself, *This time I really have to take a ride out of Salt Lake.*

An inner bubble of joy appeared as I realized I was almost finished on my cross-country journey. I had learned so much about the people of America as I had hitched about twenty-six hundred miles and had met such a vast spectrum. It had included farmers, cowboys, waitresses, store owners, young men and women, big-rig haulers and seemingly every type of delivery man, salesman, and even a few grannies and families. And in addition to one terrific Mormon, there were the bartenders and the pool players and one very sharp-eyed lesbian.

I was excited to see Nevada and California. I kept thinking how lucky I was to have hitched this far safely. As a hiker, you can anticipate some of the dangers of the road ahead of time, but you certainly can't anticipate all of them. I remembered getting out of a big rig in Des Moines by feigning an emergence bathroom stop when the driver kept popping little green speed tablets. It was a huge learning curve. Every ride carried the potential of danger—or fun.

My next ride finally got me out of Salt Lake City.

"Big Bart is what they call me," he said as he stuck out his hand when I climbed into this oversized Cadillac Sedan De Ville, with personalized "Big Bart" Nevada plates. This huge man was all smiles and was so friendly, treating me like I was his long-lost buddy.

Not another one, I thought.

"Goin' to Reno?" he asked.

"Yes sir, on my way to San Francisco."

"You can forget the 'sir.' Just call me Big Bart, or Bart."

He was a motel-chain owner and said he had seven of them, from Reno to Las Vegas to Salt Lake. He was on the last leg of the return trip to Reno and was feeling very good, as all his motels were in great shape. He wore a huge cowboy hat, with jeans and a white shirt and one of those red-and-white tied handkerchiefs around his neck, with a gold ring holding it in place. He must have been a good 275 pounds, as he filled up all of that spacious Cadillac front seat.

It was a long and, at times, twisty ride once we entered Nevada, as there were many steep mountains in the Rockies chain, and the countryside was quite rugged. Big Bart was a very successful man, about fifty years old, with a wife and grown kids. He was a nonstop talker and had a great sense of humor. Nothing seemed to bother this man. I felt that although he was loud and drove fast, he seemed to be a sincere man who told it like it was. He liked the fact that I had the balls to leave New York and hitchhike across country, with only a knapsack and seventy-five dollars. He thought that he had lived on the edge for most of his life, but this hitch of mine was a very impressive feat to him.

We developed a mutual respect.

He kept asking me how I was able to eat and sleep with "no money."

I told him about the various adventures I had and that almost everyone was generous to me. They had bought me meals and let me sleep in their campers, their homes, their trucks, their couches, their barns, and most enjoyably, their beds. I told him of the elderly twin sisters who paid me to drive them out of Yellowstone, going to Paradise Valley in Montana.

"What about your clothes?"

"I have two sets and wash one, wearing the other, at coin-op laundries."

I told him about Judith, who had washed my entire wardrobe, so I was now good to go.

"Damn," he said, "and you are lovin' every minute of it, aren't you, son?"

"Most of the time, Big Bart, most of the time." I added that I also shot a good game of pool and was able to make some money that way. I explained that I really did not need much, just some food each day, and shelter at night. "Bathrooms are the toughest part of it all," I said. "I have learned to go when I have the opportunity and not necessarily the need."

"Well, son, we are going to have a good time when we get to Reno. Do you gamble?"

"I never had the opportunity. I've never been to a casino."

This particular statement lit him up like a pinball machine. "Oh boy, this is going to be fun."

He said he would show me how to do it. He explained how casinos work, and all the different games, and the free drinks and meals and even rooms.

"Rooms?"

"Yes sir, when you win a lot of money from a casino, they give you meals and a free room and treat you real good."

"But you just won their money."

"That's right, and they want you to come back, so they have a chance to win it all back."

I reminded Big Bart that I had no money to gamble, as I was living day to day.

He just laughed and said, "We'll see about that."

We hit Reno about dinner time, and I loved the little place immediately—one main street with casino after casino, all with western names and nonstop lights. There was a big sign that bridged the main street that read, "Welcome to Reno, the biggest little city in the world."

Bart was in a zone, and it looked as if he literally was going to drool. I could not believe all the lights in this one little space. We had driven for hours, and there was only the mountains and then—pow! A neon spectacle appeared.

"Let's eat first."

"Okay, Big Bart, your town, your game."

He liked that. We went to the Frontier Casino, and he headed to the Steak and Chop House. Everyone said hello to him, like he was the mayor. We had a big steak with all the trimmings and dessert. I never saw a bill or saw him reach for money, and he just chuckled. On our way out, he said, "They owe me."

We went to Harrah's Casino next. Again, everyone greeted him by name. He walked around like a man on a mission. We headed straight to the craps table, and he told me to stand a little behind him. "Watch and learn," he instructed me.

He put down $300, and I almost fainted. At that time, you could fill up your car with gas and ride around for a week for four dollars. For anyone just to plunk down that kind of cash made me wonder just how much he had. What if he lost it? I started to sweat.

He made bet after bet, pass line, sixes and eights, hard tens, something called a yo, and it was all a whirl to me. I got the basics. You roll a number and have to roll it again before you roll a seven, but if you roll a seven first, you win. He had made his number three times in a row. Now, he handed me some chips and told me to stand next to him and do what he told me. I put down the chips, and he rolled and rolled, and they keep giving me more chips. After a while, he lost, and the dice were pushed to me.

"Go ahead; roll 'em!" he barked.

I did not know how much of a rookie I looked like, but I felt tingly all over my body. I didn't know if they could see my shakes. I gathered myself and just did what he did. I picked up the dice, shook them in my hand, and said, "C'mon, baby," and let them roll. They tumbled along the table, crashed into the front wall, rebounded, and stopped.

"Seven. Winner," came the response, and everyone at the table uttered, "Yes."

"Whew!"

The dice came back to me. I did the same thing, and it hit seven again. Now everyone cheered for me, and I felt my pressure ease a bit. I had to really stay focused. It felt like shooting at the eight ball with everyone watching. I threw for about fifteen minutes, and the table called it "a roll."

I had made my number four consecutive times and had many rolls in between that were neither my number nor a loser. The gamblers were very happy, as they were being paid along with me. Bart was the loudest, and he kept slapping me on the shoulder, while telling me to put down more chips.

"You go, son," he bellowed. When I finally lost, Bart told me to pick up the chips. I had three stacks of them, and I tried to hand them back to him. He wrinkled his brow. "What are you doing? Those chips, young buck, are yours." The smile on his face filled the room.

Bart said to the assembled at the table, "Broke his cherry tonight," and everyone gave me high-fives, back slaps, and big smiles. It felt like I was walking on air when we went to the cashier window. I gave them the chips, and they gave me $385.

"Put that in your pocket."

It was tough to not scream my lungs out.

Big Bart and I did the same at blackjack, but this time he played a second hand and said that he was playing for me, because I had no idea how to play. I watched and learned. The walk to the cashier this time netted a $135. As we walked from the window, I remembered that I had this feeling once before, when I hit the bases-loaded triple to beat Ridgefield Park in the state semifinal. I was floating with joy.

Bart said it was now time for some drinks and "entertainment." We went to a strip show, and everyone there knew him as well. We finished up the night at the rooftop bar and had some after-dinner drinks. He beamed as he looked out over the strip of lights and said that it was one hell of a fun town. "Yessiree!"

I could not have imagined that I would ever feel this good again. I had played craps in a major casino and was holding 520 of their dollars. That was almost seven times what I took to hitchhike cross-country. It was very overwhelming.

We spent the night at Bart's and in the morning, his wife, Martha, a very warm and friendly woman, made us breakfast. She kept hugging him, and he kept going on about me and my adventure. They were a happy couple. It was very rewarding to see them appreciate one another. After we told stories about last evening and had cups of coffee on his porch, it was now time to go.

I said my good-byes to Martha, and she hugged me and told me to come back again.

He drove me to a spot near the on-ramp and told me that it had been a pleasure meeting me and that I had one hell of a spirit in me. "I wish that all of your adventures will continue to be happy," he said. "Young buck, sure glad we broke you in the right way."

We hugged as two old friends. I took his card.

"Bye, Big Bart. You are a very special person and one phenomenal man. Thank you, thank you, thank you."

Three years later, I sent Big Bart a postcard from the casino in Monte Carlo and simply addressed it to "Big Bart" at the Frontier Casino in Reno, as I did not have his address with me.

I wrote, "Look what you started."

The postcard showing the Frontier Casino was waiting for me when I returned to New York. Bart said he was overjoyed to hear from me and said he still talked about me. He added, "Just keep rollin', young buck, just keep rollin'."

Thelma, finishing with Ma's lotion, said, "Mr. Ken, you one of the luckiest people I ever did meet."

Ma added, "Well, he sure did listen to that man. He's been rolling for years."

"Sure glad I did."

Heidelberg and the World's Best Job

It was harder and harder for Ma to keep her thoughts in order, and on today's visit, she remembered that I was in the US Army but couldn't remember where I served. "You were overseas, I remember, but where was it?"

"Germany, Ma, in Heidelberg."

"Oh yes, now I remember. You also had that job with that man you brought here."

"No, that was Big Mike. I worked for Robert, the Dutchman."

"That's right. Geno use to say that was the greatest job known to man."

"It definitely was right up there."

Thelma brought Ma a tray with orange juice and biscuits and said to me, "You was in the US Army, Mr. Ken, and had a second job?"

"Yes, Thelma, I was so lucky—the right place at the right time."

Heidelberg was my home from the late summer of '66 to the spring of '68. After my initial stay in the USAREUR (US ARmy EURope) hospital quarters, I moved off of the base into an apartment in

Heidelberg, above a bakery. The aromas at five in the morning were a welcome addition to my day, and the baker, Hans, would always give me anything he was making. The rent for this apartment was thirty dollars a month, which included heat and hot water and the services of a cleaning lady once a week. I learned my way around this small burg in very little time. I lived up the hill, and the strassenbahn (trolley) stop was right in front of my apartment. I bought a used Volkswagen from a soldier rotating back to the States and then had wheels for my every-other-weekend trips to Paris, Amsterdam, Brussels, or Munich.

Heidelberg was not bombed in World War I or WWII—it had no main industrial output and was spared from attack—so it preserved its original sixteenth-century buildings, cobblestone streets, and winding roads. The housing was substantial, and the Germans had added modern kitchens and bathrooms. The entire country was clean and efficient. Public areas were especially immaculate, as the Germans took pride in their jobs and community, and it showed. It was a wonderful place to live. The Neckar River curved gently around its old-city downtown area. The gigantic castle (schloss) dated back to 1294. It stood on the cliff and dominated its picture-postcard old-world appeal.

Heidelberg had a large student population, as it was known as an intellectual center. The students had many clubs and entertainment venues. One place in particular was my favorite, the Cave 54, located in one of the old bomb shelters built during the Second World War. It was turned into a club in 1954 (thus, the name).

Cave 54 was a private student club located in a residential neighborhood. The only indication it was there was a nameplate on the wall facing the door. There was a speakeasy-type slide that opened in the door, and if person at the door knew you, or you said the names of people who worked there, you could get in. The club was down a winding staircase, and there was always a traffic jam, as it was not wide enough to go up and down simultaneously—the fire hazard was very real. They did have an excessive amount of extinguishers, which reminded one of the hazards of drinking in this place.

The Cave was a live jazz venue, and Albert Mangelsdorff was the local saxophone player who wowed the crowds every week. The student population had an underground, political connection to the French students. The social unrest about Vietnam was also very strong in Germany, and this underground connection eventually led to the French/German anti-Vietnam student riots in Paris in 1968.

I made many friends in the Cave and was able to travel throughout Europe with just a name and a phone number; I always had a place to crash. I frequented other Heidelberg clubs and student hangouts. The Pop Restaurant, which served pizza—thin crust, light cheese, and a deep tomato sauce—was always a late-night favorite after the clubs closed. There were wonderful cafe spots located throughout this quaint little burg. During the day, all the students congregated at the huge Red Ox Restaurant in the old city. This is where I met my Dutch friend Robert.

Robert lived in Amsterdam and owned a European student travel business. His local representative in Heidelberg had just moved to Berlin, and Robert needed someone to replace him. I showed him I knew all the local places and had free time from Friday afternoon to Monday morning. He introduced me to the hotel owners with whom he worked, as well as the managers of all the major restaurants. Robert hired me as his man in Heidelberg, and this became the greatest job known to man.

Every other week, fifteen female college juniors—mostly American, with a sprinkling of Scandinavian—arrived by train from Amsterdam. I met them at the train station, got them booked into a local hotel, took them around, and showed them the best cafes and night spots in Heidelberg. I brought them to restaurants and got them into the student clubs. We also did some big-time shopping.

Fifteen women, every other week, and I was in charge of showing them the joys of Heidelberg. Do you know how popular I was with my Army buddies?

I also was very popular with the local restaurant, hotel, and cafe owners, who voluntarily gave me a percentage of their take for bringing customers to their facilities. It was a major win/win situation. On Monday mornings, I'd put the girls on the train for their next stop in Switzerland.

I was a draftee with a paid US Army job, with free time every Friday afternoon and weekend. Then I had that second job that paid a salary for escorting fifteen women, and I also got back-end money from the local business people—three sources of income at the same time for having fun with young women in fairy-tale castle town. I had the time of my life with this setup.

When people saw me walking around town with the girls, they would be as friendly as can be. They either wanted to meet the girls or wanted their business, and I was the conduit. It taught me a lot about how entrepreneurs operate. I loved Sundays with the girls. We would do the very German spaziergang, which was the Sunday walk. Everyone in Germany went for a long walk or bike ride on Sunday afternoon, and it was a very friendly activity, where you nodded and said hello to strangers. The men walking with their spouses would give me that "you lucky son of a bitch" look.

It was the best of times. We would lounge in the big coffeehouses, or visit the schloss, or take a local boat ride. The line of guys wanting to be my replacement was bigger than any mess hall line for breakfast. Robert was a happy man with me in charge of Heidelberg, and when it was time for me to leave the US Army, he threw me a party and gave me a going-away bonus. Now that was living.

Ma finished her biscuit and said, "That's my boy in a nutshell, always finding a way to have some fun."

"Mr. Ken, you sure was the right man for that job."

Ma said, "Absolutely. Mr. Happy, here, was in his element—young girls, money, and in the center of things."

"Yes, it was perfect for me."

Ma told Thelma, "Geno said that he was jealous that he never had a life anyway near what Sonny Boy had, and that job was the icing on cake."

Der Hund

We were all seated around Ma's table, eating Thelma's delicious sweet potato soup.

"Ma, you know who I heard from yesterday?"

"Some old girlfriend, I bet."

"No, Ma, Big Mike from Colorado."

"Who's that?"

"My old US Army buddy."

"Do I know him?"

"Yes, he came to New York twice, and we had dinner with him. He was the big guy."

"The homo?"

"Jesus Christ, Ma, will you ever stop saying that? I use to call him Der Hund."

Thelma said, "Der Hund?"

"Yes, young Germans would always say, 'Was ist los?'—their version of the American 'What's happening?' The question was never really answered, but the Germans playfully added, 'Der hund ist los'— or 'The dog is happening.' Big Mike loved it, as his last name was Hunt, and the first time he heard it, he thought they were saying he was happening. The name stuck."

"And?" Ma asked.

"He's coming to New York again. I am very excited to see him; it's been years. He's the one who played that gag on me in Mannheim."

"What gag? I forget."

I asked for another bowl of soup and then began to tell the story. ...

I met Big Mike when I was sent to work in the US Army Stockade in Mannheim, Germany. I drove the half-hour ride from Heidelberg to Mannheim once per week. Big Mike was a "lifer," as he'd been in the army seven years when I met him. He had the same job as I did, but he was with a different division. We shared a waiting room. He was a huge man from Colorado who had joined the US Army to see the world and had done well, as he was now an E-6 (a ranking for enlisted personnel) after six years. E-9 is the top, so he was well on his way there if he decided to stay. As the world around us was changing so fast in the sixties, Mike decided he wanted to be part of it. He quit the US Army when his tour was up, six months after I left Germany.

It was a chronic source of irritation to him that I had made E-5 after only eighteen months. He had put in long, hard years to get his rank, and, as he saw it, some hotshot draftee made E-5 in "no time at all." He was really envious and it showed. In spite of that, he became a good friend to me.

He was in a very difficult position. He was gay and could not talk about it, show it, or act on it; otherwise, he could be court-martialed and sent to jail. At the time, I had no idea he was gay. He knew my views on homosexuals, however, as I had told him about living in the Village, and he knew my stance against prejudice.

A few months after we became friends, he said, "Let's go out in Mannheim tonight." He said he knew a few places, so I let him take the lead. We started out in a schnitzel-and-beer joint that had great food. Then we hit a little cafe for coffee and little German cakes. I was looking at the girls, as always, and he either agreed or disagreed with my choices.

Then he asked if I was ready for some fun, and he took me to a bar that had pay-for-dance girls. This was really a lowlife sort of place that I might expect sailors in port to patronize. I told Mike that this was not for me. "I don't pay to have female company."

"Really?" he said.

I thought that a bit odd but told Mike that I met women everywhere, from bakeries to cafes, to food stores, to bus stops—anywhere people congregated. This place was for guys who couldn't meet women or were looking for sure things that they paid for.

He said, "I know a place you will like."

We drove about ten minutes to an upscale neighborhood and stopped in front of a snazzy-looking bar/restaurant. It was very appealing, with a big, beautiful oak bar and some modern paintings, which went well with the beveled glass and rich leather decor. We sat at the bar and ordered some wine. I didn't notice anything different about the place. There were guys at the bar, and music was playing. I casually commented that there were not many women here yet.

"It's early," Mike said. We had another drink and got into a long conversation. I wasn't paying any attention to what was happening in the bar.

When we finished that conversation, I looked around and saw that the bar was now almost full. I said, "Where the hell are all the women?" At that moment, I felt someone tapping my shoulder. I turned around to see a tall German man, who said, "Tanzen?"

"What?"

He repeated, "Tanzen?"

I looked at Mike, who could not hold back his laughter. He said, "He wants to dance with you."

At that moment, everything came into focus, and I said politely, "Nein, danka."

Mike just about split his pants when he described the look on my face. I now looked around and saw there were many male couples dancing. I said to Mike, "This is a gay bar."

"No shit, Sherlock."

Then I started to laugh at how stupid I felt. "Why the hell did you bring me to a gay bar?"

He looked at me and didn't answer. I looked around and tried to put all my thoughts together. When I looked back at him, he said, "I wanted to show you my world."

I still did not get it. "You go to gay bars?"

He again just looked at me as if I had no working cells in my brain. It was all about perception—if I thought he was straight, then I interpreted everything from that point of view. Now, however, I finally had my aha moment. "You're gay?"

He said, "Wanna dance?"

My jaw dropped, and my head was momentarily on tilt until it reprocessed all this information.

He said, "I am only kidding about the dance part, but yes, I'm gay."

"Why didn't you say so?"

"I just did."

Then we laughed and laughed.

"You've got a hell of a sense of humor," I told him.

"I thought I could tell you," he said, "but I had to be sure because of the serious consequences."

"I have your back. I won't tell anyone."

He then told me of five guys I knew who were gay. My jaw did its thing again. From that point on, our friendship grew, and like most relationships, if there is basic trust, then everything else can follow. Mike kept his secret and rolled along with my crazy bunch of European straight friends and US Army buddies. His cover story was that he had a girl back home, and he was being faithful. Everyone told him it was the sixties, and he should live in the now. He did but in his own way and off the beaten path from the Army crowd.

It was interesting that the straight and gay worlds were converging in Germany as they fought together against the war in Vietnam. The same process began shortly thereafter in America, as the gay rights and anti-Vietnam movement merged together to become the unified civil rights and anti-war movement.

Once I left the Army, I joined the Vietnam Veterans against the War and proudly protested with hundreds of thousands of others down Fifth Avenue and also in Washington, DC. It did not matter if you were gay or straight; what mattered was there was a terrible war to stop.

I looked to Thelma, who nodded her approval.

"Big Mike helped me so much to see how people suffered from insane prejudice, and I owed a lot to him for that."

Ma said, "I met him in the Village one time, didn't I?"

"Yes, we had dinner at the Sazerack House."

"He was a very well-mannered man, and I never would have guessed he was a homo."

"I am not even going to touch that."

"What did I say?"

"Nothing, Ma, eat your soup."

Taos and the Indians

Ma finished lunch but something was off with her today, as she was a bit detached. I knew she was bothered by something, so I addressed it.

"What is it, Ma? Spit it out."

"I have been thinking about that Nanny Alice crap, and that's not all I have to say, mister."

"Say it."

"Thelma thinks all these good things about you, and she never gets to hear my side."

"And what side is that?"

"A mother who knows her child and did a lot of worrying."

"You are now the long-suffering, caring mother, who is misunderstood by all who fail to see what a warm, loving being she is."

"Something like that."

"Please, Ma, don't push it."

Ma used her best condescending tone. "Well, Mr. Peyote, why don't you 'fess up to all your escapades during those crazy years?"

"Nothing to hide, Ma. I did it. I loved it and had extraordinary, life-altering experiences."

"You were nuts and did nutty, dangerous things. I still can't believe that you came out of all that stuff with your brain intact."

"Well, if that is a compliment, I'll take it."

"Geno said he could never do the things you did."

"I understand that, but honestly, Ma, he was a guy who lived with his mother until he was forty-seven. He and I are on the opposite side of that spectrum. I had to get away and the road was my answer."

"So it's my fault?"

"I'm not blaming you. I just had to go, see, and do whatever it was out there that was calling me."

Ma pointed her finger at me, saying, "I remember your story about the peyote button, the fire, and the Indians. It was about as far out there as you could be."

"Ever do it, Ma?"

"Of course not. It was different times for me."

"Exactly. My generation did it. We plain tore it up for years and had a hell of a lot of fun along the way. The ones who survived stopped at some point and rejoined the social fabric. Some stayed out there too long and unfortunately, we lost most of them."

"What you two talking about with fire Indians?" Thelma asked.

"Ma is referring to a night I spent in Taos, New Mexico."

"Go ahead, nut job. Tell her. She'll see how gone you were."

"Who could resist, with that intro?"

After Ben and Little Bird I spent the night with some college kids and a friendly Labrador retriever, and then I headed for Taos.

I got a quick ride out of Santa Fe, heading north to the mountains, with a farmer who got his supplies in Santa Fe. He said that Taos used to be very quiet, but hippie kids had discovered it, and now the population had grown. He liked it, because his profit was up, and they didn't cause much trouble. I told him that I had read that Taos was a very spiritual place.

"Well, they have Indians there, and they claim to be connected to the earth and spirits," he said. "This is the Saturday night that the yearly Big Fire Festival is being held on the top of the mountain. It's probably something you should see."

Taos was more rugged than Santa Fe, as it was up in the mountains, and there was only one rough road that went there. It led directly into an absolutely gorgeous little town with very quaint, artistic stores. It had the feel of Venice Beach, California, with hippie-type clothing and jewelry for sale. The difference was the Indians. They were selling their pottery, stones, jewelry, and carvings—really fine stuff. Everything was a combination of wood and stone, kind of primitive and uncut, not sanded. There were so many bright colors that my head was saying wow again. I found an Indian restaurant and had maize, a cornmeal mixture, with some fried beans and beef. I washed that down with a beer as I started to gather information about the Fire Festival.

When the sun set, it seemed like a mystical experience, as the shadows from colorful hues cut through the trees. The stars were already visible in the still-light sky, and I was ready to go to the mountaintop.

I started to walk there, but some hippies picked me up in VW bus and said this night would be a trip. Little did I know how much of a trip this night was going to be.

We arrived at the mountaintop, parked the bus, and walked onto a path that wound through an area of trees. The closer we got, the more we heard the sound of drums and bells. We reached the opening to this vast clearing. In front of me was the tallest bonfire I had ever seen. It must have been fifteen feet high and at least seventy-five feet around. It was wide at the bottom and cone-shaped at the top. Hundreds of people were dancing to live music. People were eating, drinking, and intermingling like a big-time Rio Samba festival. I was told that this was only the preliminary, as at midnight, the Indians would take over.

I walked around and took hits off the communal joint, a rolled pot/hashish combination that was the biggest one I'd ever seen. The joint was almost a foot long and had be held with two hands. The last time I saw one that big was at a hippie "be-in" at the Roundhouse in

London. I was getting into the spirit of the night when I ran smack into Gunslinger Billy.

Gunslinger Billy was the only true Hemingway character I have ever known. He was an international mercenary who rented himself out. He was also a big-game hunter and an international importer of legal and not-so-legal products. He was a skilled sea captain as well, and his drinking and A-list parties in Greenwich Village were legendary.

I was introduced to him by the Flounder, a medical student friend of mine from the East Village, in the Flounder's home in Guadalajara, Mexico. Now Gunslinger lived in a hippie commune in southern Colorado by the Sangre de Cristo Mountains. The commune was called Red Rock because of the colors of the mountains. Gunslinger Billy lived there in the summer. I had hung with him there last year, and we'd laughed that we didn't see one another as much in Greenwich Village as we did in Mexico and Colorado.

Gunslinger Billy was beside himself happy to see me, and after a mammoth hug, he told me the Red Rockers were here for the fest. The Red Rockers were mostly dropouts from California who lived on parental stipends and the profits from their commune. They sold food, clothing, and jewelry. They all lived together in a loosely integrated community where they bartered for most of their needs. The rest of the time they were stoned and playing music while they "dropped out" of mainstream America and took their acid (LSD).

Billy brought me to the Red Rockers, who were very friendly due remembering me, and to his reintroduction. I was given a peyote button, which seemed like the perfect, natural thing to do in this environment. Peyote was the hallucinogenic drug of the Indians, who used it spiritually for their rituals. I thought, And when in Rome …

I popped the button and before long, I was dancing around the fire and felt only exhilaration. At midnight, the Indians appeared in full tribal costume. I thought this was a hallucination, but others saw it as well. The drums got into me with such intensity, and the visuals were so very surreal that I had difficulty staying with reality.

The Indians were chanting, twirling, and dancing. The hippies took off their clothes and cavorted about. The bells and horns added to multisensual experience, and whatever this environment did not produce, the peyote and the beating of the kettle drums did the rest. Naked women danced with me—it really was a mixture of fantasy and reality. This event went on the entire night, until the sun came up. The fire was only smoldering ashes when I found Gunslinger and went back to his camp area to fall dead-out, wrapped in a blanket next to one of the Red Rocker groups.

I was so totally exhausted from the dancing, singing, probably screaming, and sweating out every drop of liquid from the heat of the fire and the constant intensity of the button that it was three in the afternoon before I awoke. True to form, Gunslinger Billy was up and cooking. He said, "Got your breakfast burrito right here."

I wanted water. Just water.

"I'm a lucky man," I said as I finished my tale.

Thelma was clearing the plates and offered, "That's not all you is, Mr. Ken," and her face revealed that there was a lot more to that statement.

Ma appeared vindicated and triumphantly stated, "Hah, you finally you admit you are lucky. Let me tell you something, Sonny Boy; you are so far beyond lucky. Your spirit has to be guided or protected from beyond. You should have been dead so many times from your crazy-ass shenanigans, and you just landed on your feet and went on to the next nutty adventure." She then looked to Thelma and put her arms out, indicating, See what I mean?

"That's a very nice thought, Ma. Thank you. Maybe it is karma's way of giving me something for all I lost. The yin and the yang."

"You missed the point, hotshot."

"No, I didn't."

In a lifetime, one gets certain days that exceed all the others. I have had quite a few. This one in Taos. That night in Marrakech, Morocco, out in the dark, and that night at the Carnival Masquerade Ball in Rio.

Then there was the two-day horse ride in the Montana Rockies with John Waddington. I would have three more extraordinary experiences, very much later in my life. One was when I went riding with the gauchos and saw wild horses on the pampas in Argentina. There also would be the day-long bareback ride on Mei Ka Bei, the ten-foot elephant in Chiang Mai, Thailand. My last adventure—but hopefully not my final—was most recently the fantastic boat ride in Patagonia, near Antarctica, to see the blue-ice glaciers. Oh yes, I can't leave out seeing the mammoth humpback whales in Maui, Hawaii—you never forget them.

René

Ma was fading. It was very difficult for her to keep her concentration. She now had good days and bad days. It was on an exceptionally good day, when she was clear-headed and alert, while we were sitting by her bedside, that Thelma wondered if I'd ever fallen in love in all of my travels.

Ma jumped right in. "Yes, he did, with a woman he talked about for years. That was one woman I wished I had met. I told him that she sounded like the perfect match for him, compared to all the others he ever talked about or brought home."

"Wow, Mr. Ken, you need to be tellin' me about her."

I poured us all some iced teas and began ...

It happened a long time ago, when I was hitching through Portugal and Spain, after I had graduated from Columbia. I took the trip to figure out my next life decision. I would either stay in the restaurant business in the Village, for money, while pursuing my acting career, or I would get a day job as a psychotherapist.

I was staying with two Village restaurant-owner friends, Sam and Dave, after having hitched from Lisbon to Albufeira, which was on the southern Portuguese coast on the Mediterranean. It was an absolutely fun-filled time with them, which included many people and great parties. We hung out at Sir Harry's, an English pub. All the Europeans on vacation flocked to this place, which was a noted storytelling gathering spot.

Sam and Dave were older, successful restaurant men who summered in Portugal's Algarve, where they had rented a magnificent villa.

I was torn between wanting to stay with them and continuing on my journey to Spain. I was by myself and liked it that way. I needed time to think, and I also needed time to recover from some grueling years in graduate school. Freedom, on this trip, felt exceptionally wonderful, as I was unencumbered by worries or responsibilities. I met a woman in Albufeira who wanted to travel with me, but that was not what I wanted.

I decided to leave this very wonderful villa setting, put my knapsack on my back, and head for Spain to find another Village guy, Duke, who had owned a Village coffeehouse. Sam and Dave told me he was living in Marbella or Torremolinos.

Off I went. It didn't take but twenty-five minutes to get a ride from a German couple who were going to Seville, which was 110 miles away. Hans and Lorelei were from Bavaria and like most Germans, they loved to vacation in Spain. I told them of my years in Heidelberg and how much I'd loved living in Germany. They were in their thirties and did not have kids yet, so this felt like a honeymoon for them. We were in Spain within forty-five minutes, and it seemed to get hotter by the minute as we left the Mediterranean behind.

The Spanish countryside was a bit more rugged than Portugal, as it was brown from the dry summer heat. We arrived in Seville in two hours, and I thanked Hans and Lorelei and walked around downtown.

Seville is a very old and charming city with an enormous number of parks. It is the home of bullfighting and, along with Madrid, is considered a very passionate environment to see a bullfight, as the crowd is made up of many aficionados. I found a wonderful outside cafe and was having lunch, when an obviously touristy woman walked along with her map and guidebook. She sat down at a table a few seats away, nodded gently to me, and began reading her book.

I felt a jolt when I looked at her. She was stunning, with a well-proportioned face and longish neck. She had brown hair that fell into a gentle flip. It was very uncomfortable for me to look into her eyes when I asked her first if she spoke English and if I might join her at her table. She said yes to both, as it is a common occurrence to join people sitting alone in Europe's bars and cafes. It doesn't mean anything, really, because you can just get up and leave, but all Europeans live by this courtesy at public places. Her name was René, and she was from Brussels, Belgium.

We started a very pleasant conversation. I told her I loved Brussels and mentioned the Avant Garde Theater that I had been to there. She remarked that her sister was one of the players.

Small world, I thought. I told her of Heidelberg and of my current hitch. She had driven by herself from Brussels and was staying nearby in the oldest section of town. She planned to stay a few days and was headed down to the Costa del Sol.

After fifteen or twenty minutes of talking, I asked her if we might tour around Seville together, as we'd both just arrived and that might be fun.

"Sounds good to me," she responded.

René was a graduate student in art history and was here to see the architecture and the art museums. When I said I would like to see the Fine Arts Museum, she said, "It's first on my list. It also houses works of fifteenth- and sixteenth-century Flemish painters."

She would be happy to share the experience with me, and I was glad to have her as my guide.

The Fine Arts Museum in Seville is a palace; it is exquisite. The afternoon René and I spent there was truly jaw-dropping. I love architecture, and the settings for the paintings were almost better than the paintings themselves. Having such a well-informed tour guide made it all that more enjoyable.

When I was in Brussels, I went to the Royal Museum of Fine Arts and saw the works of all the masters and especially liked Magritte. I loved Flemish painters and was impressed by their absolute command of detail and facial expression. René was so happy to find someone who could speak somewhat competently with her about art and architecture.

We had an exciting time, going room to room, and at the end of this totally thrilling afternoon, we stopped to have a café—coffee—in the garden.

There was a fiercely independent presence to René. She was strong and highly focused. Paradoxically, I sensed a vulnerability in her that was evident by her deep, soft eyes. She looked very elegant in her stylish scarf and silk blouse combination. She was poised and had an air about her, yet there was a softness that made her seem older and younger at the same time.

As the afternoon wound down, she asked where I was staying.

"I haven't looked for a hotel room yet," I said.

"I'll help you find one," she offered.

I sensed there was a question in her offer to help, just by the way she said it. I was thinking that she was trying to gauge if I was interested in her, while we were ostensibly looking for a hotel room.

I told her how really happy I was to have met her, as she was not only beautiful but extremely knowledgeable and a whole bunch of fun. I said the afternoon went by so fast that I really would enjoy spending more time with her. It was still uncomfortable for me to look her in the eyes, as it continued to give me the jolts.

She then said, "It's kind of silly to be looking for a room for you, as I have a hotel room, and we could use the saved money for tonight. That is, if you want to … and if you play your cards right."

"So your hotel room is mine to lose?"

"Exactly."

All night long, we laughed about it, as I kept asking her, like New York's mayor Ed Koch, "How'm I doing? Did I lose the room yet?"

I knew we had made a really fine connection, based on our attraction and similar aesthetic views, and that there was no way I would do anything outrageous or stupid to louse this up. So I did not worry that by the end of the night, I might wind up roomless.

We went to her hotel room to rest and clean up for the night. It was a lovely small hotel that faced west, and the setting sun was marvelous to see. I loved talking with her, as she was so sophisticated, as the Europeans can be. Her knowledge of multiple languages and different cultures made her so interesting. It was the one factor that I truly missed when coming back to the States after Europe. Americans can be so self-centered and lack the balanced view of the whole world.

We were arm in arm and laughing when we left the hotel. We went to a small, romantic restaurant, with outside tables set with candles and flowers. We drank wine and ate lightly, each feeding the other. It was very sweet. We walked past the lit-up fountains after dinner and stopped at a very lively bar to listen to some music and talk with the locals, who turned out to be not-so-local—it was summer in Spain, which meant everyone was there. I really liked René; she was very warm, open, and direct. She played no games—there was no need to, as we were attracted to one another, but neither of us said anything too intimate along those lines. We were concentrating on Spain and learning about each other.

Surprisingly, she had never been to New York and wanted to hear all about it. She liked the fact that I was well traveled and understood Europe from a non-American point of view. Her country was so small, she said, that it barely got mentioned in world news or events, and that made the Belgians citizens of what was around them. It was living in a place that people pass through on their way to somewhere else. Luxembourg was another example. Belgium was certainly bigger, and she helped me understand their mentality. They had to fight for their independence from France and that showed in their individual toughness, as it was David versus Goliath.

René spoke Dutch, French, and English and was learning German. That impressed me—what a skill. I felt handicapped with my limited knowledge of German and my college-level French.

We were tired and strolled easily back to the hotel. I used the bathroom first, and she followed. She came out wearing a beautiful nightie. We kissed and held one another very tenderly, and when we made love for the first time, I found her to be a soft, sensual lover, and she moaned ever so lightly. Her body was more of an athlete than an art student, and then she told me she was a runner. Like me. We thoroughly enjoyed making love. There was no hurry; this was one woman who loved to go slowly, and I knew that immediately. We just meshed. I had watched her eat dinner, and I knew then what kind of lover she would be. In my experience, there was a direct correlation between one's approach to food and one's approach to sex. There are exceptions, such as being too hungry, but by and large, the formula works. The spectrum goes from cautious and tense to voracious and fearless.

We slept peacefully, which was unusual for me as I had trouble sleeping when with a new partner, but that night, I slept well. So did she.

We woke up to the church bells, as it was Sunday. I waited until we were at breakfast to tell her that I wanted her to accompany me to the bullfight. I was very cautious in that request, because this was a sensitive art student who was delicate and well bred. I was sure she would not want to go.

"I have always wanted to see the pageantry of a Spanish bullfight," she said, and she went on to talk about all the stages of the bullfight, with the costumes, the colors, and the protocol of the bullfight itself.

I just shook my head at how I misread her. I was elated that she wanted to go. We strolled after breakfast and asked for directions to the bullfight. We went to the Plaza de Toros de la Madrina, which was built in the eighteenth century. It was like being thrown back in time. The classic Moorish architecture, with high columns and intricate designs, was astonishing. René explained about the four styles of Spanish-period architecture, from Moorish to Gothic to Renaissance and Baroque, and my mouth was agape all the time. This woman was a walking knowledge machine.

We settled in our seats among the huge crowd and watched seven bullfights, each getting better in class, as the main event always followed the preliminary events. The crowd was intense and appreciative, and they rated the matador and his assistants on the preciseness of their movements and the accuracy of their role in the bullfight. They did not want the animal to suffer, a paradoxical concept after we watched the picador (a man on horseback who uses a lance to draw blood from the bull's shoulder area in order to soften up the bull for the matador). If done correctly, the bull will attempt to lift the heavily protected horse into the air with its horns, thereby weakening its own neck and resulting in the lowering of the neck for the ease of the kill from the matador.

The next phase belonged to the tercio de banderillas. They were three colorfully costumed men on foot, who each charged the bull in succession and attempted to place two paper-decorated barbed sticks into the bull's shoulders, in order to further weaken the bull's neck area.

The matador now took over for the final stage. His skill was determined by the specific moves he made, while showing no fear of the bull whatsoever. After many passes by the bull, which attempted to gore the red cap that the matador twirled very artistically while covering his sword, the matador dedicated the death of the bull to the audience or a specific dignitary. He finally thrust his sword into the bull's neck. If it dropped immediately, the crowd went wild with olé and cheering. The matador then strode like only a Spanish flamenco dancer would, with pride and elegance.

The arena was a mixture of odors. Some were aromatic, which came from the flowers and well-scented spectators. Others were more circus-like, which came from the horses and bulls. Overall, we had the time of our lives at this event. René made no mention of the blood. It was, at times, a bit difficult for me, as I am no blood-and-guts guy. I don't even like car chases or action movies. She pointed out all the elaborate costumes worn by the banderilleros and the picador. Nothing came close, however, to the multicolored attire of the matador, who was considered an athlete and an artist. All and all, it was a well-orchestrated spectacle with trumpets and much fanfare.

We were very turned on by this experience, and she clutched my hand very passionately, unlike the previous night, when it was all soft and easy. Tonight would be different, and we both said it. We had a drink after the bullfight at a lovely tapas bar and decided to get something to eat. We found a traditional Spanish restaurant and had a meal of chicken and sausage with wine and a great salad. We treated ourselves to some pastries and espresso for dessert.

We returned to the hotel early to take a bath and relax. The hotel had a public balcony area, and we sat and talked and enjoyed one another. Once back in our room, we played a game about having a bullfight. We would touch certain spots and then have to back off, like they did in the ring. It drove us both crazy, and after some fantastic teasing and resisting, we made very passionate love, as promised. She was one remarkable woman. We stayed turned on all night and sleep suffered.

We woke up at noon and had to have "the talk." She knew I wanted to go to Cordoba and then head south to the coast and Málaga. I did not want a relationship, and traveling with a person sure would feel like one. But I was going to make an exception and presented a plan to her. We would go to Cordoba and spend one night there and then continue to Málaga and go our separate ways there.

All she said was, "Okay." She checked out, and we got into the car for the seventy-five mile ride to Cordoba. I assured myself that I was still on my solo adventure, except for the small detour with René.

I was not expecting Cordoba to be as magnificent as it was. René gave me the history lesson before we got there. Cordoba, at one time, was the most populated city in the world. It was built by Arabs from Syria, who also built the Great Mosque, which was absolutely breathtaking. The old city had a Jewish section with a huge synagogue. The Fernandine churches now dominated the landscape. There were bridges and statues everywhere. The parks and houses were eye-popping, and after the one afternoon, we mutually agreed to stay two days. I did not want to miss the opportunity to see this beautiful city with this extraordinary woman, who explained everything. She was beautiful, smart, sensitive, and knowledgeable and wanted to be with me. It was truly a win/win, and all I had to do was adjust the rules in my head. So I put an asterisk to hitching in Spain ("*except for the days with Rene.") I was fine with it.

We found an old hotel near the mosque. It had a top-floor room with a balcony that overlooked the Calella de las Flores, a beautiful street from the sixteenth century. If you have a romantic bone in your body, then this is the city for you. There is something beautiful to see everywhere. René had her notes and her guidebook, and she lead the way. We went all over this city, like tourists on speed, looking at the architecture, because we truly wanted to see it all. One hour it was one century, and the next hour it was another. We were going between the Arabic, Jewish, and Christian areas with glee, and she seemed to know more than the guidebook pointed out. We did the first day until the sun went down and were ecstatic about it.

We went to a hot-spot bar for dinner to mingle with the younger generation, as we'd had plenty of history and wanted to reconnect. The place we picked was perfect, because there were people from all over Europe, and we joined a bigger table of tourists. We both said hola when we entered a place and knew that whoever said it in return was announcing their intention to talk or at least to be approachable. It was a European custom, although the word changes from country to country. Still, the message is the same. It's a way people meet people who are traveling or who want to meet other people.

They thought we were a couple because we sounded alike as we talked about our day in Cordoba. They could feel the admiration and appreciation we had for this city, and we just laughed when people asked how long we had been together. (Let's see … sixty hours.) We had a nightcap and went back to the hotel. We were tired and extremely happy to have shared such a wonderful three days and two nights together. Her last comment came when she was very tired and just about to fall asleep. She asked, "How are we going to be able to split up when we get to Málaga?"

It was the last thought I wanted to have, as I had put all that away when I agreed to do this trip with her. But she was dead on—how would we deal with leaving? There were ten movies I could think of where the perchance meeting drives both of them crazy when they part. I decided not to think about it, because we had one more day in Cordoba, and I did not want to ruin it. I held her as we fell asleep.

We woke up early and after making some passionate love, we decided to go out for an early morning walk and pick some flowers for our room. The section we were staying in was so beautiful, with the colored old stones and flowered trellises. We counted the arches and loved the iron gates. We had a cup of deep Spanish coffee and a sweet roll with fruit at a small bakery that had a few outside tables.

We looked at one another intensely. We didn't say it, but each of us knew we really liked one another and were a great fit. We had our own passions about things and were very good at sharing. She was intuitive as well as reactive. I was spontaneous as well as grounded, and together, we were really good. I put my finger over my mouth, and she knew not to say it. We went back to the hotel and my "guide" mapped out the day.

Today, we would go to the art museums at a slower pace, because we couldn't rush that. She picked two that she thought were unique to this area, so we went first to the Archeological and Ethnological Museum, and in the afternoon, we went to the Three Cultures Museum, also called the Calahora Tower.

We were absolutely overwhelmed by what we saw, as Cordoba has such a rich and deep history. The one fact that set it apart from other places that had seen invasions and conquerors, like Istanbul or Jerusalem, was that they did not burn down the old to build the new. They just changed it, like redecorating, not pillaging. Therefore, its history was there to be seen. I kept thanking her for showing me all this, and she was happy to have someone interested in seeing and learning. It was truly a sharing day for the beautiful, supersmart, graduate art student from Brussels and the traveling bartender/actor/hippie/maybe future shrink/maybe restaurant man from New York.

We took a peaceful nap, as we needed to recharge the batteries. We went out about nine thirty for our last night in Cordoba. The city lit up at night so beautifully. There were lights in the trees and on the bridges. The parks had lit fountains. We got the feeling that they knew presentation was everything when it came to aesthetics. It's not just the art; it's the frame and its setting that makes the picture.

We went to the newer part of the city just to see it, and it was very lively, with a higher concentration of travelers. We found a restaurant that had dancers whirling around, but it was full, so we went to a huge outside cafe that served dinners. We talked with a French couple and a Spanish couple who actually lived there. They were taken with René because she knew more about the surroundings than they did—she knew the history. They were impressed that we had seen and done so much in just two days. We ate, drank, laughed, and had a wonderful time socializing.

We walked back through the city for the last time, stopping to dance at a plaza. An Italian couple took our picture when I bent her backward for the Hollywood kiss.

We looked out our balcony and felt the same feeling—sheer joy. This was it. We knew to enjoy it forever, because we probably would never capture this feeling in this moment again. We went to bed, wrapped in each other's arms, and made love slowly and softly until we unleashed the horses, as they say, and fell asleep, truly sated.

We slept very well, peaceful and happy. When we woke up, we had our outside-cafe breakfast and checked out of the hotel. We said good-bye to Cordoba and got in the car for the eighty-mile ride to Málaga.

Málaga and the Costa del Sol

It was early in the day, but it was already hot. We were about ten minutes into the ride when René started in. "Do you want to hear about Málaga?"

"Sure," I answered.

"It's going to be as pretty as Cordoba, because the same people occupied both cities, and it is about 2,600 years old and was founded by the Phoenicians."

She told me that it was the home of Pablo Picasso, and there were world-famous museums. Its architecture had Moorish influence as well as Renaissance. There were Arabic, Christian, and Jewish influences, and she thought this week was the Feria de Málaga, where the streets turned into a festival with wine, tapas, and Flamenco dancers.

She knew exactly what she was doing, laying it on thick. She tried to keep a straight face and just blurted out these bits of information, without attaching any meaning to the fact that we were going to split up in Málaga. I played it down, as I already knew I was not going to leave her without seeing all these wonderful sights together.

I told her it sounded very interesting, and it was something that she would really enjoy.

She shot me a look to see if I was kidding.

"Et tu, Brutus?" she said.

I laughed and told her that we never said exactly when we would split in Málaga.

We went on to discuss the reality that it would be impossible to leave one another and do Málaga separately. There would be no point to it. But were we just making it more difficult to part? We were finding every way not to do that. So I added another asterisk in my head, which now read "*except for the long side trip with René."

The word long also was undefined, so I know I still had some wiggle room, if it became too difficult to leave her. I was so captivated by this woman that I would rationalize everything away, just to stay with her, and the alarm bells were already ringing very loudly in my head.

I asked her if we were not just digging ourselves a deeper hole. She looked at me and then looked away. She thought about what she was going to say for quite a while and finally said, "We met incidentally, unprepared to find what we found in one another, and I live in Belgium and will be going back to graduate school, and you live in New York and will be going back to whatever your life takes you to there. This is an absolutely magical, wonderful experience we are having, and I could love you to death if our circumstances were different, but they are not. Why don't we love every minute together and deal with it by agreeing to understand it is now and not the future."

I love Europeans and the way they look at romance as part of life but not necessarily their entire lives. She had hit the nail on the head, and it relieved me of all doubts. I said to myself, Grow up. This is an affair, and you will have wonderful memories. Don't try to make it more than it is. She can give herself fully and know that this will not alter her life; it will just add to it. You need to do the same.

I said to her, "This will be ours to keep for however long it lasts, and then we will go back to our lives with some very wonderful shared experiences."

"Exactly."

Europeans understand affairs and do not go crazy when their political leaders have dalliances. It's part of life, love, sex, and family, and it goes together in a different formulas for Europeans. She stopped my mollycoddling of my own feelings and basically told me to enjoy them. Life would take care of itself. She was absolutely correct.

There was a quiet in the car as we processed what we had just said. These types of discussions take one out to the moment, as they cause reflection and time alteration. We let it sink in. At one point, she said, "You are a very special man. Thank you."

"For what?"

"For not running away and for being honest with your feelings and with me."

I said it was mutual. Our discussion had deepened the meaning of this time together, and I asked her to pull over. I gave her a kiss from the deepest part of me, and she felt it. It was not one of those heat kisses; it was from a place of appreciation, admiration, and understanding. We shared our first tears.

I was trying to be adult about this, because I thought, I am the freewheeler from the Big Bad Apple on a joy ride in the Mediterranean, and I was having the time of my life. Why would this experience be any different from the others? The answer was, because it was. I could not have found a more interesting and thoroughly enjoyable and attractive person than René, and I wanted to keep her. The truth was that she could handle this much better than I could, and I knew that as well. So I once again I gathered myself and added yet another asterisk—"*except for the very long side trip with René, who I will say good-bye to, even if I am in love with her."

So I said, "I hope the damn feria is there."

We both laughed and went on to discuss Málaga.

There was no longer a cloud over us, and we lightened up and planned to hit Málaga with a great shared sense of anticipation.

When we came out of the Spanish mountains, which had been a twisty, dry-earthed ride, to reveal Málaga and the Mediterranean, we both gasped. It was breathtaking to see all the white buildings with their orange-tiled roofs and the colorful floral vistas, with the expansive deep-blue Mediterranean in the background. It was almost too much for one sighting. Then we saw the sign that announced the Feria de Málaga, and we damn near peed in our collective pants. It was so exciting to see the banners and the streets shut down for pedestrian traffic. We did not mind the delay in getting around it, as we looked at everything. We parked the car, read her guidebook, and got a room in the Calle Granada, not far from the Picasso Museum. The woman at the hotel said we were very lucky, as she had just received a cancellation. All the rooms in this area were booked for the festival. We took that as a sign from the gods that this was meant to be for us. We put our stuff in the room, which had a view of the street of the very colorful, lightly painted homes and small inns. It was just perfect. The room was immaculate and had little flower vases on very old tables. The bed had a wrought-iron headboard above a decorative wooden frame.

We hit the streets running and decided to see what this feria was all about. It was huge, with booths selling Spanish clothing and religious items. It had wine-tasting areas and tapas. The music was everywhere, and we saw small groups of Flamenco dancers performing. The mood was upbeat and joyful. We had some tapas, and the sea air made everything taste wonderful. We kept hugging each other in excitement.

"Okay, Miss Belgium, get out your book, and let's do Málaga," I said.

"Gladly, Mr. New York."

I knew the Picasso paintings would be her first choice. They were housed in the Buenavista Palace, which had a section of his works. The palace was from the sixteenth century. During its renovation, workers discovered the wall of an ancient Phoenician city that dated back 2,600 years. We just gazed and gazed at the sculptures and paintings. René explained the style of the intricate details of the frames. She knew the history of the person portrayed in the sculpture or what type of oil-rock-sand mixture was used for the paint.

We spent about two hours there and decided to see the main Cathedral de Málaga, which dominated the city. She explained it was built during the fifteenth and sixteenth centuries and had Renaissance and Baroque styles. It was near the area of architectural significance that included the Castle de Gibrolfaro and the Alcazaba, a Moorish fortification that had a Roman theater. I'd been to Rome, but this thing was older and in better shape. We walked all over the area and wowed ourselves with one discovery after another.

In Europe, time frames were overwhelming. If I let myself imagine the times in which these sites were built, it became so much more significant.

We finished the afternoon and went back to the hotel to shower and rest. While René showered, I bought two cafés and some tarts. We sat by our table and let the sea breeze blow the curtains, as we'd opened all the windows. Instead of napping, she suggested we walk to the sea and lie down by the water.

"Excellent idea," I agreed, and we did just that. This was now our fifth day together, and we were a team. We took one another's suggestions, and it all flowed smoothly. I kept telling her what a gem she was and how much I was learning by listening to her. She told me that I had a keen eye and was very receptive to it all, and that made her very happy.

We relaxed by the sea and saw Málaga from that perspective, which included the mountains to the north. What a majestic city, sitting in the valley with the river running to the sea. We went back to the hotel and slept for about an hour. I had already filled one notebook; tomorrow, I would have to get another. She watched very admiringly as I journaled my thoughts and the facts of each day. She asked if I would ever write about us.

"I've always secretly wanted to be a writer," I confessed. "I have two different trips journaled and am now in the process of journaling the third. One day, I'll try to put it into a book. If I ever do, you will be someone I will explain fully."

We were ready to do the feria, which at night moved to the fairgrounds, where there were restaurants and shops that sold Spanish historical items. It was decorated with lanterns and streamers, and there were numerous small bands milling among the revelers, as well as the ever-present flamenco dancers, who wore their traditional Spanish costumes of red and red-and-black hats. The merchants sold sherry in small glasses. In the fairground itself were typical amusement rides and booths featuring games of chance.

We were told we'd missed last night's opening fireworks. People were in high spirits, and there was continual singing and dancing, which was so joyful.

We lasted about two hours and then headed to the old section for a quieter place. We found a lovely restaurant bar full of locals and tourists. We joined a couple from Morocco, and later, some Swedes sat with us. A man was playing a Spanish guitar and he was brilliant. Everyone put money in his basket as he walked among the tables.

People again assumed that René and I had been together for a long time, as we tended to finish one another's sentences, more out of excitement than anything else. Her accent was more Dutch than French, but she spoke beautiful English and only missed my colloquialisms when I spoke New York-ese. We stayed at this bar for quite a while, enjoying the conversation with the Moroccans, who were more comfortable speaking in French, with English as their second language choice. The Swedes were two guys and a girl who were making their way to Barcelona. It was a fun night, and we called it quits about two in the morning, after another walk along very old city streets. We held hands and looked up at the stars.

We slept deeply. In the very bright morning, we woke up and looked at one another across the table. We paused. each waiting for the other to speak. She held up one finger and said, "Uno mas dia."

"Si, si."

We would do one more day.

We went to the harbor and watched the boats. I saw a couple riding a scooter and pointed to them and smiled. She gave me such a hug, because she got it in a second; she must have seen it in my eyes. We found the place, rented a scooter, and drove all over Málaga. It was such a great way to get around.

We went to the Parque al Rosario after we bought some bread, wine, and tapas, and we sat under a great big tree to have our lunch—and we made out like two teenagers. We giggled and rolled around and played with one another's hair. We had a wonderful time, recounting all we had seen in these six days.

She wanted to go the pottery and crafts shops, and I wanted to see the leather-goods places, so we drove around and made one stop to see another castle before we went to the artisan section. We bought some candles for our last night, and she bought some kind of lotion, which brought a little devilish look to her face.

We dropped off the scooter and had a drink by the large harbor bar. We met some Americans from Boston who were also seeing the Costa del Sol, and we had a very lively conversation. We bantered about the pros and cons of American and European culture and the differences between countries. I was on the side of the Europeans. René took a headier, neutral descriptive position, and the Bostonians defended some American humanitarian values. We had a lot of fun.

We went back to the hotel, tired and happy and in need of a shower.

We played in the room until nine and then went out for dinner. She asked that we not make it a late night, as she wanted to come back by midnight so we could use the candles and her lotions. I couldn't say no to that. We found the most intimate restaurant we could, with a sound system that was playing softer jazz. We asked for a table outside near the door and had a delicious fish dinner with wine, as well as espresso with a shot of Tia Maria.

We walked slowly for the last hour and again found ourselves by the fountain at the castle. It was such a powerful sight, and it framed our mood, which was now a bit subdued, as we knew time was winding down. We went back to our room, and she came out of the bathroom completely naked. She lay on the bed and handed me the lotion. I lit the candles and gave her a terrific body massage. We found a TV station that was playing a musical, and it served as background. She gave me a massage, and we talked so appreciatively of one another. It was so close and intimate. We made love, looking into one another's eyes and never broke contact, which is very unusual. She gave herself to me with such intensity that I almost cried out of joy. We collapsed from sheer exhaustion and fell into the deepest sleep we had together.

When the morning came, we agreed to have breakfast and not do any drama. We wanted to dignify what we had accomplished on this magical meeting of souls. We went to a local bakery and had our coffee and fruit.

Back to the hotel, she said she would stay for a while, and I said I was going to go. I gave her my share of the hotel bill. We hugged for a long time and had one very deep kiss. I did not expect to hear what came out of me, but I told her I loved her and that she had captured my heart. I told her it was the absolute best time I had ever had and that I would be forever grateful to her for who she was and for what she had shown me. Her eyes filled up with tears, and she said I was the man she had been searching for all of her life. She would love me and our time together forever. With that said, we kissed one more time, and I left.

I made it about three blocks before I stopped and wanted to go back. I found a little bench and sat down, because I felt overwhelmed. I cried and cried. It felt like I was completely and utterly alone, and I knew this feeling. I felt the same as I did at my father's funeral. My chest heaved for a while, and then it subsided, as I slowly came to recognize that she wasn't dead and would be a part of me forever. She was right—the feelings would be part of us, and though we lived in different places and were to have separate lives, these six days were very, very special. With that feeling, I slowly recovered and wiped the tears, collected myself, took some very deep breaths, got up, walked very slowly to the main road, and headed to Fuengirola.

Thelma and Ma were both in tears. So was I.

"Oh, Mr. Ken, how could you leave that woman like that? You two was a great pair, and that make no sense at all."

Ma wiped her eyes. "Men leave all the time, Thelma, and my knucklehead son was no different."

"This is not the end of that story," I said. "Let me continue …"

Duke in Torremolinos

I walked to the beach to get the ride to Fuengirola, as it was only fifteen miles along the Mediterranean from Málaga. I was kind of backtracking because it was west of Málaga toward Portugal, but I was looking for Duke.

I got a ride from a local Spaniard who was delivering summer umbrellas and beach items. He said Fuengirola was not a big town and if I was looking for anyone, I should go by the market square, as most of the cafes and bars were located there. I asked him about Torremolinos, and he said the lifestyle was very fast, with jet-setters and lots of parties.

Being that I would hit Torremolinos first, I decided that Duke was most likely there, and I got off to see if I could find him.

The only problem was that I was only nine miles away from Málaga, and although my brain knew René was leaving, I kept telling myself that I could go back there and find her, if I did not like it here.

Torremolinos had a small downtown area that ran along the beach, and then there were a few roads that led up the small mountain to where most of the residents lived. I went to the beach first and took a swim, after changing into my swimsuit behind a clump of high rocks. The water felt great, and I just floated along, keeping my eye on my knapsack. I decided I would spend the afternoon asking around to see if I could find him. If I hadn't found him by five o'clock, I would head to Fuengirola.

After my swim, I went to a few cafes and asked a few people if they knew him, as I gave his unique description. No luck. I stopped in a very popular bar and asked the barman, who said he did know Duke and that he'd be here, sooner or later.

I continued to search the town and found the biggest cafe in a beautiful garden area by some boutiques. When I saw all the pretty girls shopping, I knew this would be his hangout. I walked in and out of the very lovely shops; it was a little after noon. I sat at a table and ordered a sandwich. I looked over to my right ... and there he was. He was sitting by himself, reading La Monde, a French newspaper.

I finished my sandwich and took my coffee with me. I carefully stayed out of his vision and sat directly behind him. Duke was irascible and was known for having good days and bad days, so the approach had to be just right.

From behind him, I called out, "Hey, Duke."

He never turned around, but he said, "Who wants to know?"

I offered my credentials. "Ken, from the White Horse, friend of both Mikes. I recently spent eight days with Sam and Dave in Albufeira."

With that, he turned around and lowered his sunglasses. He looked at me for a long time before a wry smile appeared across his tight lips. When he recognized me, he motioned for me to join him. "Can't get away from you Village cats."

Duke was older than Sam and Dave; I guessed him to be in his late forties. He owned the second largest coffee house in the Village after the Figaro, near Bleecker Street. I had met him about ten years earlier, when I was hanging out at Googie's Bar, which was just down the street. I knew the owners, Benny and Phil, and the three of us would have coffee at Duke's. Duke always wore black and a signature medallion around his neck. He was a tall man who shaved his head long before it became fashionable to do so. It wasn't hard to find someone with that description. At times, Duke was difficult to be around, but he was known to be terrific to his friends. I was not his friend, just a Village compatriot he knew by face. He was friends with Sam and Dave, though, and he asked how my time was with them.

I told him of the Sir Harry's event, and we started talking. I told him I had hitched from Lisbon and was just coolin' it on the coast for the summer, as I had just finished grad school and had to decide if I wanted to continue in theater or "go straight."

He asked if I knew Jack E.

"Why do you ask?"

"Because that is one crazy guy who also had to decide if he wanted to act."

"Jack and I are close friends," I said. "We've done theater together."

Then Duke and I started naming a bevy of guys and gals that we knew in common. The more I talked, the more he placed me, and he eventually remembered my coming in to his place with Benny and Phil. When I told him I'd cooked at David's Pot Belly on Christopher Street, he really opened up, because David and he had been longtime friends.

"It's amazing that we knew the same people and really never hung out together," Duke said.

Here was my chance and I took it. "Well, motherfucker, we can do that now."

He laughed and then called the waiter over and asked what I was drinking.

"I would like a Duke's double espresso, with lemon, no sugar, and leave the spoon in."

That did it. He shook his head and asked how I could remember a thing like that.

I had watched him drink that when I was a teenager and thought at the time, that is a very cool dude.

He still owned the place in the Village but no longer wanted to work it. His checks were sent here. It was fun getting to know him, and I now could match stories, sharing my own experiences from all the places I had worked in the Village.

I asked him about Torremolinos. He said it was "outta sight," and he would show me around. Later that afternoon, he asked if I was looking for a place to crash.

"But of course," I replied.

"I have a big house, and you can grab a room."

"Thanks, Duke."

"But I will need my own space," he added.

"Your moods are legendary."

"Fuckin' A," he replied.

I was home.

Duke explained the scene to me. It was more of a literary thing for him now, as he was hanging with a French crowd that read poetry and had "gatherings" each night at another cafe.

"Not just a hook to meet women?" I asked.

He laughed and said, "Well, that too," but he really was reading French poetry.

"So Le Monde is not just a cool cover?"

"No, I can read French." He started rattling off the Le Monde he was carrying to prove he could read it.

I went back to his sprawling place with him. It was not on as grand a scale as Dave and Sam's, but this was one cool house. It had a small fountain in the courtyard with a sitting swing. The rooms were bright, big, and airy. Duke had quite an art collection on the walls. There were books everywhere, and it was apparent that he was a heavy reader. The kitchen was impressive, as it looked like restaurant quality.

He was noted for being more of a loner, and so I told him I really appreciated his letting me stay with him, and I would not get in his way.

He smirked and said, "Well, thank you, white man."

We both laughed. He had a wickedly cutting sense of humor, and I could see he was quite bright, yet there was a dark side to him that lived just beneath the surface.

Everyone had seen his tirades and screaming fits in his coffeehouse, and I wondered if that was brought out by New York and business or if it was just his character. Time would tell. I was honest with him about money and said I had enough to cover some expenses, but it was limited, and I was hoping to make it last. He said he didn't think "a post-grad student who was hitching" was rolling in it, and he would cover my food.

"Mighty nice of you, kimosabe," I replied. "And the catch?"

He wrinkled his brow, and his semismirk returned. Then it turned to a small smile when he told me that "Butch did better with Sundance."

My being twenty-nine would be an asset for him with the younger women, and that made perfect sense. I was his wingman.

"No free lunch," he said. We had a deal.

I put my stuff in a big room on the second floor and prepared for what appeared to be a very different kind of week than the one I had just had with René.

Duke was not Sam or Dave in terms of popularity. The phone did not ring once from the time when I got there until we left for dinner. I guess that is why he agreed to bring me on board. Duke had a standoffish vibe, but when he put out energy, it worked. When he was in one of his moods, however, everyone backed away. I was going to see which Duke I got here in Torremolinos.

He brought me to a very quaint Spanish restaurant on the hill going down to the town. It had a back seating area that was not visible at all from the street, and we had a bisteck dinner that was superb. The waitress called him Señor Duke, and he was good to her. We proceeded to go to town. He brought me to the Cafe Andalusia, where he said hello to some people. I was going to establish myself right away so he would not feel burdened with me.

I approached the bartender and struck up a conversation, asking about what was happening in Torremolinos. The waitress joined in, and they said I should meet their friend Gil, who was seated nearby. I introduced myself to Gil, and he spoke of the feria going on in Fuengirola and Málaga and said the scene in Torremolinos was mainly private parties. I told him of Albufeira and Sir Harry's, and he said he knew that scene. He said there was a get-together later for friends of the Andalusia, and I could meet him there later. He scribbled the address on a piece of paper. As I thanked him, I said I was going back to be with my friend Señor Duke.

"You know Señor Duke?"

"I am staying with him."

"Bravo," he said. He looked past me and waved to Duke.

I told Duke that Gil just had invited us to an Andalusia get-together later.

"You work fast," he said. "I haven't heard about this one yet."

"Wanna go?"

"I want to go to my scene first," he said. "We can use that as backup."

That was okay by me. I just wanted to establish some independence, and I had done that.

We went to the cafe where I had met him. At night, they set up a mock stage, which was really just a small platform with a microphone and a chair. Duke didn't say hola when we got there, but I did, and we received about six responses from the cafe crowd. Good start, I thought. We sat around for a while, and Duke made the rounds, talking to people at various tables, and then the poetry reading began. Mainly it was English, but there was Spanish and French as well. People would just go to the mike, sit down, and read their poem or someone else's.

The crowd in this small plaza started to swell, and people filled the empty seats. I asked two women standing near us if they wanted to join our table, and they sat down. Duke smiled. They were French Canadians on holiday, like everyone else. Duke was pleasant but not overly friendly.

Duke went up to the stage next and read one of his original poems in English. It was about seeing and not seeing, being and not being. It got the best applause of the night so far. I thought it was very good—surprisingly good.

We all talked together for about two hours as people came and went. Those women left and others followed. Some guys from Turkey joined us—they were hysterical. One of them went up to the mike and sang. After he'd finished, he was told it was only poetry, and the place laughed like crazy. I could see how each night here could be different, depending on the crowd. I could see why Duke liked it.

At about one in the morning, we went to the get-together than Gil had suggested. It was at a place on the hill similar to Duke's. Duke knew a lot of the people there, and he got into a conversation with an older woman. I stayed for about an hour but then told him I was calling it a night. He gave me the key and directions to his place. I left and walked slowly back to his hacienda.

I wondered where René was. I knew if she was up, she would be thinking of me, as we had made a pact to look at the moon at one o'clock and talk to one another. It was past one o'clock, but I was thinking of her.

I was going to be all right in Torremolinos, as it was jam-packed with people, but the conversations with René that were in my head were starting to take over, and I just let myself have them. I got to Duke's and when I got into my bed, the damn moon emerged from behind the clouds and was visible from my bed.

"Good night, René, sweet being that you are. I am here … I am here."

Thelma was shaking her head at me, because to her, I should have never left René. Ma picked up her tea and said, "I have never heard him talk that way about anyone else. He was really smitten with that woman."

Fuengirola and Marbella

I had the basic landscape for what it was going to be like in Torremolinos with Señor Duke. During the next few days, we rolled out around noon and had our café downtown. Then we might spend the afternoon at the beach or catch up with some people in the late afternoon and figure out where the party was going to be for that night. It included going to the cafe and reading the poems, meeting people, telling stories, laughing, and doing a lot of drinking or pot smoking. The regulars were always around, and by the third day, people were recognizing me—that was very comfortable.

I read some poems that I wrote one night as my old existential self got hold of my pen, and I wrote some funny Theater of the Absurd riffs, which, surprisingly, were well received. It led to some younger women coming to our table, and Duke lit up like a kid in a candy store. He was able to spend the night with a midtwenties girl from Austria. I kept thinking about René.

Duke and I really had a good time with one another. I never saw the moods that had overtaken him in the Village days. He was glad to have my company and told me that I was good for him—I think that that meant I lightened him up a bit, and he laughed more. He could be a bit deadpan—that was a common burnout symptom of Village night people. They had done it all, seen it all, and everything got a bit tainted after a while.

I told Duke on the fourth day that I was going to Fuengirola for a few days and would come back. He offered me a ride. I reminded him I was a hitcher with no money, and he chuckled.

The ride to Fuengirola was easy, as it was six miles. A young woman in a Fiat gave me the quick lift. She said Fuengirola was similar to Torremolinos, and many of the same people could be seen in both places.

The beach was bigger and nicer than in Torremolinos, and I even used the changing room that was provided, a freebie service. I strolled around and decided I liked the town, as it was very well maintained and very crowded. In the afternoon, while I sat eating a light sandwich, I heard a New York accent from a table a few yards away. There were three guys talking and telling jokes. They were arguing about some place in the Village where they had gone but could not remember its name. One guy made up names, and the others just laughed and broke balls. So I walked to them, told them that it was called the Cafe Wha!, and kept walking to the restroom. When I returned, they asked me to join them. They were three Jewish guys from the Upper East Side, card-playing sports fanatics who bet on everything and were faster and more quick witted than anyone I had met on the trip. Randy was the pack leader, and Harvey and Mike were the sharp-witted foils. Think Seinfeld, Kramer, and George.

We fit like fingers in a glove, and when I told them about the White Horse, they said that I had to hang out with them. When I told them I was traveling, Randy said, "You have to stay with us. We have this huge house."

Randy, Harvey, and Mike would be my nut-job hosts for three of the funniest and craziest days I had in the Mediterranean. They went to the beach and joined every blanket with three girls or more. They walked through town, advertising their names and where the party was that night. They were accepted as fun-loving and carefree.

Their house was one major piece of disarray, as they could never get it together long enough to plan anything well. It was a chaotic pile of dishes, clothes, books, and magazines thrown everywhere, and no one cared. They had a good music system that played their cassette tapes, which was the extent of the technological music revolution as that time.

At Henri's, one of the bigger cafes, I borrowed Duke's poetry scene and had the owner set up a faux stage, and it worked. Once we started to read some poems, a crowd gathered, and the owner loved it. I used my old improvisational theater bit to have the audience tell dreams, and then I made up different endings and took suggestions from the audience. The more you drank or smoked pot, the funnier it was. Quite honestly, I loved the minirecognition that I received from those three nights. Randy and the boys were very supportive and ran around telling people of the new theater participation night at Henri's. Europeans are quick to join in, as they love being in the moment.

I met and talked to many women during the three nights at Randy's, but I did not want anything more than that. I was content at night to just be by myself and talk to René before closing my eyes. She would have been ecstatic if she had seen me in my improvisational theater element. In my head, I told her about it anyway.

These were the years before there was such a thing as a cell phone, and I wondered how different all relationships might have been if we'd had the ability back then to connect by text or phone from wherever we were at the moment.

After the last night of "Dream Theater," as the owner called it, the boys and I went to the Fuengirola Fiesta. They danced and sang with the Spaniards, and we sipped espressos and sherry with anyone sitting at big enough tables. We ate hamburgesas and went to the ball-throwing games and shooting galleries. There was a rifle target booth with moving ducks and flying birds. The barker told us that if we shot down all the birds and ducks, a pop-up target would appear, and if we hit it, it would take our picture while shooting. He loaded my rifle with the pellets—only fifty shots. I told the guys not to bet against me, because I had won a three-day pass during basic training in the US Army and earned a sharpshooter medal with a real M14. If the rifle shot straight, this was a done deal. That set off Mike and Harvey, and they put down five dollars each to say I was full of crap. Randy looked at me, and I said, "Really, I can do this."

Randy put down ten dollars on my side.

I drove them really nuts when I said, "My father told me to never bet on a sure thing, and this is a sure thing."

They started cackling and even got passersby to join in the bet.

I asked the barker, "How often does the target get hit?"

"It can be done, sir," he answered.

"Okay, let's roll."

I shot down every one of the floating ducks and missed only one shot while getting the flying birds. The red-and-white circle target popped up, and I hit it dead on—and the camera flashed and took my picture.

Randy was giving the others a whole lot of abuse when the barker handed me a card with a number on it and said, "Come back tomorrow for your picture."

"You have to be kidding," I said. There were Polaroids in those days, but this was a roll of film that had to be developed. "But I am leaving tomorrow! Randy, you have to get this picture and send it to me."

"Sure, just give me your address before you go."

I felt the chances of this guy going back the next night to get my picture were slim and none. The odds on not losing my address were even greater, and the overall odds of his going there, getting the picture, not losing the address, and putting the picture in an envelope with a stamp and mailing it to me was about 100 to 1. We finished up the night with a late-night sing-along at Henri's. I went to sleep, laughing. René, in my head, thought it was funny too.

At noon the following day, I said good-bye to Randy and the guys and asked him to really try to get my picture. He said he would. I left Fuengirola and went to Marbella.

(After the trip was over, and I had returned to New York, my phone rang, and it was Randy. He was back in New York and had looked me up in the phonebook. He said, "We are having a party and you are invited—and oh yes, I have your picture." I went up to see them, and we had a great time telling the Fuengirola stories. And the son of a gun really had my picture.)

The ride to Marbella, like all rides on the coast in the Costa del Sol, was probably the easiest in the world. So many people traverse between the cities that there is a constant flow of traffic day and night. I got the forty-five-minute ride from some German guys in an Audi. They were from Leimen, and I almost popped a gasket, because that was the next town to Heidelberg. We talked about "home," and it made me feel good that all the places I knew were still there and in good operation.

After we said auf wiedersehen, I walked along the beach and stopped at a cafe. The town was not much different from the other sun towns, except the Marbella harbor was connected to a long wharf with many restaurants. The beach was bigger than Torremolinos and Fuengirola, and there were many colored umbrellas that made it look like a quilt.

I had written down some budget hotels at Randy's and was on my way to look for a room when I saw it. There it was, parked on the street: the blue Renault with the Brussels plates. She was here. My heart started fluttering, and I almost got lightheaded, as I don't think I took a breath. I absolutely did not know what to do. I had so many thoughts that I could not process them all at once. Should I stay here and just wait? What if she is with another man? What if she doesn't want to see me? What should I do? Oh, my God, I am going crazy. If I leave and come back, and the car is gone, I will go absolutely nuts. I better calm down. I know—I will leave her a note and put it on the windshield.

I calmed down and thought about what to say. This really can't be. She is really here. She was most likely going to Granada and that was about eight days ago. I could walk around to all the hotels near the car and ask if she was there. No. I will just leave her a note and pick a place and time. But I do not know any place. I will go find a place near here and then come back to the car. But she might leave in between. I was starting to lose it. I know—I will tell her to meet me right here at six in the evening. So I wrote the note. I actually wrote two notes and put one in the door seam and the other under her wiper blades on the front window. It was ten in the morning.

I did not want to leave the car, but it was crazy to just sit there, because she was probably gone for the day. I made sure the notes were grounded as well as possible and then decided to go down to the beach and think about this. I changed in the public bathroom, rented a towel, and lay in the sand. After what seemed like three hours, I saw it was quarter to eleven. I was restless and unable to stop my head from going in every direction. I really thought this was a perfect time for a joint, but I did not have one.

I left the beach and decided to explore the town to distract myself. I went into the very tasteful shops and found a bookstore. I started to read, and that helped a little. I walked back to the car to see if it was still there, and it was. This was not working. I had to get control of myself, so I decided to do some yoga. I went back to the beach and found a spot a bit away from the crowd. I went through my stretching and centering exercises. It took a while, but my breathing quieted, and so did I.

I decided to go talk to people. I would trust that if René got my notes, by six o'clock tonight, I would see her. I did just that. I found some French people from Paris at a café, and we talked for at least an hour. Then a couple from Madrid helped pass the time. I went back to the car, and it was there—and so were the notes. I knew now that she was going to be at least one more day, as she had not checked out, and that helped me relax. To say it was a long, long day is an understatement. I did not get a room, based on the hope that I would see her. Even if she did not show up, I could go back to Randy's as an emergency, or I could go back to Duke's. I even had time to get a room here in Marbella, or I could sleep on the beach. The last few hours were actually better, as I knew she was here. I was hoping, however, that she would not be with another man. That would not be good.

When six o'clock finally came, I went to the car. The notes were gone. I looked around but did not see her. The next minutes were very hard as I tried to stay calm. What if she is not going to come? How long should I stay here? It was now ten past six, and my mood was darkening with fear. I told myself I'd wait five more minutes and then leave her another note. Why didn't she answer my note? Maybe someone else took them off the car, and she never got them. My head was spinning at record speed. I would not be able to deal with knowing she was here and didn't want to see me. I waited another five minutes, and with my hopes fading and reality setting in, I started walking away when I heard behind me—someone running. I turned to see her running toward me, yelling, "Ken! Ken! Ken!"

She leapt into my arms, nearly knocking me over. She kissed me a zillion times while trying to say she was sorry for being late and was afraid I would leave. We both talked at the same time for a few minutes until we started laughing. I said, "Let's not talk," and I just held her until we heard our hearts start to come back within normal range.

I asked, "Are you free?"

With her cutting-edge sense of humor, she said, "Yes, I haven't yet started charging."

After ten minutes of "I can't believes," and "whys?" and getting a quick summary, I said that I was the luckiest man in the world to have found her again.

She said she only got my notes a little after five thirty and just raced to the hotel to shower and change, but she had left her key in the room and had to go back. The hotel man had taken forever, and that's why she was late.

"We should get a drink by the harbor and catch up," I said, and off we went. The feeling I had as we walked to the harbor was utter joy, and I did not know whom to thank. If I were a religious person, this feeling would have been addressed to God.

I told her about Torremolinos, and Duke, and Fuengirola, and Randy and the guys, and the theater piece. She was as happy to see me as I was to see her. She had gone to Grenada, and she told me about the Alhambra, the Moorish citadel, and all she had seen there. She went to visit a friend at the university and had stayed with her. She had been in Marbella two days and was going to leave tomorrow.

We walked the town and had a delicious dinner in a courtyard restaurant of one of the bigger hotels, and then we went to some lively bars with dancers and singers. Later, we sat by the harbor, and she just rested her head on my shoulder as we filled in all the blanks from our eight days apart. I told her I'd been with no one else since her, and she said she hadn't even thought about it for herself. I asked her what it was like after we parted, and she said it was a very up-and-down time. She, like me, had cried quite a bit after I left and then lectured herself on being a big girl and practicing what she preached.

I told her about the moon at Duke's, and she said she had sent me messages through it also. This was bonus time for us, and we felt the same way. The asterisk was unnecessary, as I did not have to convince myself of one thing. This was what I wanted to do, and we would just spend more time together. We went back to her hotel, and she went right for the lotion. The familiar smell was so exotic. We were together again. I did not know what I had done to be this fortunate. As we finished our lovemaking and were in one another's arms, she said that she loved me and that she was the happiest now that she had ever been. I welled up, and she gently kissed the tears. It doesn't get any better than this, I thought. I was in love and felt it everywhere.

In the morning, we talked about what we would do. I wanted her to see the theater piece in Fuengirola and said we could go back to Duke's in Torremolinos, as I had a room there. I did not want to bring her to Randy's, as that was a zoo. We spent the afternoon on the beach after she checked out, and we then drove to Fuengirola. She wanted to see the galleries, and we spent the early evening in and out of them, along with some bookstores and boutiques. We had a light tapas meal with red wine and went to Henri's. Randy and the boys were not there, but the owner was all over me, and it felt good, in front of René, for him to say such complimentary things about me. He had no idea I had left, as it was really just the next night. We set up the little stage, and I started talking to the crowd. Sure enough, people started gathering and before long, people were telling their dreams, and I got the place in full swing. René was the loudest with applause and screams. The crowd had a lively group of northern Germans, and they jumped right in. I was very comfortable with them and made some funny "inside" German references, which they loved. It was a wonderful evening.

René and I were in the car when she looked at me from behind the steering wheel and said, "How many more parts of you are there?" She said it was so exciting for her to see me do my thing.

"That is why I think I should stay in theater and not become a shrink."

She kept shaking her head, with a smile from ear to ear. It made me feel on top of the world.

We drove to Torremolinos, and I brought her to Duke's cafe as the night was winding down. He was there, and I told him, "This is René. I found her again in Marbella."

"Enchante," he said and kissed her hand. We toasted each other, and later, we all went to Duke's. René loved the place. It felt good to bring her to that room, and I showed her where the moon was the night after we had parted. She repeated my line, "I am here. I am here."

This felt like the best French romance movie ever.

Thelma, very animatedly clapped her hands. "Oh, Mr. Ken, I am so happy you found her again."

"Just his lifelong string of uncanny luck, Thelma," Ma said. "This does not happen to other people."

"I was elated to have found her again."

The Last Good-Bye

We awoke to the birds chirping at Duke's place, It felt special, having René here with me. I made omelets, and we sat in the courtyard, having coffee. We knew Torremolinos was not a big cultural city; it really was a tourist beach town. We decided that we would take a day trip, as she said there was a wonderful little town built on top of the rocks of a mountain, called Ronda.

It took us about an hour to get there. Once again, she was an absolutely spot-on travel guide. Ronda had fields of sunflowers surrounding it. We went to the Puente Knave, a mountaintop clearing, which overlooked the entire valley. It was a spectacular view. In this picturesque little town was a huge statue of El Torero, as it was built as a companion to the huge bullfight ring that was two hundred years old. We saw Los Tajos de Ronda, which were individual buildings built on their own rock foundations but separated by erosion, each seeming to have its own little mountain.

A bridge was built to span two mountains so that the structure beneath the bridge went all the way to the basin, with flowers climbing all the way up the side of the walls. It was a beautiful afternoon. We had lunch in the plaza by the bull ring. We sipped some wine and went for a walk along the mountain ridge until we were all alone in a huge field of flowers. We made love in the sun, and I put the flowers in her hair. We were so happy and carefree. It was a time for me when the world stood still. There were no politics, no schedule, no real responsibilities. It was a time out from the world of work and study that would be our futures. But for this moment, in this field, with this woman, I felt as happy as I had ever felt in my life. It was one of those moments that made me want to feel as much as I could and absorb everything from every way possible. I yelled to the mountain that I loved this woman, and the echo resounded three times. We damn near fainted.

We spent the rest of the afternoon in the village and painted some rocks with some children who were having a feria party. It was magical.

We drove back to Duke's and planned to stay in and make a meal at home. She and I would shop and make Duke an arroz con pollo dinner with salad and wine. He was all for it, and he invited a woman named Teresa, whom he had met while I was in Fuengirola. The evening was a big success. During dinner, he asked if I remembered the Arab filmmaker from Morocco who went to NYU. That kid, Mohammed, was now grown up and back in Marrakech, and he had a pipe store/cafe kind of thing.

Duke said it was a happening scene there, and he was going in two days and asked me to come with him. René and I would have one more day, as she had to start back to Belgium. So I told Duke I would go.

René and I sat in Duke's swing for a long time, just talking and holding hands. It was so wonderful, spending time with her. The more I knew her, the deeper my feelings for her became. We went to bed and spent most the night just talking, while we burned candles and used up all of her lotion.

We slept very late. It was almost noon when I heard Duke barking, "Where the hell are the fucking omelets?" After breakfast, we walked to town to go to the cafes, and René found a historical society building. We went in to read about Andalusia and look through all their picture albums. She bought a hat with a large brim and posed for imaginary Spanish postcards pictures. We walked to the harbor and went out for a small boat ride with a couple that knew me from Duke's cafe readings. They were Spanish and were just testing out the motor repair. It was a lovely one-hour ride on the Mediterranean.

René was so beautiful when she stood by the mast, with her hair blowing in the sea breeze. The sun was shining through her white dress to reveal the silhouette of her body—it was a sight to behold. This woman was the whole package: brains, style, and beauty. I was a goner.

We walked back up the hill to Duke's, showered, and hung out with him as we planned tomorrow's trip to Morocco. René and I knew tonight was to be our last—for real. Classes started for her in four days.

We all went downtown for the last poetry readings, and René told Duke about me and the Dream Theater bits in Fuengirola at Henri's.

"What?" Duke asked.

She explained what she'd seen, and Duke was beside himself.

"You sonna bitch! You ripped me off!"

"I didn't think you owned the world's creativity. The cafe format is yours, but the dream bit is mine. Besides, imitation in any form is flattery."

He really was just breaking chops and was quite happy to hear that I had found something that was fun. René went on and on about how good I was at it and that she also thought I should continue in the theater and not become a psychotherapist.

We drank and ate and talked with the cafe crowd. Later, we said our good-byes to everyone and walked one last time by the water. I was not going to wait until the end of the night, so I told her right there and then that she was the most lovable woman I had ever met, and I could spend the rest of my days with her. "Why couldn't life be based just on feeling and not reality?"

She kissed me deeply and said how happy I made her and that every time, for the rest of her life, she would associate Spain with me and the memories, feelings, and love we shared would always remain in her heart.

We walked back to Señor Duke's for the last time. When we got there, he said there was a change in plans, as his cousin and wife were now coming in from Amsterdam the next day, and he would not be going to Morocco.

He gave me his plane ticket and told me to go by myself.

I thought for a moment and said, "Why not?"

René and I went to bed, and there was no sadness this time. We knew what it was like to leave one another, and we knew what it was like to find one another again. We said if we could not do life without one another, then we would be together, somewhere, somehow. If it never happens, it was because this time in Spain was meant to show us that love was possible for us individually, and we would have a way to measure it in our futures.

We put our hearts, souls, and bodies together for the last time, and in the morning, after breakfast, I walked her to her car. We hugged and kissed with all the love and appreciation that was inside us, and when it was time to go, I simply said, "Good-bye, Brussels."

"Good-bye, New York."

She drove away and waved her arm out of the window until the blue Renault was out of view.

I never saw her again.

Thelma was crying, and I was wiping my tears, when Ma said very softly, "You had a real love there, Sonny Boy. You should have found a way."

"I know … I know."

The Hardest Road

Of all the roads I have traveled, the most difficult was the one back to Ma. Initially, we did have our baseball connection, which provided some of the best early memories we had together. Then it was lost, because of my father's death.

We fought continually, as her perfectionism and critical nature became overbearing for me, and I tried to stand up to it, only to realize, after trying many different ways to deal with it, what really was best for me was to get away from it.

During my twenties, I was angry at her, while struggling like hell to regain my balance from my college failure and my chronic poverty. The US Army helped in so many ways to restore my self-confidence. My connection to Ma then was mainly through the postcards and some letters, except for that one wonderful call I made from Paris. We met infrequently in the Village or at her apartment on the Palisades. We did the holidays.

Columbia provided me with a base for my future, and I was now strong enough to start to see her again. But Ma was Ma, and her scrutiny of me still hurt. I realized that for whatever reason, I still loved her, but spending time with her still subjected me to her dark side.

I sought therapy for myself, as I had chosen to be a psychotherapist and really needed to understand the process from sitting in the other chair, as well as addressing my own emotional issues, which I knew were going to be difficult to face. I had individual as well as group therapy, and the experience was life-affirming for me, as I started separating what was my issue and what was Ma's.

By my late thirties, I had finished therapy, and I now had an apartment/office in the city and had bought a big house in the suburbs. I was focused on my career. I was rising in the ranks of the American Group Psychotherapy Association and was teaching in their institute. I was now a field supervisor for Columbia and Yeshiva Universities. I then completed a certificate program in family therapy from the Philadelphia Child Guidance Clinic and was involved with the Association for Advancement of Family Therapy in New Jersey. I had married, and we had our son when I was forty-two. It was time to approach Ma again. I mainly wanted her to be a grandmother for my son, Josh, and, three years later, for my daughter, Aly.

That did not work either, as Ma was now Alicia and was off to see the world. I just about gave up on ever getting what I needed from her. We spoke on the phone, but it was still awkward and uncomfortable. She had her life with Geno, and I was involved totally with being a father and a therapist. I loved taking my kids to New York City and showing them all of what New York was about. I was involved with being my son's baseball coach and watching a million of my daughter's soccer matches. I even got on stage for my kids' yearly elementary school play fund-raiser. But the issue with Ma was always with me.

At age sixty, I went back into therapy yet again to address the issue about my mother once and for all. I was determined to have a relationship with her, despite all the scars. What I uncovered in the final analysis was that I loved her on my own, but I was still reacting to her and kept being sidetracked by her issues.

The most difficult part of this for me was realizing that I had a part of her in me. I saw myself in her at times, and that was really what I was running from. I hated feeling that pain. Once I could separate that and just work on myself, I changed for the better. I was no longer angry at myself, and most important, I was no longer angry at her. I had become who I really wanted to be, and now, free of her dominating persona, I would approach her once again. This would be my last attempt.

So I started taking Ma out for lunch, just her and me. Of course she bellyached about everything, from where I parked the car, to the bad service in the restaurant that I had picked, or whatever thought crossed her mind at the moment. But the magic was, it no longer got to me. Her comments about my hair, or my clothes, or my cologne just bounced off me. I directed the conversation to have her tell me about herself and her life. I was certainly good at that. We started to really enjoy these talks, and they formed the basis for the rest of our time together.

I had found the way to get her back, not so much as a mother or traditional nurturer, but as the person l had loved all those many years ago. I was totally surprised by the amount of feeling that returned for her. Her influence on my life had been profound, and now I could finally enjoy it. She had taught me to do no harm and to care for the world around me. She encouraged me to see that world. She had taught me honesty and responsibility. I knew I was strong because of her. We were able to laugh together, and she started to enjoy going out and talking with me. We went to great restaurants and to dives. Sometimes we packed a picnic lunch. She would call and ask when I was free to take her out. I enjoyed her and loved our time together. Geno then got sick and died two years later, and that brings you up to date, except for what happened next.

The Switch

Ma was getting increasingly confused as the weeks rolled on. Her appearance had really deteriorated, even as Thelma tried in vain to maintain it. Her hair was unkempt and looked slept in. She refused to wear her wig. Her thoughts were rambling and, at times, scattered.

Visits to her were more and more painful, as I watched her slowly fade into her own inner world. She never failed, however, to recognize me, which was always a reward. At least she knew I was there for her, and no matter what, she always reached her hand out to me. She never was big on hugs or kisses, but she always held my hand. It was tender.

Our conversations were shorter now, as she could not follow a thought for too long. Thelma told me that Ma slept a lot and her feistiness was almost completely gone. It was hard to see this strong, independent world traveler and prime-time hard-ass reduced to a whisper of her former self.

On my next visit, I noticed something very different about her. She beckoned to me to come closer, and as I did, she sat up and looked at me with her most intense stare.

I remembered that stare, and it immediately shot a bolt up my spine.

With a stronger voice than I had heard in weeks, she said, "I can't walk any more, can I?"

"Why do you ask?"

"Don't give me that therapy crap. Just answer the fucking question."

"No, Ma, you can't."

"For how long?"

"It's been about eight months."

"Jesus Christ, Kenny, I didn't want this."

"I know, Ma. I know."

She continued, "I see it all now, and it's terrible—for you, for me. This is no fuckin' life."

It was hard to argue with her, because she was right. I was supposed to take her out back, which is something she had always told me, but when it actually came to it, no one can really do that.

"Well, Sonny Boy, this is it. No more. I'm done, and I want out. I am going to flip the switch."

We both knew exactly what she was saying, as we'd watched Pop-Pop flip his and die within fifteen days.

"You sure, Ma?"

"Would you want this?"

"No, Ma, I am like you. I would want them to take me out back as well."

"I had a great life, Kenny, and it's now my time, before I forget what I now know and become a fucking vegetable."

It was a moment of surreal clarity, like the ones you read about in the dementia books. She was aware of her situation for the first time since her stroke. She was completely clearheaded, strong, and resolute.

"I love you, Ma."

"We have come full circle, my boy, you and me."

"Yes, we have."

"You gave me more than I deserved, and I want you to know I love you for turning into such a good man and for taking such good care of your fucking old mother."

"Well, as much as I hate to say it, I have you to thank for that, Ma."

"Fuckin'-A right." And with that said, she gave me a very rare hug and kissed me on the cheek. "Good-bye, Sonny Boy. I love you."

"Go in peace, Ma."

"I have no regrets, Sonny Boy. I lived a good life and am only sorry I won't see your kids when they have children. But it has to stop sometime. We don't live forever, and my time has come."

"So this is it?"

"Yup, this is it." And with that moment of honesty and connection, we said our last words to one another, and she waved good-bye and closed her eyes.

That was a Thursday. On Saturday morning, I got the call from Thelma. "She gone, Mr. Ken, she gone… she passed in her sleep."